Development
and Management

**Selected essays from
*Development in Practice***

Introduced by **Tina Wallace**

A Development in Practice Reader

Series Editor: **Deborah Eade**

Oxfam GB in association with
The Open University

First published by Oxfam GB in association with The Open University in 2000

© Oxfam GB 2000

ISBN 0 85598 429 5

A catalogue record for this publication is available from the British Library.

Available from the following agents:
USA: Stylus Publishing LLC, PO Box 605, Herndon, VA 20172-0605, USA
tel: +1 (0)703 661 1581; fax: + 1(0)703 661 1547; email: styluspub@aol.com
Canada: Fernwood Books Ltd, PO Box 9409, Stn. 'A', Halifax, N.S. B3K 5S3, Canada
tel: +1 (0)902 422 3302; fax: +1 (0)902 422 3179; e-mail: fernwood@istar.ca
India: Maya Publishers Pvt Ltd, 113-B, Shapur Jat, New Delhi-110049, India
tel: +91 (0)11 649 4850; fax: +91 (0)11 649 1039; email: surit@del2.vsnl.net.in
K Krishnamurthy, 23 Thanikachalan Road, Madras 600017, India
tel: +91 (0)44 434 4519; fax: +91 (0)44 434 2009; email: ksm@md2.vsnl.net.in
South Africa, Zimbabwe, Botswana, Lesotho, Namibia, Swaziland: David Philip Publishers,
PO Box 23408, Claremont 7735, South Africa
tel: +27 (0)21 64 4136; fax: +27(0)21 64 3358; email: dppsales@iafrica.com
Tanzania: Mkuki na Nyota Publishers, PO Box 4246, Dar es Salaam, Tanzania
tel/fax: +255 (0)51 180479, email: mkuki@ud.co.tz
Australia: Bush Books, PO Box 1958, Gosford, NSW 2250, Australia
tel: +61 (0)2 043 233 274; fax: +61 (0)2 092 122 468, email: bushbook@ozemail.com.au

Rest of the world: contact Oxfam Publishing, 274 Banbury Road, Oxford OX2 7DZ, UK.
tel. +44 (0)1865 311 311; fax +44 (0)1865 313 925; email publish@oxfam.org.uk

The views expressed in this book are those of the individual contributors,
and not necessarily those of the editor or publisher.

Published by Oxfam GB, 274 Banbury Road, Oxford OX2 7DZ, UK
Printed by Information Press, Eynsham, Oxford OX8 1JJ, UK

Typeset in Melior
Oxfam GB is registered as a charity (no. 202918) and is a member of Oxfam International.

Contents

Contributors

Michael Bailey is a Senior Policy Adviser at Oxfam GB, following over 20 years' work with several British development NGOs in Latin America and the Caribbean.

Simon Bell is a Systems Lecturer at the Centre for Complexity and Change at The Open University with a focus on developing countries and transitional economies.

Ato Brown is Waste Management Specialist at the UNDP-World Bank Water and Sanitation Programme in Kenya and previously worked with the Swiss NGO, SKAT.

Norma Burnett is qualified in Town Planning and Social Administration and has been working with the Assiut Burns Project in Egypt.

Joanna Chataway chairs the Development Policy and Practice Research Group at The Open University and has a particular interest in Central and Eastern Europe.

David Crawford, Michael Mambo, Zainab Mdimi, Harriet Mkliya, Anna Mwanbuziu, Matthias Mwiko, and Sekeite Sekasua are based in Health Projects Abroad, a British NGO that works in Tanzania.

Deborah Eade worked for 10 years in development and humanitarian work in Mexico and Central America has published widely on these issues. She is Editor of *Development in Practice*.

Alan Fowler is a development consultant and senior staff member of the Oxford-based training institution, INTRAC, where he specialises in organisational management issues within the voluntary sector.

John P. Grierson is Senior Specialist in Enterprise Development for FTP International in Helsinki and previously worked with the Swiss NGO, SKAT.

Richard Heeks works on information systems and development at the University of Manchester, with particular reference to the public sector and to NGOs.

Tom Hewitt is Director of The Open University's MSc in Development Management and co-editor of its latest course book.

Hazel Johnson is a Lecturer at The Open University and chairs the postgraduate course *Capacities for Managing Development*. She has carried out research in rural livelihoods and food security in Southern Africa and Central America.

P. Kassey Garba is a Senior Lecturer in the Department of Economics at the University of Ibadan in Nigeria and specialises in gender issues.

David Lewis is a Lecturer at the Centre for Voluntary Organisation at the London School of Economics where he convenes the MSc in Management of NGOs.

Carmen Marcuello works in the Department of Economics at the University of Zaragoza in Spain.

Chaime Marcuello works in the Department of Sociology at the University of Zaragoza in Spain.

Martin Onyach-Olaa coordinates the Programme Management Unit in the Decentralisation Secretariat at the Ministry of Local Government in Uganda.

Lina Payne is a Social Development Adviser at the Department for International Development (DFID) in Bangladesh and was previously Oxfam GB's Social Policy Adviser for eastern Europe and the former Soviet Union.

Richard Pinder works on voluntary and community sector involvement in community care in Sheffield and has a particular interest in inner city regeneration.

Doug Porter is Regional Technical Adviser to the UN Capital Development Fund, working with decentralised governance programmes in East and Southern Africa.

Stephen P. Riley was, until his death in 1999, Reader in Politics at Staffordshire University.

Dorcas Robinson is Development Adviser to Health Projects Abroad and a member of the Executive Committee of British Overseas NGOs for Development (BOND). She is currently studying at The Open University.

Purna Sen works at the Gender Institute at the London School of Economics and is on the management committee of Southall Black Sisters and on the advisory board of the feminist NGO, Change.

Ines Smyth is Programme Manager for Oxfam GB's Human Resources Development Programme in East Timor and was previously Policy Adviser for Gender and Capacity-Building.

Marielle Snel is an urban and regional planner based at the Water, Engineering and Development Centre (WEDC) at Loughborough University.

Babar Sobhan is undertaking research at the University of Cambridge and has worked as a consultant to various NGOs and official donor agencies.

Ramya Subrahmanian is studying at The Open University and has extensive experience in gender, development, and human rights work in southern India.

Alan Thomas is Director of the Centre for Complexity and Change at The Open University and a Senior Lecturer in Development Policy and Practice. He is also centrally involved in the OU's postgraduate programme in Development Management.

Tina Wallace has studied and taught at universities in Uganda, Nigeria, and the UK, and has worked with a range of development and refugee rights NGOs. She is now based at Oxford Brookes University.

David Wield is Head of Discipline in Development Policy and Practice at The Open University and has a particular interest in the processes of industrialisation in Africa.

Gordon Wilson is a Lecturer at The Open University where he chairs the undergraduate course *Third World Development* and its postgraduate counterpart *Development: Context and Practice*, specialising in technology in the small- and microenterprise context.

Preface

Deborah Eade, Tom Hewitt, Hazel Johnson

The articles in this *Reader* are taken from a special issue of *Development in Practice* (Volume 9, numbers 1&2) that was commissioned and assembled by guest-editors Tom Hewitt and Hazel Johnson of The Open University (OU). Drawing largely on the content of two of the core courses in the OU's programme for the degree of MSc in Development Management, the volume brings together an unusual collection of essays on and insights into the ethical dilemmas and real conflicts posed by doing 'development management in practice'.

The *Reader* reflects the view that 'development' is not exclusive to developing countries, and that 'management' refers to far more than merely operational or bureaucratic matters. Thus, development management encompasses *'the management of intervention aimed at external social goals in a context of value-based conflict'* (Thomas 1996:106). 'Intervention' in this sense means influencing social processes, rather than using resources to meet goals directly. 'External social goals' are achieved by actions in the public sphere, directed outside a given organisation rather than internal to it. Social goals are of course often contested: opinions differ about what they are, as well as how to achieve them. Since individual social actors seldom have more than partial control over a given development process, value-based conflict is an intrinsic part of development management.

The definition of development policy and its subsequent translation into practice constitutes a set of processes — not just tangible inputs and outputs — that are themselves shaped by the relations and dynamics between a multiplicity of interests, which are in turn represented by state and non-state organisations and associations. Policies and strategies are the products of inter-related pressures and processes: political action (arising from movements and ideas); state action (influenced by the former); non-state political action; and private responses. These pressures and processes are all played out within institutions (norms, values, and practices) that filter and mediate their outcomes. It is therefore only in retrospect that we can know what strategy(ies) emerged.

Negotiation over policy is at the heart of public action for development. Thus development managers and their organisations are as much a conscious and central part of public action as other players are; they do not simply act on development from the outside. And although the uncertain nature of public action and its outcomes means that one cannot predict exactly what kind of expertise will be called for, development managers do need distinctive skills and understanding, in order to cope with and respond to 'tension, conflict and [re]negotiation' (Wuyts 1992:280). The question of management *for* development as opposed to management *of* development, and whether indeed there is anything distinctive about 'development management' is explored by **Alan Thomas**, in a paper that acts as a springboard for some of the central ideas and practices featured in this *Reader*, namely the following:

- *The management of specific tasks in development interventions.* This may include the conceptualisation of such tasks and the ways in which tools and techniques can be used in a process-based way (see both **Simon Bell** and **David Wield**); or it may involve approaches towards building institutional sustainability through stakeholders negotiating agendas for action in development programmes (see **Hazel Johnson** and **Gordon Wilson**). In a complementary fashion, the composite paper 'Day in the life of a development manager' charts some of the routine and non-routine concerns in managing development tasks, while papers by **John P Grierson** and **Ato Brown** and by **Marielle Snel** consider such negotiations in the context of public-service provision.

- *Management oriented towards development ideals.* Chapters on a range of themes and practices, all based on experience from various parts of the world, describe the tensions between development ideals and the realities of practice. **Ramya Subrahmanian** analyses some of the contradictions inherent in attempts to decentralise the delivery of primary education in India, asking 'what if local preferences run counter to policy interests?', while **Dorcas Robinson** explores the policy arena of health-care delivery in Tanzania and asks whether different agendas and actors can in fact join together in an effective programme of action. **Jo Chataway** and **Tom Hewitt** cross the North—South divide by comparing the experiences of Poland and Tanzania in their respective attempts to develop non-linear and learning-centred approaches to technological change. Shorter pieces about difficulties and achievements in seeking to orient management towards development ideals include the papers by **Richard Pinder**, **Norma Burnett**, **Purna Sen**, and **Lina Payne** and **Ines Smyth**.

- *Management in a development context.* The management of development organisations that try to achieve external social goals, and perhaps to represent or lay claim to certain values, is the focus of another set of case studies. With reference to Bangladesh, **David Lewis** and **Babar Sobhan** focus on whether trust can be built between bilateral donors and the Southern NGO recipients of their aid, and on challenges to Northern NGOs arising from the expansion of direct official aid to those in the South. **Michael Bailey** addresses the problems of local fund-raising among civil-society organisations in Brazil. How can they increase and diversify their incomes, and what are the compromises they may have to make in doing so? What role can foreign donors and aid agencies play in fostering financial autonomy among Southern organisations?

The latter set of papers in particular reminds us that the question of resources, especially money — where it comes from, the conditions attached to it, how much there is, to whom it is (to be) given, for what purposes, and for how long — is never divorced from the business of development and, therefore, of development management. For organisations that depend on external resources, this may amount to the management of scarcity: how to retain one's integrity and core values when these are being eroded by lack of funds, or tangled up in the strings attached by the donors; and how to be most effective when resources are inadequate and sustainability is far from certain. For those responsible for deciding how to allocate resources and/or manage grants budgets, the question is how to manage the power that derives from relative wealth: how to define core values and honour ideals in making choices between competing demands — critical decisions that will affect another organisation's whole future; and how to be effective when power relations obscure an understanding of what is at stake for the beneficiary organisations whose survival and direction are under threat. Although these dynamics are present in any relationship between someone who gives and someone who receives, they are particularly marked in the context of what is today often called the 'development industry'. While this industry involves a vast range of actors — from governments to grassroots organisations, from multinationals to home-based enterprises, from academic think-tanks to groups proposing radical change — (international) NGOs are distinguished by their attempts to bridge the gap between the North and the South and in some sense to interpret the tensions inherent in seeking to do so. (Here, 'North' and 'South' serve as proxy terms for those institutions that are in a position of power and those that depend in some way upon them, and not just as synonyms for industrialised and developing countries. It is important to recall that there are many thousands of voluntary-sector agencies all over the world that channel government grants or public donations to deprived or marginalised sectors in their own societies, while at the same time seeking to influence public policy and sensitise public opinion.) Within the particular context of aid, however, international NGOs can choose simply to transmit the norms, values, and culture of the North to the South. But as civil-society organisations in their own right, such NGOs and their counterparts may also be in a position to hold up a critical mirror to the North, from the perspective of those who are marginalised.

Within the broad arena of development, international NGOs almost by definition cut across the three main areas of development management with which this Reader is concerned : namely, the management of specific tasks in development interventions (for instance, service-provision), management that is oriented towards specific ideals (as expressed in NGO 'mission statements' and policies), and management in a development context. Because of what NGOs can show us about how these various aspects of development management both influence and are influenced by the aid chain, **Tina Wallace** opens with some sobering reflections on the changing ways in which these various roles and the tensions they generate are themselves managed. Back in the 1960s and 1970s, when the development NGO sector was smaller, less competitive, and more voluntarist in nature, 'management' was often seen as a perjorative term; at best irrelevant, at worst incompatible with commitment — not something for which the average supporter collected funds, went on sponsored walks, or responded to appeals and adverts.[1] However, with the increased competition for public donations, and the rise in official assistance being channelled through them from the mid-1980s onwards, the NGO sector urgently felt the need to professionalise itself.[2] This coincided with a period when the certainties that had guided much post-war thinking about development began to crumble along with the Berlin

Wall, and then to capsize in the tidal wave of economic globalisation, the rolling-back of the state, and advances in information technology. That the roles of government and the private sector were changing so rapidly, and so profoundly, compelled all development agencies — NGOs included — also to rethink their own *raison d'être* and direction. Corporatism, strategic planning, and formal accountability became the order of the day; a way to contain if not to understand the complex environments in which development and humanitarian programmes now had to function. Having discovered a particular brand of corporate management, however, many Northern NGOs and official development agencies began to seek spiritual and practical guidance not from within their own unique and multicultural experience, but from the orthodoxies of the for-profit sector (Powell and Seddon 1997; Lewis 1998). Ironically, many observers and insiders fear that in nailing themselves so firmly to the mast of strategic planning and market-led approaches, NGOs risk casting their central values and accumulated wisdom — their distinctiveness — overboard.

The recognition by development agencies that, in order to be effective, people and resources must be managed makes a welcome change from the 'muddling through' of an earlier era. Development management is about making choices, and this is possible only if decision makers' roles are clear and if the organisational culture (and structures) encourage accountability and transparency. Assumptions and values *do* need to be challenged: complacency is not an option for NGOs, any more than it is for businesses that must compete in the market place, or for governments that are accountable to the electorate. But as Tina Wallace (1997) has suggested, the turbulent environment to which their conversion to a particular brand of professionalisation was a response has been surpassed by the welter of cultural and structural changes, strategic reviews, and often losses of staff that so many international NGOs continue to inflict upon themselves.

The question is one of balance as well as overall direction. No healthy institution can allow its professed values to be a smokescreen for unprofessional and poor performance. Nor, however, should development agencies, governmental or non-governmental, concentrate so much on their own management that they lose sight of where they really stand in the overall picture. Reputations cannot be taken for granted in an increasingly competitive environment, and development agencies now have to cultivate a high public profile as well as seeking to achieve excellence. Thus even household-name UN agencies and multilaterals invest huge resources in producing annual flagship reports, fearful that, as Michael Bailey puts it, 'lights under bushels are invariably short-lived'.

But when does publicity-seeking become an end in itself? How far do NGOs and other development agencies still believe that they should be working for their own extinction, or be actively seeking to transform their relationships with their local counterparts into genuine partnerships? Without strong values to inform them, planning and evaluation quickly become bureaucratic ends in themselves. Processes then lose their dynamism, documents are viewed as reality, and aid is thought to be synonymous with 'development'. All too easily, management gets reduced to managerialism. Addressing these tensions, Tina Wallace asks how far the methods brought in from the business sector are suitable for, or even compatible with, the values of empowerment and commitment to social justice that NGOs as well as other social actors would claim. Perhaps only history will reveal why development agencies in general, and the NGO sector in particular, have at the close of the twentieth century shown such a collective lack of confidence in their uniqueness; and so little capacity to look to their own experience, their own ideals and values, as a basis for generating development- management tools that might enable them to deepen and broaden their impact, and to become genuinely accountable for it.

Though it is caricatured as being top-down and bureaucratic, management is basically a process of getting things done by the best means available. However, this *Reader* shows that development management is more about dealing with the messiness of intervening for change, with the importance of feelings and intuitions, with uncertainty and risk-taking, with handling conflict and diversity, with mutual respect, with what is *not* said or is *not* visible than it is about establishing concrete facts and objectively verifiable indicators, quantifying achievements, or seeking to put reality into neat packages labelled 'projects'. Development management is, then, concerned not with exercising control or counting beans, but with seeking to act on an understanding of how change processes intersect with power, and of how best to shape these processes in favour of those who are excluded from resources and decision making.

Notes

1   A notable exception is the NGO Management Network, which began in the 1980s, well before most development agencies thought they had anything to learn in this field.

2   In the UK, and partly because of historical assumptions about the voluntary nature of charitable work, NGOs imply in their publicity that they can deliver development more cheaply than can governments or official agencies. Thus, they compete to keep down their declared overheads, as though spending on management were synonymous with inefficiency. Low overheads are thus still a criterion against which public opinion measures an NGO's effectiveness. However, the professionalisation of the sector has involved a shift towards paid staff and away from the appearance of 'do-goodery'. Since such spending has always been embedded in other budget lines, accurate figures do not exist. However, it is probably true to say that no major NGO today spends less on itself than it did ten years ago. This would not be problematic if the donating public regarded NGO spending on competitive salaries, modern communications, and international travel as the best way to achieve the goals for which they gave their support.

References

Lewis, D. (1998) 'NGOs, management, and the process of change: New models or reinventing the wheel', *Appropriate Technology* 25(1).

Powell, M. and D. Seddon (1997) 'NGOs and the development industry', *Review of African Political Economy* (71).

Thomas, A. (1996) 'What is development management?', *Journal of International Development*, 8(1): 95–110.

Wallace, Tina (1997) 'New development agendas: changes in UK NGO policies and procedures', *Review of African Political Economy* 24(71): 35–55.

Wuyts. M. (1992) 'Conclusion: development policy as process' in M. Wuyts, M. Mackintosh, and T. Hewitt, *Development Policy and Public Action*, Oxford: Oxford University Press in association with The Open University.

Introductory essay
Development management and the aid chain: the case of NGOs

Tina Wallace

NGOs have become key in disbursing aid money to organisations and individuals in the South: how they conceptualise and manage such funds has a profound effect on the nature of the development they can promote. Recipients of their aid may find that the terms and conditions for accepting it have changed, and not always in ways which promote the values NGOs are best known for, including transparency, participation, and partnership.

It has long been agreed that NGOs form part of civil society, and that civil society is distinct from government (the state) and business (the market). While we lack precise definitions, NGOs are usually seen as an integral and institutional form of civil society. NGOs are bearers of values which they openly promote through their literature and fund-raising, and they define themselves as very different from the other two sectors. The three sectors are often delineated in terms of triangles or circles; analysts scrutinise where their function and roles in development are distinct and where they overlap. While this representation helps to clarify the separateness of the three types of institutions, it is blind to the values, dynamics, and politics between and within the circles:

> ... as a matter of fact, a distinctive feature of this perspective is its preoccupation with dilettante methods — ahistorical models and magical geometric shapes, of triangles, circles and arrows in lieu of the analysis of historical relations. Thus it is not surprising that instead of political economy... the services of management science are summoned to define and explain 'civil society'. (Acharya 1999:4)

While 'development management' as presented in this volume seeks to accommodate the idea of complex negotiation between a range of social actors, many NGOs have bought into a narrow concept of managerialism. Drawing, often uncritically, from the experience of the other sectors, especially business, they have taken on outmoded thinking and ignored the original purposes and context of these models. I shall argue that there are inherent dangers for NGOs in taking on apolitical 'managerial' — and at times discredited — approaches to the way they define themselves, organise their procedures, and conduct their work. Behind the adoption of language and methods borrowed largely from the business sector, changes may be taking place which, rather than enhancing the work of NGOs, may be pushing them into roles which contradict their stated values, mission, and vision. As they receive increasing funding from donors who support them precisely because of their claimed flexibility, responsiveness, and closeness to the ground, the procedures and approaches they have accepted in disbursing this money have often become a threat to these positive characteristics.

Focusing on NGOs is important when looking at issues of development management for a number of reasons: NGOs are now key players in the development process, and it is important that the ways in which they work should be scrutinised in a professional way. They are very vocal players, voicing critiques of the work of others and promoting their own views on good development practice. It is therefore critical to explore the extent to which the values and practices they espouse in development are reflected in their own organisational structures and to see how this in turn affects their development practice. It is clear that other kinds of institutions that promote democracy or participation are often themselves undemocratic and suffer a participation deficit (for instance, the European Commission or the UN). Third, NGOs have a duty to stand back and be self-critical both to examine how far their own practice promotes the values they espouse, and to look at whether the way in which they operate does or does not enable them to engage positively with the lives of poor people.

Defining NGOs

There are now literally hundreds, even thousands, of NGOs in most countries around the world. They have exploded in number, and some have grown greatly in size; many British NGOs, for instance, now have annual incomes of more than £80–100 million. They differ in size, in sectoral focus, in ways of working, and in religious affiliation. They are so diverse that whatever is said of one kind of NGO can be contradicted by looking at another one elsewhere. To avoid becoming entangled in discussions of typology, this paper will focus entirely on UK-based NGOs, and on the most prominent and larger ones among them. However, much of what is said applies more generally across the NGO sector in both the North and the South; and there is clear evidence of growing convergence among many NGOs and between the NGO sector and other development actors, especially donors.

The role of institutional donors

The role of institutional donors (for example, bilateral government donors and multilaterals such as the European Commission, the UN, or the World Bank) has grown significantly in relation to British NGOs. Today, donors are not only the source of money but increasingly of ideas and conditions which directly affect the NGO sector — initially primarily NGOs in the North, but now also large NGOs in the South. Down the funnels through which the money is channelled come a range of procedures, understandings, and the latest 'development thinking', all of which have a major influence on NGO policy and practice; some funding is completely tied, and the NGOs become straightforward implementers of bi- and multilateral aid programmes, rather than independent development actors. Some aid is less 'tied', but still carries with it certain conditions.

Over the years, the theoretical underpinning of official aid has shifted considerably, and understandings of what development is and how to promote it have changed radically. In the early days of post-independence, the focus was entirely on the role of the state in promoting agricultural and industrial change, and on training public officials to behave in ways appropriate to developing modern, economically flourishing states. This focus on the state and agents of the state was gradually eroded by the poor economic performance of many countries and replaced by the belief in markets as the mechanism for delivering efficient and effective development. Structural adjustment programmes (SAPs) brought with them a wave of liberalisation requirements, including the 'rolling back' of the state, trade liberalisation, devaluation, cuts in public spending, and the privatisation of key state functions in line with the macroeconomic analysis promoted by the IMF and the World Bank. NGOs began to attract the attention of the donors in two ways: because they were criticising the effects of structural adjustment on the poor (though not necessarily analysing or opposing the basis on which SAPs were built); and because they were seen as an alternative conduit for aid which would allow for development funds to be channelled to certain countries without offering financial support to the state. The state by this time was seen as inefficient, corrupt, and over-staffed.

While NGOs were raising important issues about the impact of SAPs on people living in poverty during this period, it should be noted that since the collapse of the Berlin Wall the NGO sector has offered no serious challenge to, or rejection of, the neoliberal model of economics. The debates have been essentially carried on within an implicit acceptance that many aspects of SAPs are essential in order to restructure failing economies. More fundamental critiques of SAPs have come from feminist economics than from the majority of UK-based NGOs which lobby the World Bank on these issues. Indeed, many NGOs have benefited from their own lobbying about the effects of structural adjustment by receiving funds from the Bank to ameliorate the worst effects of these programmes for the poor in certain countries, especially in Africa.

NGO funding increased significantly during this period, partly because NGOs became part of the privatisation agenda. Donors and NGOs identified many areas of mutual interest in terms of development; but this growth in funding did not come 'free'. In return for money, gradual changes had to be made to NGO development practice in order to bring this more into line with the procedures and approaches of the donors. NGOs continued to be critical of much donor practice, while at the same time receiving ever more money from official sources and being shaped by these. There was continuing dialogue between the two — indeed, donors were also influenced by the NGO sector. Hence their discourse started to reflect the language of NGOs in concerns about sustainability, the need for participation, a focus on gender, and agreement on the need for special provisions for the poorest who were affected by SAPs.

The language of the donors is currently shifting again, with a growing recognition of the importance of the role of the state in development, not as an implementor, but as an enabler and regulator. The ideology of rolling back the state is being replaced with a focus on partnerships with the state; conditionality is giving way to 'comprehensive development frameworks'. The emphasis is on working with like-minded governments to create a policy development framework to be delivered by a range of institutional actors. There is a renewed focus on poverty and, to a lesser extent, on rights as the overall goal of development work. In this scenario, NGOs, especially Northern NGOs, are still being seen as a key channel for development aid, but only as one of a range of possible conduits for implementing development goals. Other actors include private consultants, markets, local groups, community-based organisations (CBOs), and local government. It remains to be seen whether budgets previously allocated to NGOs will be squeezed as they start to compete with other civil society players including the churches, unions, women's movements, as well as with development actors from both the business and government sectors.

The increased communication between NGOs, donors, and governments has led to a growing homogenisation of language; this is the language of strategic and business planning, efficiency, accountability, cost effectiveness, and impact; but also of sustainability, participation, facilitation, enabling frameworks, capacity-building. Several questions arise, which will be addressed here. How far have donors changed NGOs' agenda and processes of development practice, as well as their language and procedures? To what extent are NGOs still independent players? How compatible are these two languages, one of (development) management and the other of social change? If they are incompatible, what are the implications for donor-dependent NGOs? The other set of major questions — to what extent NGOs have changed the understanding and working of the bilateral and multilateral donors, rather than merely their language, and what other factors encouraged donors to take up issues of participation and civil society involvement — are for another time.

The changing face of NGOs

British NGOs have diverse origins and have changed significantly over the past three decades. Many which started as refugee-relief, child-welfare, or solidarity organisations have developed into multi-million agencies, processing money given by institutional donors as well as by the public. They have grown from small voluntarist groups into bureaucratic organisations with clearly defined hierarchies, roles, and responsibilities; many employ professionals in their headquarters and in their offices around the world. Towards the end of the 1980s there was a growing concern within many NGOs that they were facing problems arising from a lack of focus and of procedures and structures to maintain their work. At the same time, donors started to channel more resources through the NGO sector, both in order to by-pass the state in many countries and for ideological reasons. NGOs became part of the 'privatisation' of aid agenda in keeping with the dominant politics of the time, and donors exerted pressure on them to become more rigorous, more professional, and more accountable.

There was clearly a need for NGOs to make internal organisational changes and to address issues of policy and procedure as they grew, both as the early founders moved on and were replaced by new directors, and as the development world changed around them. The question is: why did the NGO sector borrow so heavily from procedures developed in the business sector and even within the US military, rather than building on their own experience in order to develop new approaches and methods?

Business organisations and the military are very different types of organisation with quite different aims: one is measured by profit rather than performance (and the two are not as closely related as the literature suggests), the other by success in arenas of war. The limitations of military strategic planning were recently highlighted in NATO's involvement in Kosovo, where poor information and understanding of local conditions turned a three-day onslaught into a war of several weeks. To what extent do these 'borrowed' management practices enable NGOs to fulfil their stated aims of empowering poor people, building civil society, addressing rights — including women's rights — or promoting sustainable poverty reduction, all of which require a deep understanding of the people and contexts in which they are working? How compatible are they with the approaches that have grown more directly out of NGO experience of working with people, for example participatory methods of research and planning, and participatory video?

The pressures for change

Links between funding and approaches to development

The pressures for change were to be found not only from the donors, but also within many NGOs themselves. Staff were dissatisfied with lack of clarity about their roles and responsibilities; issues such as where decisions could be made in UK-based NGOs that worked internationally were unresolved, and fragmented visions existed of what the organisation was about, especially in those NGOs which expanded fast during the 1970s and 1980s. Some of the field staff and Southern partners also advocated change in terms of devolution, resource allocation, and decision-making.

But a major pressure for change did come from the donors. The donors are rarely discussed in the paradigms that are represented by circles and triangles, yet they have had a massive impact on the shape and workings of many British NGOs and on the sector as a whole. Vastly increased sums of money have been spent through UK-based NGOs around the world, in both development and emergency work. Many NGOs which prided themselves on never taking more than 10 per cent of their funding from institutional sources in the 1980s are today much more coy about discussing their percentages; moreover, percentages can be calculated in many ways, and NGOs often deliberately cover up the volume of aid from institutional donors.

Table 1 Money channelled through UK-based NGOs from the Department for International Development (DFID) 1987–95* (in millions, rounded to £ sterling)		
Budget lines	**1987–8**	**1994–5**
Emergency work	£19,581	£83,093
Joint Funding Scheme	£ 8,424	£34,360
Geographical desks and other	£ 5,635	£42,320
Total	**£33,630**	**£161,773**

Note: In 1987, no money was channelled through geographical desks; by 1990 this had risen to £1,176,800. As DFID has decentralised budgets and increasingly pays money directly to NGOs in certain countries, compiling figures of grants and contracts through the regional offices has proved impossible , but it is certainly rising all the time.

The Reality of Aid 1997/8 (Eurostep 1998) calculated that US$281.7 million went through British NGOs in 1995–96, US$184.8 million of which was bilateral aid for NGOs to work as part of the British government's aid programme, compared to half that sum (US$96.9m) for grants to fund NGOs' own projects.

The key donor for UK-based NGOs is DFID (formerly the ODA) which funds them in several ways. A flexible form of funding was available through the Joint Funding Scheme (JFS); this was responsive (matching) funding which allowed NGOs broadly to set their own agendas. The JFS is relatively small at £35 million a year and has recently been transformed into the Civil Society Challenge Fund, the impact of which is not yet known. Since the Hodges Report (ODA 1992), government funding has been given to NGOs directly to assist in implementing Britain's bilateral programme in various countries; NGOs have thus become implementers of the UK government aid programme. This is not flexible funding, but funding to be either a direct contractor for clearly defined parts of the DFID programme, or for accountable grants, the terms of which are negotiable within the strict parameters of the DFID strategic plan for each country. The bulk of the growth of donor funding for NGOs has come within this part of the bilateral programme, along with the exponential growth in emergencies funding.

The influence of this direct government funding has been immense: it has put increasing pressure on NGOs to become 'accountable', professional, to demonstrate their efficiency and effectiveness, and to show their impact in terms of poverty reduction. NGOs have been required to use procedures developed for the bilateral aid programme. Hence, NGOs have adopted approaches such as strategic planning, project-cycle management, and logical framework (logframe) analysis, even where they have felt that these are not in keeping with their way of working or their concepts of development processes.[1] Even the JFS, which started as a flexible fund, moved on to train NGO staff in DFID methods of planning and implementing the project-cycle from the mid-1990s. University-based advisers have made more demands on the NGOs that request funding, and most have promoted formal systems of planning, monitoring, and evaluation in cooperation with DFID.

The increase in institutional funding has been profound, but many NGOs still have access to voluntary contributions and 'untied' money for their work; in 1996–7 their voluntary income was estimated at twice their 'tied' income (US$569.2 million compared to US$281.7 million in donor money). Thus other pressures must have added to this donor push for NGOs to use procedures commonly accepted within government and business for developing their vision, planning their work, and disbursing their money through projects.

Changes in NGO management and staff

Trustee boards have been one such factor in changing NGO practice. Through the 1980s and 1990s, many people from the private sector were deliberately brought onto trustee boards to bring a new perspective and new skills to the NGO world. They have repeatedly asked that NGOs work in ways familiar to them, find ways to demonstrate their impact, and prove that they are worth funding. Many trustees have no knowledge of development; some even pride themselves on this. They see the management of development as the same as any other form of management, requiring certain disciplines, skills, and procedures which are relatively uniform across the three sectors. Under the influence of trustees and external consultants, one UK agency has developed a set of training modules for management competencies which draws heavily on generic management principles and is to be uniformly applied to all managers across the world.

This pattern of applying management principles from one sector to another, using private sector experts as trustees and consultants, has also been a dominant factor in reshaping the public sector in UK, raising similar questions for staff working in health, education, and social services. To what extent *is* 'management just management'? And to what extent do we need management approaches that are developed specifically in relation to the organisation's purpose — be that development, education, or health — and tailored to the cultural context in which management is practised?

The 1990s also saw the rise in the number of private sector staff employed by NGOs, initially in the finance departments and marketing, then in information technology (IT), policy, and planning. They have brought with them very different values and perspectives from those held by most of the staff who are responsible for running the development programmes. Clashes have occurred between marketing and advertising staff, campaigners, and advocates on the one hand, and field programme staff on the other. Private sector management consultants saw a new niche in becoming management consultants to the burgeoning NGO sector, and many leading NGOs shared the experience of being reviewed by one of a handful of companies that specialised in working with the non-profit sector. Their techniques and approaches were all drawn from standard business management practice and theory.

Many parts of the university system have also begun to draw on the same pool of ideas, especially those found in the new public sector management; and development studies programmes increasingly include management studies and business studies. While some have grappled with the issues of whether NGO management is unique, others have adopted business management techniques almost wholesale, perhaps adding some cultural sensitivity. Some of the academics who teach these management courses have no direct experience of working in development in Africa, Asia, or Latin America — and do not see this as a problem. They are teaching 'basic standards' which they understand to be universally applicable. In addition, as student numbers have dropped and financial stringency has become increasingly common within those UK development studies departments which are self-financing, ever more resources for academic research and consultancy come from the same set of institutional donors. Inevitably, the language and understanding of development being promoted by these academics to some extent reflect the interests of the funding agencies. Few academics feel that they are in a position to 'bite the hand that feeds them' at a time of real competition for shrinking resources in academia. Rather, they try to respond positively to donor concerns that development ideas be translated into easily used planning tools, measurable indicators, and impact assessment guidelines.

These pressures, combined with the fast-changing funding context in which increasing numbers of NGOs compete for the same or declining resources, and competition becomes acute, led many NGOs to adopt management packages from the private sector and apply them to their development work. The changes that have taken place in most NGOs in the UK have been driven more by the desire for financial growth, for maintaining access to large donors, for meeting bilateral and trustee demands, than by trying to learn from their own experience, to develop their own strategies and processes, and to promote good development practice. It is interesting to speculate what NGOs might look like if half the resources spent on professional Northern management consultants and 'off the peg' management training in tools developed outside the NGO sector such as strategic planning and logframes, had been spent on operationalising concepts drawn from within their own practice. This experience would offer important lessons such as how to work effectively with those whose voices are hardest to hear, to plan from the basis of local realities in a way which responds to their needs, to find ways of combining local and external knowledge into real forces for development, and to empower women and men who are excluded by current local, national, and international contexts.

Does this matter?

Many may be shaking their heads by now, asking why any of this matters. There can be no harm in adopting practices which promote clarity of thinking, apply logical analyses to problems, streamline project implementation, and raise levels of accountability. These are all worthwhile goals, but many questions arise when business concepts are taken into development. Businesses which talk about accountability are often quite closed organisations, and their primary motivations are to maximise profit and market share and to maintain market dominance. While many NGOs feel comfortable with a focus on market share and dominance of the NGO sector, others do not; and none of them would want to be accountable only to a small group of 'shareholders'. NGOs know that they need to serve a wide range of stakeholders, but they are adopting approaches which are not designed for multiple accountability. Are procedures for accountability to donors and trustees the same as, or even compatible with, accountability to beneficiaries? To what extent are 'market surveys' and the search for ways of assessing public opinion relevant to NGOs, which after all must listen to, learn from, and plan in the light of the needs of their Southern partners and beneficiaries? While Epstein et al. (1991) have advocated the benefits of consumer-survey approaches to development beneficiaries, most NGOs have rejected this because they see the shallowness of these methods when advocating beneficiary participation, bottom-up planning, and responsive frameworks.

In addition, these discussions ignore the reality of the relations of dominance within aid processes, and the potentially disempowering and alien discourse of formal tools. Long and Long (1992), Scoones (1993), and Chambers (1986) all show the negative impact which positivist, rationalist, Western epistemologies have on local people's knowledge and what counts as knowledge. This can be extended to analyse what space beneficiaries can find and what language they can use in order to enter the debates set by strategic planning and project-cycle management systems. Systems for upward accountability which are framed within the business concepts of proving efficiency, effectiveness, and value for money, have become far more developed than have tools used for downward accountability to beneficiaries. Indeed, they may have become additional barriers which prevent local people from access to development processes that directly affect their own lives.

There is a value in applying logical analysis to problems, but whose logic is used? Whose information guides the completion of project documents? Who sets the criteria by which a project will be judged a success? Can participatory processes really change the structural factors that shape projects for agencies, and intrude into the neatness of the project-framework language of inputs, outputs, and indicators?[2] Complex evaluations have highlighted the reality that what constitutes success for an NGO's headquarters, or in terms of the project document, may differ from definitions of success by its staff on the ground; these may themselves differ from the criteria used by the partner organisation; and women may have different understandings of success from men within the same village and even household.[3] When insisting on measurable impact within two to three years, what happens to risk-taking, to working on the difficult, sometimes almost intractable, problems which often underpin the causes of poverty for some groups of people? How does learning take place when the focus is on showing concrete achievements? How are the unintended consequences of the way a project is framed and the indicators set handled?

Two examples from the public sector in the UK illustrate the thorny issues that arise in measuring effectiveness by focusing on demonstrable impact, and at how these concerns can militate against the very changes desired. Each service has had to select a range of indicators against which to assess their work. When the police service selected 'clear up' rates for crime as a key indicator, there was no improvement in crime detection, because these issues are complex and long term. Instead, police officers started to make routine visits to prisons and to cross-examine prisoners about other crimes they might have committed so that these could be declared as closed. The effect on crime on the streets and on crime deterrence was zero, but numbers had been recorded and impact assessed. There are myriad examples of this kind in all public services; for instance, cutting hospital waiting lists can be done in many ways apart from actually seeing and treating patients faster and well. Speed can push out quality; people can be deleted from lists on grounds of poor health, disability, or age; people can be seen but not treated. The NGO sector has undertaken no serious assessment of how measurable impacts are possibly skewing public service work, although it is embracing similar concepts of measurable impact, often uncritically.

Three concrete examples will serve to highlight some of the tensions and dilemmas raised by the wholesale adoption by some NGOs of policies and procedures derived from outside. Many in the NGO sector, and some observers, feel that these approaches can undermine their stated commitment to changing social relations, confronting structures of oppression and exclusion, building local capacity, enabling participation of the excluded, and may force them become short-term contractors, service providers, or project implementers working to plans drawn up by institutional donors.

Illustrating the tensions

Working for management or social change?

Research carried out with 17 UK-based NGOs during 1996 highlighted several areas of tension for staff in Northern NGOs (NNGOs) as well as Southern NGOs (SNGOs). These included the real tensions between staff based in the North and working to Northern paradigms drawn from the business sector, and staff in the South who felt that their perspectives, analyses, and understandings were irrelevant to the organisational changes being made in relation to management and development practice:

> Muchunguzi is not the first to describe how SNGOs lump all international agencies together as donors (multi-, bi-laterals and NNGOs) but because his statements are based on extensive SNGO

contacts they carry weight highlighting this as a crucial point in current development relationships. SNGOs did not experience the diversity of NNGOs (something NNGOs stress all the time) but experience them all as having their own clear agendas and procedures which shaped the work. SNGOs feel imposed on, often ignored and their cultural values and concepts are devalued. The feelings expressed were very strong. Smillie echoes these themes, and talks of the swelling chorus of complaints from SNGOs about their exclusion... and the lack of Northern accountability to the South. (Wallace et al. 1997:108)

There were also tensions between those preaching the limitations of seeing projects as synonymous with development and the fact that the current management tools were in fact increasing the focus on projects and project management and impact, rather than looking at alternative ways of promoting social change.

Gender was one issue which highlighted many of the inherent tensions between those advocating a managerial approach and those preferring a more analytical and social relations approach to development work. While many agencies have formal gender policies and implementation plans, and although most agencies agreed that 'gender mainstreaming' was essential, in reality few of the political issues of power relations between women and men had been addressed, either internally or within the NGOs' programmes. Few NGOs support local women's movements; many had no equal opportunities policies, and women were not represented at the top either in the directorate or on the board of trustees. Little money was spent on gender equity in relation to overall budgets, much of it on no more than 'add-on' women's projects, or on microfinance and income-generation projects for women; very small sums were given for work on women's rights (Wallace 1998).

Structural change in three major UK-based NGOs

A second example comes from a recent meeting of the UK Development Studies Association's (DSA) NGO study group in Oxford, which looked at the structural changes taking place in three major UK NGOs, and at how these structural and managerial changes relate to the different visions of the respective organisations. Interestingly, all these NGOs have a strong independent financial base but have accepted increasing amounts of institutional donor money over the years because of their desire to grow, to raise their profile, and be 'market leaders'. The pressures on these particular NGOs probably come less from the donors in a direct sense, and more from their high-level and constant discussion with donors about development issues and their wish to remain significant players on the development stage. They all have businessmen among their trustees, and these trustee boards are predominantly male. These three NGOs interpreted their understanding of how to best achieve development for poor people, and their own roles, very differently.

The meeting asked the following questions: As UK-based NGOs undergo major restructuring, what vision is shaping the organisation and its management? To what extent do the current structures and practices enable them to fulfil their vision of development and change? In answering these questions, there were close similarities between two NGOs, while the third was being driven by contrasting sets of values and commitments. This was a useful reminder that NGOs are not changing identically across the board. There are, nevertheless, growing convergences between many NGOs which in the past were starkly different (as the two sharing a similar analysis once were), and most are converging with a range of official donors and increasingly using a shared language. This language can now be read in government documents, public sector reports, private sector policies and plans, and NGO papers. It draws on concepts and approaches that were once see as the unique preserve of NGOs. Hence both government and the private sector now talk about the need to consult, for participation, and for being 'learning organisations'. These concepts are seen as easily compatible with the language of new public management (NPM), but experience throws doubt on this conclusion.

In relation to their restructuring processes, two of the leading British NGOs stressed the need for structures and management which would enable their organisations to retain and extend a high public profile, work efficiently, and increase their impact. Both manage their work from the UK; their new strategic frameworks are developed and set from the centre — with greater or lesser degrees of consultation and participation of staff, and almost none of Southern partner organisations. Management control and overarching decision-making remain at the centre, in a context of devolving certain functions to regional or country offices. The concepts and ideals driving the change processes included the need to develop a global programme and to have a recognisable and consistent 'global branding' (whatever the local context) so that people around the world recognise the product as belonging to a specific NGO. Other concerns included the need to cut running costs; a desire to develop the organisation and strengthen management, ostensibly for the purpose of accountability, but also implicitly for control; the felt imperative to work across boundaries and transcend country contexts or parameters (although the reasons for this regional rather than local approach remained unclear); and the need to redefine and clarify the strategic intent and character of the NGO and its programmes.

The presentations were couched in terms of the need for staff to understand and work within the agreed objectives for strategic change, and to implement comprehensive management functions at the regional levels in order to meet the centrally set targets; these would ensure that everyone's work would meet the needs of the entire organisation — including marketing, advocacy, and fund-raising as well as the development programme. Within the agreed overall strategic objectives, decisions can be made about allocating resources at the regional and even national level; however, these must retain the organisation's 'brand' style and organisational coherence, in order to ensure the development of a distinctive profile for marketing and fund-raising purposes. There was a fear of regions' and countries' autonomy and even secession if power and control were devolved. There was a marked anxiety about having diverse responses to seemingly similar problems across different countries, which was thought to fragment and weaken the organisation's power to lobby for change on the wider stage.

The aim is clearly to show that the NGO adds value, that it has impact, that it is making a difference, and especially that it has influence. This is being driven partly by the trustees and auditors and closely corresponds to the growing trend for 'accountability' in the public sector, leading to the development of targets, indicators, and impact assessment. It is also driven by the ambitions of many top NGO staff to be influential in the world of development policy and practice, to 'punch above their weight'. These NGOs are trying to integrate their development projects with advocacy work, to 'scale up' their impact, to make their mark; they are keen to play their role in shaping policies at the highest level. While there is tremendous pressure on development work to demonstrate quality and impact through developing and using measures of effectiveness, little credible work has been done on how effective advocacy work is, whether NGOs are being co-opted and compromised in their advocacy work (because of their relationships with powerful players such as governments or the World Bank), or to what extent a change in policy actually has a positive impact on the lives of the poor around the world.[4]

The speakers talked about 'selling the vision' to staff, about 'getting staff on board', about the problems faced if the values of some staff appeared to conflict with the current trajectories. They talked about the need for highly skilled staff to be recruited on 'competency-based frameworks'; some staff, however committed and experienced, may not find a place in the new order. One NGO had managed its change process in a way that gained staff support, while the other was grappling with a demoralised and discontented staff in some departments and country offices.

While these NGOs are clearly taking their concepts and approaches from the world of business, they appear to be out of step with much of the recent business literature which talks about the need to embrace values, to empower and value staff as the key organisational resource, and to find ways of managing them and structuring them that will allow them to perform to their best potential. The issues for successful business are no longer total control or total devolution but rather managing diversity, coordinating variety, releasing potential:

> both over-centralised (over-integrated) and over-decentralised (over-differentiated) companies perform to significant degrees. Differentiating and integrating need to be synergised or reconciled. The corporation with the best integrated diversity is the one which excels. (Trompenaars and Hampden-Turner 1998:171)

There is a great deal of interesting business literature that deals with issues of how to work cross-culturally, of how to motivate staff to perform well, and of how to encourage learning and positive change, which are not reflected in this dominant model of contemporary NGO practice. It appears safe to say that, when borrowing from the business sector, many NGOs are acting uncritically and also missing some of the most recent and potentially relevant ideas to be found there.

The third NGO had a different starting point, one which in the past might have been felt to be the more distinctive approach of a Northern NGO, although it also fits with some current thinking in the business literature. Its restructuring was driven by the need to see how it could best support the work on the ground in the South, how it could shift the balance of power from the North to the South and closer to the people, and how it could decentralise and hand over power to those most affected by development processes. The shape of the organisation and the role of the central office became very different when that vision and those values were used as the starting points. Certainly there are as yet unresolved problems about how to retain a coherent organisation within the growing diversity of country strategies and regional approaches which have been shaped to fit specific contexts, and how to prevent regional directors from creating their own unaccountable fiefdoms. Accounting for money raised in the UK under the existing governance laws of NGOs remains problematic, although field offices are developing new decentralised procedures to encourage local responsibility and accountability. The overall focus here is more on enabling staff to find management systems which enable them to do good work, rather than on supervision and control.

This NGO felt that its tentative steps towards shifting the balance of power and decision-making, even incrementally, towards to the staff and partners in the South, had unleashed energy and commitment among staff and partners in various countries and was leading to new ways of working and new relationships. They were seeking new ways to structure the NGO and management systems which could enable poor people to benefit more by involving them in developing the NGO's agenda. Different decisions had been taken in relation to management systems because delegation was prioritised over control, and local needs were chosen over global approaches; finding ways to learn from experience to promote better change processes in the future was seen to be important.

The three NGOs' restructuring processes differed according to the driving motivation behind the organisational change. It is hard to see how to reconcile the two approaches taken: one is driven by a concern to try to lessen unequal power relations with Southern partners, to shift the centre of gravity, if only a little, towards the South, to allow locally derived solutions to problems rather than adhering to 'coherent and consistent' responses. The other has as its driving force coherent organisation and management, the management of objectives that are set at the centre, and the need to show effectiveness to donors and supporters. This sits uneasily with concerns about locally derived solutions, the participation of partners and beneficiaries in planning, monitoring and evaluation, and listening to the voices of women as well as men.

Two ways of mainstreaming gender

The third set of examples is drawn from a conference on mainstreaming gender in policy and planning run by the Development Planning Unit at London University. Here again there appeared to be two discourses; some participants saw them as existing in healthy tension and not in conflict, while others experienced them as being in direct contradiction. On the one hand were several presentations from agencies, including UN and government agencies and NGOs, detailing their gender-mainstreaming policy and strategies. These presentations included discussions on their strategic planning processes, the ways they had found of persuading policy makers to take gender seriously and include it in planning, and the different processes of implementation. The latter included the appointment of focal points on gender around the organisation, or universal staff training in gender; plans included complex sets of consultations and training on gender and the need to include gender within project logframes. The concerns were to ensure the allocation of organisational resources, the monitoring of gender, the development of measurable indicators, and proving positive impact. The speakers were all familiar with the language of NPM, including the need to prove efficiency, value for money, meeting targets, benchmarking, and demonstrating impact.

These were all valid and interesting presentations, but at the heart of them was a perception that in the context of gender, unequal social relations can be changed through planning, management, and monitored implementation. None of these presentations addressed the personal issues facing women within their organisations, nor did they look at the extent to which women were promoted, or were able to perform well, within the dominant organisational culture. The personal was excluded in favour of the professional. There was little analysis of the political and cultural barriers to promoting gender equality in the development arena.

Another set of voices grew during the conference, raising questions about the politics of gender relations, the power struggle inherent in confronting gender inequalities, the fact that struggles can be won and later reversed. These people felt that progress towards adopting a gender-sensitive approach is neither linear nor straightforward, that the work is marked by struggle, that is it exhausting, and that the issues go far beyond the technical approaches of 'managing gender mainstreaming' within an organisation. While those involved in mainstreaming work themselves recognised many of these issues, and talked of the evaporation of gender between the policy commitment and project implementation, and of the problems of keeping gender on the agenda, their analysis was couched in management language, not the language of social relations, transformation, struggle. It was perhaps no coincidence that those who rejected the language and process of management for addressing gender equity were those who came either from countries where the politics of social change are well understood — South Africa, Philippines, India — or from the feminist tradition in the North, from women who have been involved in struggles around gender for many years, and from younger women who were involved in issues such as rape and violence against women, issues which are highly contentious and heavily politicised.

One result of using the language of strategy, change objectives, logframes, and impact assessment appears to be the depoliticisation, almost the sanitisation, of development. While there is reference to the context and the possible barriers to change, these are often minimised or (over)simplified in programme and project documents. Development is often seen as linear, as a rational and managed process, rather than one of engagement, struggle, facilitation, and of enabling people to take control of their environment. The language used may be more suited to the work of service delivery, although even in that context, issues of access, rights, or control require more dynamic analysis; it appears ill-suited to the work needed to address the causes and structures of poverty and inequality — yet these are the causes most development NGOs espouse.

Conclusions

There is diversity within the British NGO sector, but there are trends showing a growing similarity of language, procedures, and concepts of development with those of institutional donors and decision-makers within governments, the UN, and the World Bank. There are clearly tensions between the growing 'professionalisation' of development, the NGO adoption of 'new public management' practices and approaches, and the increased focus on upward accountability and communication on the one hand, and the commitments within these organisations to participation, downward accountability, local empowerment, and gender equity on the other. The managerial paradigm — which in the NGO sector still has the project as its primary focus and method of disbursing and accounting for funds — runs a real danger of being remote from the social, political, and economic realities and processes that take place at country and local levels, and of ignoring cultural patterns and local understandings.

The growing centralisation of some UK-based NGOs contrasts with the language of devolution, and is running behind the decentralisation agenda that is currently driving many governments. In many NGOs, power is becoming concentrated in small senior management teams and trustees who are shaping the vision and ways of working. Their targets for change are usually institutions and those in power in the North, and their advocacy work involves intense and direct interaction with people who hold power and influence in the North. Far less emphasis is placed on national or local processes and decision-makers, yet these also have a profound effect on keeping people in poverty. These NGOs implicitly subscribe to 'globalisation', seeing the world as increasingly shaped by forces that are external to individual countries. This focus on communicating with those with money and power in the North is not matched by efforts to hand over the work or to develop real partnerships that would enable NGOs and people in the South to tackle those causes of poverty which are embedded in their own societies.

The few British NGOs that are trying to decentralise power see the sources of inequity and poverty as being rooted in social and economic relations at the local as well as the global level, and believe that working at the micro level is important for changing unequal social relations for poor people. It is an approach which emphasises capacity-building, self-development, empowerment; and involves taking a back seat, becoming a supporter not a leader, starting to hand over power, and developing systems of accountability downward to beneficiaries rather than only upward to donors and trustees. However, these NGOs are hampered in shifting the balance of power by the rules governing financial accountability for UK-based charities, and also by the procedures they use which are largely dominated by a project focus and rational planning approaches, including logframes.

There is an argument which says that these very different approaches are not in opposition but can sit together and work in synergy; so there is talk of bottom-up and top-down strategic planning, of participatory logframes, of participatory impact assessment sitting alongside milestones, indicators, and targets set by NGOs. However, the evidence is lacking that the managerial and technical approach to development and the demands of addressing long-term issues of social change can combine and work together. Evidence from a 1999 conference on NGOs went the other way: many writers and NGOs based in the North placed great emphasis on global processes, the increasing homogenisation of the world, and the need for clear responses which are identifiable 'brands' etc.[5] This caused a major outcry from many participants, often Southern-based, who stressed the diversity, differences, and complexities according to geography, history, gender, race, and religion that mark processes of subordination. There are no 'one size fits all' solutions. If change is to be sustainable it has to be location-specific, owned by the people, rooted in their experiences and understandings, and meeting their criteria. The gulf between these two broadly accepted development paradigms was wide at the conference, and remains wide in practice.

Notes

1 This emerges from research done with 17 UK-based NGOs presented in Wallace et al. (1997).

2 An argument well put by Cleaver (1998).

3 The ODA evaluation of NGO projects undertaken by Surr (1995), and impact assessment work carried out by ACORD, highlight these issues very clearly.

4 Jenny Chapman (1999) shows that for advocacy work to be effectively translated into changes on the ground requires work at all levels, and work at the local level with the people who are intended to benefit, are essential for turning policy into development practice.

5 'NGOs in a Global Future' conference convened at the University of Birmingham, 10–13 January 1999.

Bibliography

Acharya, J. (1999) 'State, Civil Society and NGOs', paper presented at the conference 'NGOs in a Global Future', Birmingham, 10–13 January 1999.

Chambers, R. (1986) *Normal Professionalism, New Paradigms and Development*, IDS Discussion Paper 227, Brighton: IDS.

Chapman, J. (1999) 'Effective NGO Campaigning', briefing paper, London: New Economics Foundation.

Cleaver, F. (1998) 'Paradoxes of Participation: Critique of Participatory Approaches to Development', paper presented at conference on participation, Bradford University.

Epstein, S., J. Gruber, G. Mytton (1991) *A Training Manual for Development Market Research (DMR) Investigators*, London: BBC World Service and Hassocks: Innovative Development Research.

Long, N. and A. Long (1992) *Battlefields of Knowledge: The Interlocking of Theory and Practice in Social Research and Development*, London: Routledge.

ODA (1992) 'Report of Working Group on ODA/NGO Collaboration: The Hodges Report', London: ODA.

Eurostep, Actionaid and ICVA (1998) *The Reality of Aid: An Independent Review of Development Cooperation*, London: Earthscan.

Scoones, I. et al. (1993) *Rural People's Knowledge: Agricultural Research and Extension Practice*, London: IIED.

M. Surr (1995) 'Evaluations of NGOs Development Projects: Synthesis Report', Evaluation report EV 554, London: ODA.

Trompenaars, F. and C. Hampden-Turner (1998) *Riding the Waves of Culture: Understanding Cultural Diversity in Business*, London: Nicholas Brealey.

Wallace, Tina (1998) 'Institutionalising gender in UK NGOs', *Development in Practice* 8(2): 159–172.

Wallace, Tina, S. Crowther and A. Shepherd (1997) *Standardising Development: Influences on UK NGOs' Policies and Procedures*, Oxford: Worldview Press.

■ **Tina Wallace** *is a Senior Research Fellow in the Business School of Oxford Brookes University and a visiting lecturer at CENDEP. She has also taught and carried out research for many years at the universities of Birmingham (UK), Ahmadu Bello (Nigeria), and Makerere (Uganda). Her NGO experience spans from addressing refugee issues at World University Service (WUS) and race relations work in the UK, to running first the gender and development and then the planning and evaluation departments at Oxfam GB. Her major publications include Changing Perceptions (1994), an edited volume on gender and development, and Standardising Development (1997), on which this essay is largely based.*

What makes good development management?

Alan Thomas

Introduction

In a previous paper (Thomas 1996) I asked 'What is development management?' I was looking for a counter to 'the idea that management principles are universal, so that, whatever the context, management can be taught using the same learning materials'. Arguing that 'the nature of the task determines the appropriate version of management', I found that the answer to my question depended on what view I took of development. If development is viewed as a long-term historical change process, then development management may be taken to mean the management of any type of task in the context of development. If, however, development is seen in terms of deliberate efforts at progress, then development management would be characterised as:

> the management of deliberate efforts at progress on the part of one of a number of agencies, the management of intervention in the process of social change in the context of conflicts of goals, values and interests. (Thomas 1996:106)

Thus the two approaches to the definition of development lead to different ideas of what is meant by development management, which might be summarised as *management in development* and *management of development*. I went on to list a number of conceptual and skill areas which would be important particularly for management of development, which, I argued, emphasised 'areas and approaches less well covered in traditional subjects like development administration', so that 'there is indeed a substantially new field here' (ibid.:109).

I have since begun to think that the arguments I put forward did not go far enough, on at least two counts. First, I may have demonstrated how to determine when it is development management rather than simply management which is taking place. However, this may not be enough for us to recognise when development management is being done *well*. Surely if development management really is distinctive, then *good* development management will be distinctively different from simply good management in a development context? It now appears to me that my 1996 paper was limited in that it did not address this question directly. In that paper I attempted to unite the 'command and control' and 'empowerment and enabling' views of management into 'the simple idea of management as *getting the work done by the best means available*' (ibid.:100). This in turn led me to define development management in terms of what is needed to carry out development tasks successfully. Since I engaged no further in discussion of *how* best to undertake development management, the implication was that good development management, like good management in general, simply means succeeding in the task at hand.

Second, I have become increasingly uncertain whether I really did succeed in making the case that there is something distinctive about development management. Let me emphasise that I have not changed my mind on this point. With others, I have spent the intervening period devising learning materials on development management aimed at helping students develop skills and competences in the areas listed. I have met many students, who are usually simultaneously practising development managers, both from Europe and from Southern Africa, who have found these materials both intellectually stimulating and of practical use. There is indeed something distinctive and substantially new here. Again, the limitation of my previous approach seems to lie in my excessive reliance on defining development management in relation to a view of development in terms of specific development interventions as a distinctive type of task. My uncertainty is over whether it is really the case that what is distinctive about development management derives entirely from the nature of the task.

In the 1996 paper I mentioned a somewhat different approach to defining development management in one or two places without really carrying the argument through. In this different approach, *development management* would signify a particular *style* of management rather than merely management of a particular kind of *activity*. I have come to think that this corresponds to a third approach to defining development itself, and the view of development management entailed is at least as important as the other two. In this third approach, development is neither historical process nor a set of deliberate intervention tasks but a particular kind of *orientation*, an orientation towards progressive change. Ideally, this development orientation guides *all* the activities of development organisations, not just specific development interventions. This approach has several things in common with the idea of development management as the management of interventions, notably the importance of value-based conflicts. Whether one thinks of managing specific interventions aimed at positive change or an orientation towards progressive change which guides all the management of all activities, what is thought positive or progressive will clearly vary according to subjective beliefs, ideology, and interests, and thus give rise to such conflicts. However, the new approach has the potential to make development management more broadly applicable, and thus seems worth pursuing at least a little further.

Thus we can define development management as management undertaken with a development orientation, rather than management in the context of the development process or the management of development interventions or tasks. I will dub this third view of what is meant by development management: management *for* development, to add the previous two: management *in* development and management *of* development. This extends the matrix produced in my 1996 paper, as follows:

Development as:	*Development management* as:
1 historical change process	management *in* development (management in the context of the development process)
2 deliberate efforts at progress	management *of* development (management of development efforts)
3 orientation towards progressive change	management *for* development (management with a development orientation).

I am not suggesting that my previous emphasis on the management of development tasks was wrong. However, I do suggest that a task-oriented approach has limitations. It does not help us to recognise the special characteristics of good development management, and it does not really provide the best counter to the notion that management principles are universal. I would argue that a combination of all three approaches is needed. To this end I intend to develop further the idea of development management as a style of management, of 'management for development'.

Limitations of task orientation

Previously, I had argued that 'there is something specific about those tasks which may be called development tasks' (ibid.:101). I identified four distinctive features of development tasks (ibid.:106):

- external social goals rather than internal organisational ones;
- influencing or intervening in social processes rather than using resources to meet goals directly;
- goals subject to value-based conflicts; and
- the importance of process.

In effect, these 'features' are aspects of the context in which development interventions are undertaken. In particular, they are mostly about the goals of development interventions. In practice, all kinds of tasks may be required to meet development goals. There are certain kinds of activities which are likely to be central to development management defined in this way, and which correspond to some of the conceptual and skill areas identified in the 1996 paper. These include, for example, negotiation and brokering, policy analysis, and the appraisal of the likely impact of proposed interventions. However, when broken down into detailed tasks these activities cannot be said to be specific to development management; similar tasks occur in any management context, although the goals may be quite different.

A task-oriented approach to development is reflected in the ubiquity of logical framework planning and its variants, in which development interventions are planned on the basis of devising a logic by which tasks or activities will lead to desired outcomes and thence to the achievement of set goals. The tasks tend to be evaluated by indicators which show simply how fully they have been carried out, while the achievement of outcomes and goals is evaluated by measuring pre-determined indicators specific to them; and if tasks are completed without achieving the goals this is attributed to deficiencies in the assumptions made about the logical connections between them (Gasper 1996).

Thus, with this approach, once it is decided what activities are needed, it is then simply a matter of getting the tasks completed. The management required appears not to differ from that required to get similar tasks done in any context. However, there are several limitations to an entirely task-oriented approach. First, the concentration on defining what is required, and then getting the tasks completed by the best means available, appears to downplay the possibility that the *way* a task is performed may affect the outcomes and hence the achievement of goals. For example, a micro-finance institution may have fieldworkers whose tasks include regularly collecting repayments from women's groups. Completing this task could be done quite mechanically, with the fieldworkers themselves doing most of the calculations and organising the required meetings. If, however, the collection is done via a mechanism that involves active participation by the women themselves, it may be more likely both that the women gain confidence and self-esteem and that repayment levels remain high, even with less frequent contact from the fieldworkers, thus contributing better to long-term goals of empowering women and financial sustainability.

Of course, management theorists have already been debating limitations to task orientation in conventional management, so that this in itself is not distinctive to a discussion of development management. Indeed, in the 1996 paper I referred to the discussion by Paton (1991) of task orientation (which he calls the 'instrumental' aspect of management) and noted (ibid.:101) that:

> this *instrumental* aspect of management needs to be complemented with a realisation of the importance of the expressive aspect of management, in which values and ideas are promoted as part of how an organisation (and its members and managers) defines itself (and themselves), not just as one way of getting things done.
> (Emphasis in original)

This points to a second limitation of task orientation. Not only does it downplay the importance of how a task is done as opposed to just getting it done anyhow; it ignores the importance of acting consistently with the organisation's own values in order to reinforce those values and thus the organisation's culture and sense of its own worth. For example, an international NGO may undertake a campaign to raise funds from the public in the Northern country where it is based. Finding images to use on posters and television for its campaign may be undertaken as a task with just the images themselves and their effectiveness in mind. However, for many such NGOs it is important that images are chosen which show respect for those depicted in them and are used with their consent, since mutual respect and self-determination are among the development values adopted by the NGOs, and it is seen as crucial to their integrity as development agencies that they act consistently with their values.

There is a third limitation, which has similarities with the first two but goes beyond them. It relates to the two aspects of public action (Wuyts et al. 1992; Thomas 1997). Public action means not only acting to meet public need but promoting values which define what is regarded as public need and how it is regarded. Development management surely also includes promoting values, in particular what is to be regarded as development, in this way. Again, conventional management also includes promoting values. However, while business management promotes the values of business, I would argue that good development management should promote the values of development.

One might try to reconcile this with a task orientation by arguing that political activity devoted to contesting the definition of public need in a particular arena is also a kind of task to be undertaken, noting that 'the importance of process' is one of the features of development tasks. However, such 'tasks' are so contingent on the activities of others and their interrelationships that it becomes virtually impossible to analyse them in terms of whether they have been fully completed and evaluating their outcomes by pre-set indicators. For example, there are many areas of public concern now accepted as such largely because of the efforts of NGOs and other development organisations, including the rights of indigenous communities, the need to combat environmental degradation, child rights, and many others. These are not accepted because of specific interventions undertaken by the organisations concerned to make them so, but because they consistently built those concerns into the way they reacted to events and took opportunities, over a long period. Development management must include managing values within and between organisations so that they are promoted over a period in cases like this.

Management for development

Thus, while accepting that development management often means managing deliberately designed development interventions and hence ensuring that the required tasks are done 'by the best means available', I have also noted some important limitations of relying entirely on a task-oriented approach.

Management *for* (rather than *of*) development implies a style of management in which any and every activity is undertaken in such a way as to enhance development. It applies both to activities which are designed as a deliberate development intervention and to other activities. Thus, for planned development tasks, it implies considering the way they are done, not just getting immediate results. The 1996 paper mentioned empowerment as a value which might be expressed in the choice of how activities are carried out: 'in some circumstances, to empower members of an organisation or community is more important in its own right than getting any particular job done' (ibid.:103–4). If empowerment is taken as part of a particular value-based definition of development, then managing in such a way as to empower would be an example of managing for development. In the example of the micro-finance institution given above, this could be a justification for using participatory mechanisms, even if there were no benefit in terms of improved repayment rates.

There are also plenty of tasks undertaken by a development organisation which are not specifically part of a development intervention. On the one hand there are tasks of organisational maintenance and day-to-day administration. On the other, there are occasions when the organisation's developmental values are called more clearly into question by unexpected changes in circumstances or by the actions of other organisations, so that a reaction is required which entails new tasks. Once again it is the way in which an organisation reacts to such opportunities and unforeseen challenges that demonstrates the extent to which its management can be termed *development* management in the sense of management which is always *for* development.

An extreme example here is furnished by a development organisation in a complex emergency. Providing relief in a quickly changing situation exacerbated by violent conflict makes it almost impossible to work for development when there is so much to be done in terms of response to immediate need. Nevertheless, it may be possible to maintain values such as mutual respect and a belief in people's right to and potential for self-determination, and to take what opportunities exist to put these values into practice. A less extreme example would be how an organisation undertaking an awareness-raising campaign responds to an unexpected opportunity for publicity. Once again, management *for* development would ensure the same care was taken about values of mutual respect and so on as with carefully planned elements of the campaign.

It may help here to conceive development at several levels, with a degree of linkage between them. First there is the level of individual human development, often thought of rather mechanistically in terms of training, but also including notions such as empowerment which can apply both to staff and to 'clients', or members of communities with which an organisation is working. There is organisational development, which incorporates the more specific discipline of organisation development (OD) with its emphasis on learning, reflection, and processes of intervention and change at the group and organisation levels (see, for example, Schein 1969; Argyris 1971). Then institutional development is distinguished from organisational development by involving directed change which takes place outside any one organisation (Cooke 1997; Fowler 1997), particularly when progressive change in institutions in the sense of norms and values accompanies change in the organisations and organisational forms which carry those norms and values. Finally, development at the societal level may be thought of as resulting from the combination or accumulation of changes or development at lower levels. In proposing that development management is a style of management which embodies particular development values, one is suggesting that the values which would underpin one's vision or model of a well developed society should also underpin one's actions at the lower levels. Thus, for example, an ideal developed society may be seen as one where every human being's potential can be fulfilled, as in the suggestion by Dudley Seers that 'the realisation of the potential of human personality ... is a universally acceptable aim', in his celebrated article 'The meaning of development' (Seers 1979, first published 1969). The implication is that development management means managing, as far as possible, in such a way as to enhance the potential of those one is working with directly, and developing organisations that carry similar values, even if this is not the most straightforward way of getting a particular job done.

When development management is thought of as management *of* development, that formulation contrasts it, implicitly at least, with the management of other types of activity (the production of goods and services, organisational maintenance, administration, public relations, etc.). However, if we conceive it as management *for* development, the implicit contrast is with management for other purposes, notably with management for profit. And just as the idea of profit as a 'bottom line' can guide any and all activities and regulate the linkages between levels, so too the idea of development as an ultimate good can potentially be applied at all levels and be used to relate good practice at one level to the others. Thus, management for profit implies linking the way people are managed in terms of 'human resource' to managing organisations in such a way as to generate maximum dividends to owners, and eventually to a view of society in which output and added value are the ultimate measures of good. Similarly, management for development relates managing people to bring out their potential, to organisational development aimed at the regeneration of positive values and to a view of society in which development values such as maximising the potential of all individuals and groups are upheld in their own right.

One may ask if management for profit and management for development can be combined. I would answer that this may be possible in some circumstances. Indeed, a development orientation may be a positive benefit to business organisations, in terms of developing both their staff on the one hand and their relations with governments and development organisations on the other. However, there will also be circumstances where the two will clash, and where the way management is carried out will depend critically on what values are given precedence.

The notion of development management as management which aims at development consistently at all levels does not do away with disagreement over the meaning of development. The values to be incorporated into development may differ markedly between development organisations even when they are involved in similar areas of development work. For example, some organisations supporting micro-finance initiatives do so by promoting western-style entrepreneurialism, while others specifically promote women's empowerment. In both cases, the organisations concerned might reasonably claim to be performing what I have called 'management for development' by building the values of, on the one hand, entrepreneurialism, and, on the other, empowerment, into the way they conduct their activities at all levels.

While there is not likely to be agreement in detail on one particular version of development and its underlying values, there may be some general principles in common between them. One is the notion of *progressive* change, which I take to mean not just change towards one's particular ideal but change which builds on previous development and in turn lays the basis for further development. Capacity building and organisational learning are both very important concepts within this type of view of development. Development management, then, is not just a question of getting the task at hand completed by the best means available. It also means simultaneously building the capacity to undertake future tasks, and learning how to be able to cope with what at present are unspecified tasks.

A normative definition of development management

I can now come back to the new question which I posed in the title of this paper: what makes *good* development management? Thinking in terms of management *for* development allows us to evaluate development management in its own terms. In other words, the more it lives up to the essential idea of being *for* development, the better it is.

This is tantamount to a normative definition of development management. Development management *should* be management *for* development, that is, oriented towards development, and, one might argue, it only really deserves the name if it lives up to this ideal.

By contrast, think how we have to evaluate management *of* development. This implies assessing how well development tasks have been done. On the whole, there are two possibilities. One is that the criteria are internally determined, in the sense that the development intervention was designed with its own objectives and pre-stated means of verification, as in the classic use of logical framework planning. The drawback here is that apparently simply being less ambitious makes it easier for development management to be done well. Alternatively, the criteria by which the achievement of development tasks are judged may be externally determined, as when standards of efficiency are applied which might apply to the same or similar tasks in any management context. For example, fundraising, or the delivery of relief services, may be evaluated by criteria such as the amount of money raised per unit of resource spent, and the cost of supplying a defined service in a particular location. Such criteria may appear to give an objective basis for assessing how well development management is carried out by one development organisation compared to another, but the values underlying the criteria are not specific to development and could apply just as well to fundraising for an élitist university or to relief supplied by the military. However, such an approach certainly has its appeal, as witness the spread of contracting for the delivery of services in the development field, which clearly implies that the criteria for the satisfactory completion of the development tasks concerned can be defined even before the organisation which takes on the tasks becomes involved.

Using the normative definition of development management, as management which should be oriented towards development, certainly ensures that good development management is not the same as just good management. But doing this has its own limitations and dangers. One limitation is that development management in this sense is not always possible. For example, supplying food or rebuilding infrastructure after a natural disaster, or reacting to adverse publicity or to a proposal which you believe will cause environmental damage, are cases where an immediate focus on a task may be called for which does not allow for specific promotion of a development orientation. I argued above that in a similar case, such as a development organisation working in a complex emergency, it may, nevertheless, be possible to bring developmental principles to bear on the work being done, so that what I have called 'management for development' may still be attempted. However, although this is an ideal, it seems necessary to admit that it cannot always be realised in such situations.

As for dangers, one is similar to the problem just mentioned, with internally determined criteria for assessing development management, when thought of in terms of tasks to be completed. What count as being oriented towards development is relative to how the particular organisation conceives development, and a weak definition may make it relatively easy to appear to meet the criteria. Perhaps more importantly, there is the danger of a completely relativistic approach, where development management in a particular organisation is good if it succeeds in promoting the developmental values of the organisation concerned, even if those values are contested or even abhorrent to others.

There is a clear need for some external validation of what is done in the name of development management. At the same time, unlike the concept of profit where arguments are mostly about how to measure it or how it is created rather than about what it is, there is no universal definition of development and the debates about it readily take the form of value-based conflicts. As noted above, development management includes managing activities aimed at contesting the definition of development and at promoting particular values. In my case, I would promote the ideal of enabling all human beings to realise their full capacity, though even with such a broad definition there is still plenty of room for disagreement about priorities and about ways and means of achieving even part of the ideal. Nevertheless, as a version of 'people-centred' development (Korten 1990), this fits with my suggestion above that development management should be thought of in terms of positive linkages between development, capacity building, and learning at individual, organisational, institutional, and societal levels.

Finally, no discussion of development management is complete without some mention of power. The 1996 paper differentiated between development management carried out on behalf of those in positions of power and on behalf of the relatively powerless. In the former case either the 'command and control' or the 'empowerment and enabling' mode of management might be employed, depending on the nature of the task, whereas in the latter case 'empowerment and enabling' was preferred because of the particular need of the powerless for empowerment before they could take part in development. This paper has argued for a view of development management as management *for* development, where development links personal development of individuals with a broader view, which includes the ideal of enabling all human beings to realise their full capacity. Thus, I have effectively been arguing that the empowerment and enabling mode of management is particularly appropriate for development management, irrespective of the particular task at hand, something which the 1996 paper put forward only for the special case of development management on behalf of the powerless.

Does this imply that the normative definition of development management gives precedence to development management on behalf of the powerless? I stop short of giving an unequivocal 'yes' to this question. On the one hand, those with power are not the most likely to support the equitable, people-centred view of development I put forward above. Thus, managing development interventions which they might promote might not be managing for development in the sense put forward in this paper. On the other hand, no management can achieve much, however strong its orientation towards development, without some access to power to carry out at least some activities.

In conclusion, it seems most useful to consider development management as including both the management of the specific tasks involved in development interventions (management *of* development) and the normative idea of management oriented towards development ideals (management *for* development), as well as the more straightforward notion of management in a development context (management *in* development). The clearest examples of *good* development management will be those which use the enabling and empowerment mode of management to achieve development goals for the relatively powerless. However, the majority of cases will be more ambiguous, with value-based conflicts, contestation over the definition of development itself, and power struggles. Development management will often remain an ideal rather than a description of what takes place.

References

Argyris, C. (1971) *Management and Organization Development*, New York: McGraw-Hill.

Cooke, B. (1997) 'The theory of ID and OD: a comparative review for practitioners', mimeo, Manchester: IDPM, University of Manchester.

Fowler, A. (1997) *Striking a Balance: A Guide to Enhancing the Effectiveness of Non-Governmental Organisations in International Development*, London: Earthscan.

Gasper, D. (1996) 'Analysing Policy Arguments' in R. Apthorpe and D. Gasper (eds.) *Arguing Development Policy: Frames and Discourses*, London: Frank Cass in association with EADI.

Korten, D. (1990) *Getting to the 21st Century: Voluntary Action and the Global Agenda*, West Hartford, CT: Kumarian Press.

Paton, R. (1991) *Managing with a Purpose* (Book 1 of OU course B789 *Managing Voluntary and Nonprofit Enterprises*), Milton Keynes: The Open University.

Schein, E. (1969) *Process Consultation: Its Role in Organization Development*, Reading, Mass.: Addison-Wesley.

Seers, D. (1969; 1979) 'The meaning of development' in D. Lehmann (ed.) *Development Theory: Four Critical Studies*, London: Frank Cass.

Thomas, A. (1996) 'What is development management?', *Journal of International Development* (8)1: 95–110.

Thomas, A. (1997) 'The role of NGOs in development management: a public action approach', Paper for International Conference on Public Sector Management for the Next Century, University of Manchester.

Wuyts, M., M. Mackintosh and T. Hewitt (1992) *Development Policy and Public Action*, Oxford: OUP.

Tools for project development within a public action framework

David Wield

Introduction[1]

The growing professionalisation of development management has grown out of, and involved, acceptance of new public management approaches. These include goal-setting — increasingly quantitative — with outcomes overtly described and evidently achievable, in the name of efficiency and financial and/or managerial accountability. In terms of project design and implementation, this suggests the use of technical tools such as Logical Framework Approach (LFA). LFA tools were originally developed and used as design tools for 'blueprint' approaches, and as such they have been highly constraining, quantitative, and boundaried. More recently, as many development agencies, particularly NGOs and aid agencies, have addressed the pressure to 'professionalise', they have adopted such tools. However, these agencies have at best exhibited an ambivalent attitude to their use and their applicability to the complex and uncertain realities of development practice.

The paper looks at ways of thinking about the LFA in various types of application. There have been many well-publicised attempts to use the LFA in process-based ways.[2] However, with the countervailing pressures for project management to become more managerialist, these interesting efforts can be threatened. We consider the process-based use of the LFA and argue that this should not be lost in the drive for professionalisation, and that such application is useful to practitioners in complex, value-driven, and qualitative contexts. We also consider the limitations of the LFA from a public action perspective, where public means a wide range of institutions — not only government institutions but aid agencies, NGOs, community groups, collectives, and political movements.

Development management and tools

Development management is a process that includes the social definition of needs and it is embedded in public action. Development management is more than policy implementation in a rigid sense. Rather, it involves activities that steer and facilitate intervention towards the identification and meeting of human need. This style of management 'differs from the simple idea of getting the work done by the best means available' (Thomas 1996: 101). It means steering effort outside the particular organisation for which one works. Since there are never enough means available, it involves balancing resources, often from many sources, all with different needs and priorities. Agencies, institutions, groups, and individuals may never completely agree on what has to be done. Ideas such as influence, steer, facilitate, and sustainability point to the overriding importance of process and continuity. And development management involves learning lessons and feeding them back into practice.

Thus, among development agencies, there is fundamental doubt and considerable cynicism about whether LFA tools can possibly be relevant to process-based management, given that they appear to promote the very project-based styles, with a tendency to technocracy and non-participation, that many agencies believe weaken the overall effectiveness of development interventions.

Development projects and development processes

Development management takes place in a variety of development contexts and institutions, always involving a range of agencies and individuals (i.e. a diversity of stakeholders). There is a tension between the need to focus and clarify development interventions in manageable ways, often artificially simplified, and an understanding of the limitations set by such a narrow focus on boundaried projects, interventions, and activities. Interventions take place in a complex, highly populated landscape of human activity.

One starting point for such initiatives in development is the project. At a simple level, this allows a complex series of processes to be broken down into an organised set of tasks which follow a decision to implement a project. There are great variations in what constitutes 'a project', including:

- the installation of a single new piece of equipment;
- the introduction of a single new job category;
- an agency expanding its activities to another location;
- the development of a whole new sector of activity.

Because of this diversity of scales it is important to develop approaches that, in effect, step back from a project and see it in its full context as part of a longer and broader process. The importance of this is illustrated by a comment made by one practitioner/academic:

> Moving from ideas to action (at whatever level) is one of the trickiest issues [in development]. It requires identifying what actually needs to be done once one has the bright idea, who will do it, and how they will be accountable. Failure to spell this out can be intentional or unintended. For example, government departments often come up with grand plans without concretely working out the institutional base, the impact on incentives, and the power relations that will result. Donor agencies and governments alike, especially recently, talk to stakeholders at great length but the who's and how's are unspecified and vague. NGOs also waste a lot of time and effort in this way. Result — all the lovely discussion and plans for participation come to naught.

Policy and action: projects and environments

How then, in a process-based way, can we situate the intervention (project or whatever) within the 'highly populated landscape'? Considering the relationship between policy and action, and between projects and the wider activities of operations and institutions (i.e. its environment), another practitioner said:

> There is a tension between the need to focus projects and interventions and the need to appreciate the complexity of the environment of the new activity. It is obvious that at any one moment the focus may be entirely at project level with no sense of its context. Conversely, those responsible for implementation, may feel they have little control over decisions outside their project.

The following quotations further illustrate the tension:

> For example, in a very unstable environment the managers will probably need to adjust project design more often, and there will be a different planning and management approach than in a more stable

environment. Account has to be taken of the breadth of impact of a particular project — and the full range of factors that may affect its course — and of the long term character of change. There are major differences between, and concern with, development processes more broadly — which are likely, at the very least, to involve several projects over a significant period of time, and most likely a complex interaction between different individual projects. (NGO employee)

Most practitioners/project managers are focused on, or perhaps even blinkered by, the project level. Many are so busy managing 'their' project that the wider picture is lost. It is also perhaps a reflection on the fact that most project managers feel little responsibility for, or influence over, events outside their project. In reality, there is often a lack of influence. (Aid agency employee)

Projects: Are they discrete, technical initiatives to achieve defined objectives, or should they be viewed as socio-political processes in which competing and collaborating actors seek to achieve stated and unstated objectives? (Academic)

Policy as blueprint or as process

This tension is always there, a reflection of the conflicting images of what projects are.[3] The tension can be described, perhaps simplistically, as that between blueprint and process. The term blueprint comes from engineering images of detailed drawings showing exact product specifications, suggesting 'that projects need to be systematically and carefully planned in advance, and implemented according to the defined plan' (Cusworth and Franks 1993: 8) — perfect imagery for both state-led and scientific management approaches, but not for the idea of multi-agent, complex, process-based approaches. The process approach, on the other hand, 'allows for flexibility in project design: although wider objectives must be defined from the outset, project inputs and outputs ... are not set in stone .. and lessons are learnt from past experience' (ODA 1995: 104). It seems clear that the polarised either/or approach to blueprint versus process is not the way ahead. Rather, it may be 'a question of which form of blueprint or process, in which circumstances, and even of what means may be used to integrate blueprint and process approaches' (Hulme 1995: 230).

So, account must be taken of the breadth of impact of a project, of the relationship between projects and ongoing activities, and of the development processes of which it is part. Projects take place in a sea of linked activities that involve multiple agencies 'an aggregate of organisations which are responsible for a definable area of institutional life' (Anheier 1990), where 'the objectives of individual organisations involved in a project do not necessarily add up to, and coincide with, those of the project or the target group', and where issues are 'complex, ill-structured, interdependent and multi-sectoral'.

In practice, many managers and practitioners prefer working with relatively tight routines and blueprints, but they also recognise that these, in fact, exist within processes.

Influencing environments

Such a recognition implies that a simple boundary between the project and its environment is not that helpful. Smith et al. (1981) developed a framework that recognised the environment as more complex than 'all the elements outside a project, or outside an organisation, that cannot be controlled'.[4] They use a three-level model of the environment. In the centre is the *controlled* environment, then what they call the *influenceable* environment — those activities and institutions which can be influenced by the project or organisation but not directly controlled. Outside this is the *appreciated* environment, which includes activities and institutions that 'can neither be controlled nor influenced by its management', even though their actions affect project or organisation performance.

Such an approach overlaps with that of Vickers' appreciative system (1965; 1970). This is a process whose products conditions the process itself, 'but the system is not operationally closed ... the appreciative system is always open to new inputs' (Checkland 1994: 83–84). Research in the evolutionary theory of technological change strongly suggests that during periods of rapid innovation, the boundaries between businesses (or firms) and their environments are in constant flux (Amendola and Bruno 1990).

Projects and ongoing public action

There is, then, a tension between the need to focus projects and actions and the need to appreciate the complex environments in which interventions take place. Many development practitioners think of their work as project-based and development as a series of projects and programmes — a vast interlocking series of them. In many parts of the world, projects are an increasing element of development activity. Not only has there been a major decrease in state activity, but much of that activity has been turned into projects — a process of projectisation. In many countries and sectors, there has been a major decline in routine, ongoing activity and a corresponding increase in support for NGO activity (sub-contracted with short time-frames). Aid agency funding, much of it on a project or programme basis, is increasingly important. Many large loans and grants have thus been projectised. But, despite the recurrent debates on the disadvantages of projects as instruments of development intervention, no effective alternatives have emerged, and projects are likely to remain a basic means for translating policies into action programmes (Cernea 1991).

Nevertheless, many development practitioners work in organisations that facilitate and coordinate many different actions simultaneously, rather than having prime responsibility for one project. For example, at a local level, someone in charge of primary health may be responsible for pulling together many projects (that in turn link to many different agencies) into some sort of coherent whole. Their work includes balancing the need for overall coherence against the need to keep up the enthusiasm of project workers. Or rather, the need to combine coherence of action with punctuated intervention. One serious problem in many locations is that the work of project intervention is separated from that of building or preserving coherence — that is, different people do the different tasks, with one type of work (the project work with donor funds) valued more highly than the routine, ongoing activities which try to continue in the face of diminishing budgets. Such balancing involves serious tensions between many different organisations, all with different cultures, resources, and agendas.

Understanding the LFA in a public action perspective

We have argued so far that development issues are generally complex and messy. They usually involve problems that are strongly interconnected, and multiple agencies. They cannot easily be reduced into neat individual problems that can be resolved within one organisation — they require those involved to go outside their organisation, to where they may have little leverage to implement change. Untangling the different casual processes is not possible solely by following a set of routines.

If tools are used as process-tools, the extent to which they can assist in steering and forging coherence of action in situations with multiple actors and many interests can be assessed. So it is with the LFA.

Framework planning is a tool used to improve clarity and focus in the planning of interventions. The tool, which has many different forms, was established as a structure to assist project planning, but has grown into an approach that can aid the process of consensus-building in project design and management. The LFA has become ubiquitous in the development business, defying those who prophesied its demise as simplistic and just another form of technocratic management by objectives. The basic idea of the tool is to provide a structure to allow those involved in projects to specify the different components of activities, and carefully and causally relate the means to the ends. The framework aims to aid logical thinking about the ways in which a project or other intervention may be structured and organised. It also allows the different groups associated with the intervention to participate in discussions and decisions about it and its underlying assumptions, and to continue involvement as the project develops and changes. Coleman argues that the approach 'is an "aid to thinking" rather than a set of procedures' (1987: 259). Framework planning can be used in a mechanistic manner. There are anecdotes of framework plans being developed in hotel bedrooms by visiting consultants after a day or two's discussion with those most affected by the intervention, or even just with those in favour of it. One practitioner said: 'Consultants are not given much time but expected to come up with a project document and log-frame (framework plan) as part of their terms of reference. This means that a log-frame is sometimes constructed by the consultant alone, which is not intended. If handled badly it can set back an intervention severely'.

There is no shortage of analyses of the LFA in terms of its efficacy as a blueprint and/or process tool. The ambivalence and cynicism mentioned earlier has been encapsulated in a range of good publications.(5) We will not rehearse these arguments here. Rather, the question we consider is how the change from state-led to multiple-actor involvement in development can be reflected in, and inform, micro-level project design (see Table 1).

State-led development implies that a single actor is able to implement or at least to control implementation. The 'public action' perspective assumes, on the other hand, plurality of financing, and multiple actors with plurality of interest. With state action it is easy to imagine that there is a *public interest*, which the state's role is to reflect and act on. This implies a concept of planning with a single actor doing things. The implications for project design and planning are that techniques are required for identifying, prioritising, and evaluating such action. The big problem for development and project planning was how to plan development more effectively so that the state could better achieve those tasks that were its responsibility. The development planning and project appraisal literature from the 1950s onwards shows a gradual improvement in these techniques. The 1970s and 1980s brought a massive growth in programming tools and social and qualitative techniques, so that:

> ...there is now a much wider range of techniques and procedures available for policy analysis. Models can more easily be designed to match the constraints and policy objectives of individual countries, rather than using a standard framework. Also, the shift towards simulating market outcomes means that policy analysis has shifted away from the setting of targets to the comparison of instruments and programmes (Chowdhury and Kirkpatrick 1994: 4).

This categorisation of public interest is simplified of course, but if we consider it from the perspective of the new policy agenda (NPA) it becomes much more complex. The public interest is contested by different interests and different stakeholders. The idea that there can be coherence of planning cannot be assumed. Who should act in the so-called public interest? NGOs? Donors? Local government? The state? If they all act independently in the same sector, how does it all add up? Under these conditions, the old concept of project appraisal is insufficient. Techniques can be used for assessing individual projects, but, overall, how does it pull together? In the 'old', blueprint approach to planning, an unchallenged single actor can plan by allocating resources it controls. Now, with concepts like 'planning as steering' and 'influencing behaviours to get agreed outcomes', a new approach to project design is needed. What would be its characteristics? Intervention as a process means consensus-building and giving priority to coherence so that 'things add up'. The implication is that tools and techniques are needed to seek such consensus and coherence, and that tools are also needed to illustrate and display the results of one actor going it alone in a multiple-actor situation. The right hand column of Table 1 is an attempt to express this situation.

Table 1 State-led and multiple-actor development policy, and implications for planning and projects

	'Old', state-led approach	'New', public action approach
Type of actor	State-led single actor	Public action by multiple actors with plurality of interests
Public interest	Yes, the state knows what public interest is, and acts on it	Public interest is not immediately obvious. Definition of 'public' interest' contested. Different interests, different stakeholders
Planning	Planning with one actor. Techniques needed to identify, prioritise, evaluate actions	Coherence cannot be assumed. Who should act? NGOs? Donors? State? If they all act, how does it add up?
Problem	How to do it better?	How best to steer and influence behaviours of various actors?
Tools	Project appraisal, cost benefit analysis, etc.	Techniques to build coherence. Tools for seeking consensus for coherence of action. Tools to illustrate and display the results of one actor 'going it alone', e.g. participation analysis, stakeholder analysis, framework planning as process. And so on.

The LFA as process-tool?

So, the LFA can be a blueprint tool restricted to matrix box-filling, but evidence from a range of cases we have analysed suggests that, as one part of a range of tools, it can assist practitioners faced with managing complexity but also having to state goals for which they are accountable.

However, a straightforward strengths and weaknesses analysis of the LFA does not really capture the complex practice of the approach. Rather, it is the ways the LFA are used which are important. Ironically, as Gasper has well described it is the ZOPP (objectives-oriented project planning system) method which, while using the LFA in a process-based way, has also stuck to the most top-down, managerial style of implementation

(Gaspar 1996: 15). Although it has the rhetoric of participation, it ends up being one of the most imposed tools in development policy and practice. Similarly, some of the most interesting uses of the LFA have been as part of a raft of tools used as and when needed. However, some agencies have tried to turn the raft of tools into a prescriptive list of 'must dos'. And all the time the LFA, has become increasingly used by agencies worldwide.

In our teaching (with, so far, around 250 practitioners), we emphasise that the LFA and other tools are approaches that have and will continue to evolve, perhaps into something quite different; and that the tool is not a 'precious thing' — it can be treated roughly and used in whatever ways assist with the process of clarifying and focusing. It is not a 'pure' method. We use a range of well-known tools, and also emphasise the importance of power and contradiction at various levels — macro, meso, and micro. Table 1 is an expression of how we have conceptualised the relationship between tools and 'new' approaches within a public action perspective.

Reflections

To date in our use of the LFA for teaching purposes, at least three issues have arisen which illustrate its limitations as a stand-alone tool.

Form over substance

In the aid business, form often substitutes substance. In the case of the LFA, the victory of form over substance can be 'the filling in of the matrix', or it can be the tyranny of the manipulated 'participation'. One practitioner had this to say about one particular participatory tool, Participatory Rural Appraisal, 'PRA leads to genuine participation and ownership. One of the problems ...is that agency staff or consultants are not properly trained, and in fact start creating short cuts in the methodology. Hence the "quick and dirty" type PRA work that is now very common.'

But if public action is contested, as we have argued, and if 'public interest' is plural, there must be an analytical framework to handle it. So, in that case, there are some key aspects of LFA which are essential.

These are the tools that give an analytical handle on *public interest as contested terrain* — in situations of multiple interest, tools are needed that help identify the 'stakes' and 'interests' in particular activities and interventions. But more, tools are needed to ensure that 'you get somewhere' — that a platform for action emerges. So, for example, tools are needed that show stakeholders the results of pursuing self-interest, and that subordinating some interests can improve the overall solution for most stakeholders.

To argue for the identification of interests is not to argue for an ideal or perfect consensus where none exists. Indeed, the identification of interests is needed to develop an understanding of a blocking or controlling interest — which could well include the donor — that would need to be confronted. In the framework plan matrix, the column of measurable output may be a donor's controlling device, for example, which means, 'I will only fund this project if it has these predetermined outcomes'.

The LFA can also be used to bring out disagreements and so used in a process to investigate the possibilities for collective action. It is only by identifying such interests that coherent action can be forged, and that is what makes it so difficult. The search for coherent action will almost always involve institutional change. And transformation is not only an organisational question, but also a political issue. A cynical response to that might be 'Who said it was going to be easy?' Analytical tools are certainly required to improve the conceptualisation and practice of making connections between, and sense of, complex personal interactions.

Assumptions

The second issue for reflection is that of assumptions, the vital importance of which is always emphasised in the LFA. The success of an intervention depends on being clear what is likely to constrain it. However, there is another side to the need for serious analysis of the assumptions that may adversely affect an intervention. Assumptions can also be seen as things you have to work on and change.

A slavish adherence to the LFA would focus on making the most of the constraints rather than on changing them. LFA experts would argue that that is precisely why there need to be iterations of the LFA in a process-based way, but there are numerous examples where the emphasis on assumptions has cemented a constraint rather than trying to change it.

Breaking boundaries and constraints is, of course, quite normal in the steering of development activities. It is also an important aspect of strategic management. Michael Porter (1990) for example, a classic author in this field, has analysed these issues both at a business (firm) level and national level. He argues against the idea of comparative advantage — that nations always produce what they can produce most productively with, for example, some producing low-value products like cotton while others produce computer software. He argues instead that comparative advantage — and thus competitive advantage — can be reshaped by national and firm-level action.

Although Porter is writing in the context of business or national competitiveness, the same argument can be made for other types of organisation. One way of building advantage is to work on the constraints and continually improve. This key notion in innovation theory is as relevant in development projects and programmes as it is in firms. Those who study 'the behaviour of the firm' are constantly looking to understand why some 'adapt' to their environments more favourably than others. Similarly, some organisations and programmes appear to be able to engage in 'adaptive behaviour'. A narrow focus on framework planning can deflect from the need to work on the assumptions and constraints associated with an intervention. Adaptive action can widen the scope of an intervention and increase its effectiveness.

Conclusion

In working on this practitioner-based material, a metaphor kept springing up — one that has been well used in management and development circles to signify both survival and evolution. Ironically, a metaphor that is much used in social constructions of Africa — that of the dance — emerged also at the Harvard Business School in the 1980s with Moss Kanter's *When Giants Learn to Dance* (1989), a study of corporate attempts to transform organisations and institutions. In writing on Africa, it is used as a metaphor for survival, as, for example, in Stephanie Urdang's book on women's survival strategies in Mozambique, *And Still They Dance* (1989). The different uses of the metaphor — dance as flexibility and dance as survival — come together quite nicely when we think of how to improve learning from interventions, and how to use tools without being dominated by them. In multi-actor environments the ability to steer in complex yet practised movements and at the same time to continue to dance — to be 'active' and evolve new, creative forms of movement — lie at the heart of notions of public action.

Notes

1 This paper results from reflections on approaches to teaching these tools within a public action perspective, and has benefited from the large quantity of practitioner insights and feedback, some of which is cited throughout. Thanks particularly to Marc Wuyts for insights and discussions, both on our joint attempts to teach and at the same time critique cost benefit analysis in the 1970s, and on the relationship between the LFA and the moves from state to public action. Thanks also to David Daniels, Des Gasper, Mark Goldring, Caroline Harper, David Hulme, Penny Lawrence, Carolyn Miller, Berit Olsson, Gita Sen, Graham Thom, Adrian and Timlin for their contributions, some of which are inside 'quotes', and especially to my colleagues Dorcas Robinson and Simon Bell who assisted with the production of teaching materials for The Open University's Global Programme in Development Management.

2 See for example, INTRAC/South Research (1994) and Gasper (1997).

3 Hulme (1995) provides a useful analytical framework in which to examine such tensions.

4 I am grateful to David Hulme for this insight on Smith et al.

5 See, for example, Coleman 1987; Gasper 1997; INTRAC/South Research 1994; Biggs and Smith 1998.

References

Amendola, M. and S. Bruno (1990) 'The behaviour of the innovative firm: relations to the environment', *Research Policy* 19: 419–433.

Anheier, H. K. (1990) 'Private voluntary organisations and the Third World: the case of Africa', in H. K. Anheier and W. Siebel (eds.) *The Third Sector: Comparative Studies of Non-Profit Organisations*, New York: de Gruyter.

Biggs, S. and G. Smith (1998) 'Beyond methodologies: coalition building for participatory technology development', *World Development* 26: 239–248.

Cernea, M. (1991) 'Using knowledge from social science in development projects', World Bank Discussion Paper No. 114, Washington DC: The World Bank.

Checkland, P. (1994) 'Systems theory and management thinking', *American Behavioral Scientist* 38: 75–91.

Chowdhury, A. and C. Kirkpatrick (1994) *Development Policy and Planning: An Introduction to Models and Techniques,* London: Routledge.

Coleman, G. (1987) 'Logical framework approach to the monitoring and evaluation of agricultural and rural development projects', *Project Appraisal* 2: 251–259.

Cusworth, J. W. and T. R. Franks (1993) *Managing Projects in Developing Countries,* Harlow: Longman.

Gasper, D. (1997) 'Logical framework: a critical assessment, managerial theory, pluralistic practice', ISS Working Paper.

Hulme, D. (1995) 'Projects, politics and professionals: alternative approaches for project identification and project planning', *Agricultural Systems* 47: 211–233.

INTRAC/South Research (1994) *A Tool for Project Management and People-driven Development* (2 Vols), Oxford: INTRAC and Leuven: South Research.

Kanter, R. M. (1989) *When Giants Learn to Dance: Mastering the Challenge of Strategy, Management and Careers in the 1990s,* New York: Simon and Schuster.

ODA (1995) *A Guide to Social Analysis for Projects in Developing Countries*, London: HMSO.

Porter, M. E. (1990) *The Competitive Advantage of Nations*, London: Macmillan.

Smith, W. E., F. J. Lethem and B. A. Thoolen (1981) 'The design of organisations for rural development projects: a progress report', World Bank Staff Papers No. 375, Washington DC: The World Bank.

Thomas, A. (1996) 'What is development management?' *Journal of International Development* 8(1): 95–110.

Urdang, S. (1989) *And Still They Dance: Women, War and the Struggle for Change in Mozambique*, London: Earthscan.

Vickers, G. (1965) *The Art of Judgement*, London: Chapman and Hall.

Vickers, G. (1970) *Freedom in a Rocking Boat: Changing Values in an Unstable Society*, London: Penguin.

Institutional sustainability as learning

Hazel Johnson and Gordon Wilson

Introduction

This article is concerned with how negotiations between stakeholders over action on development can enhance institutional sustainability. It argues that institutional sustainability is based on a three-point agenda for negotiation which provides a framework for action and performance assessment, and hence a means of learning and innovation. We see learning and innovation as key to institutional sustainability because development is a dynamic process, not simply a set of desired targets or goals. However, learning and innovation often involve steering a course through conflictual social relations in which relative power and strength of interests will be evident. Learning within and between development organisations and other participants in development processes is not automatically consensual, while negotiating conflict creatively can also be an important source of innovation.

Our three-point negotiation agenda for institutional sustainability involves: (i) the ability to investigate *assumptions* behind action; (ii) agreeing roles and responsibilities — or establishing forms of *accountability* over action between actors and their constituents; and (iii) being able to *attribute* the outcomes of action (and therefore enable further learning and innovation). Engaging with such an agenda implies participatory management and open rather than closed systems (Murray 1992). It also implies moving from a goal-oriented to an action-oriented approach to interventions (Carley and Christie 1992).[1] Such an approach is also in line with Guba and Lincoln's (1989) proposal for 'fourth generation evaluation' reviewed by Marsden et al. (1994). Fourth generation evaluation consists of two key elements: *responsive focusing* (allowing the boundaries of the evaluation to be set by the constructions and interactions of its stakeholders) and a *constructivist methodology* (providing the wider frameworks within which meanings are constructed). Out of this process emerges an '*agenda for negotiation*' (ibid.: 30).

Guba and Lincoln's agenda is based on what is not resolved during the dialogue of the evaluation process, whereas we advocate an *a priori* agenda. We do so because simply allowing an agenda to emerge exposes stakeholders to a potential tyranny of 'structurelessness' where the content of the agenda can depend on the positions taken by powerful stakeholders, positions which may be more or less 'enlightened'. An *a priori* agenda, however, provides a basis for continual negotiation of action and learning.

The framework we propose is both a blueprint and a process, in that it is a framework for a process approach. The link between blueprint and process is that the detailed content of the framework/blueprint is itself processual in that it is subject to change and innovation via its application. Our discussion of the development of the framework/blueprint engages us in a process of our own: that of staged model-building. The debate about blueprint and process approaches (as well as whether learning does or does not take place in development interventions, whether blueprint or process — see, for example, Hulme 1989) has become an integral part of development management discourses. In practice, development managers weave between the two, with emphases on one or the other approach. These tensions are evident, for example, in the use of logframe (logical framework analysis) in planning, implementing and evaluating interventions, and of processes such as participatory action research (e.g. PRA, PLA, PAR). Thus, the framework we develop below, and its contribution to institutional sustainability, cannot be seen simply as a set of tools or be applied mechanically. The relationship between blueprint and process is a tension to be acknowledged and managed.

We first look briefly at some concerns and debates about the concepts of sustainability, sustainable development, and institutional sustainability, and then at how such concepts can be used in practice as broad parameters for establishing an agenda for negotiation and action. We then disaggregate the negotiation agenda and show how it can contribute learning and innovation within and between development organisations in the context of their interventions. We conclude with some qualifiers about participation, consensus, and conflict.

Constructing institutional sustainability

Our argument that institutional sustainability is based on people's capacities to learn and innovate is derived more generally from our views of sustainability and sustainable development. These two concepts have been interpreted extremely widely and have lent themselves to many areas of analysis, and policy rhetoric and design. One question is what useful meanings can be given to these concepts. Another is whether and how they can inform the management of development processes, or development management — in particular whether and how they can be used to provide a framework for learning and longer-term action.[2]

The literature on sustainability and sustainable development is extensive.[3] Concerns about the relationship between environment and society, or environment and development, often focus on how social forms and practices act to the detriment of the environment, whether in practices associated with industrial development (including in agriculture) and profit-oriented activity, the supposed short-term nature of poor people's survival strategies, or the environmental effects of social upheaval and war. From a primarily environmental focus, sustainability/sustainable development has taken on many meanings from informing a critique of economic policies and practices to the nature of social organisation, values, and behaviours in society at large. The concepts of sustainability and sustainable development are often used interchangeably largely because of this widespread inflation of their meanings (Mitcham 1995). In his perceptive analysis of the strengths, weaknesses, and operationalisation of the concepts of sustainability and sustainable development, Lélé (1991) points out that attempts to combine concerns about environmental degradation, development objectives, and the participation of different people (especially 'the poor') in development planning results in unrealistic consensus-building across widely differing social forms, power relations, and conflicting interests. Lélé states:

> In short, SD [sic] is a 'metafix' that will unite everybody from the profit-minded industrialist and risk-minimising subsistence farmer to the equity-seeking social worker, the pollution-concerned or wildlife-loving First Worlder, the growth-maximising policy maker, the goal-oriented bureaucrat, and, therefore, the vote-counting politician' (ibid.: 613).

Sustainability and sustainable development have become a form of discourse about development in which many perspectives on change can be located, even though they embody different views about means and ends. Thus, questions such as: what is being sustained? why? and, for whom? remain areas of contention, as do relative emphases on the environmental and the social. In spite of (and because of) this inflation and diffuseness of meaning, we do not suggest that the terms be abandoned but rather that they be used to frame and enable debate and negotiation between stakeholders in development. Such a process can provide the backdrop for sharing values or discovering areas of disagreement and difference of values and understandings, all-important if action is to achieve its goals and have a longer-term perspective.

In this article, we inevitably incorporate some of our own values about sustainability/sustainable development. However, they act as an 'example framework', the precise content of which may be drawn differently by others. For example, Mitcham (1995: 323) suggests that sustainability/sustainable development 'can insinuate... core principles into new areas... Sustainable development need not require growth, but it does imply an input-output management'. Input-output management can be seen as balancing (and replenishing) the use of resources, whether physical or human. However, we choose to see it as a relationship between action (input) and learning and innovation (output) for future action (further input), while recognising that such an action-learning cycle approach to intervention needs to be attached to some substantive meanings and values about means and ends.

Box 1 Sustainable development and sustainability

Characteristics (or tasks) of *sustainable development* may include:
- developing sustainable resource use;
- building sustainable livelihoods;
- reducing vulnerabilities;
- enabling empowerment;
- increasing equality;
- increasing self-reliance.

Sustainability may include:
- continuity;
- an extended time frame;
- the potential for activities to be self-supporting;
- the development of capacities;
- the realisation of capacities through performance;
- learning as an integral part of developing capacities and assessing performance.

Source: adapted from Johnson and Wilson (1996: 17–18).

In a recent teaching text at The Open University, we gave some 'working characteristics and tasks' to the concepts of sustainability/sustainable development (see Box 1). They are not our own original list but comprised from existing debate and were suggested as parameters for guiding monitoring and evaluation, or performance assessment. However, in practice such 'working characteristics and tasks' are a negotiating point between stakeholders.

It is this process of negotiation of meanings of sustainability/sustainable development and the subsequent process of negotiating and carrying out a performance assessment agenda which, we suggest, can lead to learning and innovation and hence institutional sustainability. This view is based on the idea of institutions as 'complexes of norms and behaviours that persist over time by serving collectively valued purposes', which can either be diffusely practised or structured into organisations (Uphoff 1996: 8–10). Thus, we argue that a combination of (i) negotiation over meanings of sustainability and sustainable development as a framework for action, (ii) negotiation of an *a priori* performance assessment agenda linked to this framework, and (iii) a participatory and open involvement in this agenda by stakeholders, can lead to (iv) learning and innovation. This is a process through which collective and purposeful norms and behaviours can be developed and changed over a sustained period of time, both in shared practices and in the coordination and cooperation of organisations. In other words, this process is an approach to thinking about — and acting on — institutional sustainability.

At this point, it is worth adding a note about 'participatory and open', to which we return in our concluding comments. It is often suggested that sustainability/sustainable development requires participation and that participation can in turn lead to empowerment. A valid critique is provided by Lélé (1991) who points out that participation has replaced concepts of equity and social justice in sustainable development discourse. Lélé states that while the concepts of equity and social justice highlight issues such as resource distribution and use — that is, structural inequalities which lead both to poverty and to environmental degradation — the concept of participation is neither equivalent (particularly in the many ways in which it is discussed and operationalised) nor can it be a substitute. One might add to Lélé's analysis that unequal power relations between different stakeholders (as well as within organisations and communities) are likely to be a serious obstacle to certain forms of participation. This is a complex arena about which there is now a considerable literature. Lélé's and other critical writing (see, for example, Brown 1997; Mosse 1994) have opened up the discussion on the role of experts and 'outsiders', of social and cultural differentiation in development, and have contributed to rethinking the relationship between blueprint and process.

Operationalising concepts

If one were to take our distinctions between sustainable development and sustainability, as shown in Box 1, it might be concluded that sustainable development comprised a set of ends while sustainability was substantially about means. However, the distinction between means and ends is not evidently clear-cut, and it can also change over time. Thus, for example, a sustainability goal for an aid organisation may be the longer-term self-sufficiency of the recipients of aid; however, the goal of self-sufficiency may be a means to a different and even longer-term end for the recipients. Equally, empowerment of a given group of people may be an end in terms of improving the social position and control of that group, but it also may be a means towards further ends such as a development of new livelihood opportunities or having a voice in local or national policy.

Thus, looking more closely at these 'working characteristics and tasks' suggests that:

- means need to be taken into account as much as ends;
- means have an important role in whether ends are achieved or not;
- both means and ends require continuous negotiation and agreement between actors and organisations in any given context.

This leads to our first model (see Figure 1), in which the relationship between sustainability and sustainable development, and means and ends, is seen as a process of participatory learning and innovation.[4] Figure 1 appears more like a grid than a set of flows (inputs and outputs) or feedback loops. In this representation, the meanings of sustainability and sustainable development and the suggested distinctions between means and ends are a starting point for negotiation: they offer a way of giving direction to action and/or agreeing anticipated outcomes. The precise content of the cells are thus subject to negotiation between stakeholders. There is also a central cell which is apparently unrelated to others in the grid but which is the location of processes which enable the other cells to be linked to each other: participatory learning and innovation (which can lead to new forms of control and empowerment) is the kernel of institutional sustainability.

Figure 1	Institutional sustainability as a negotiation grid		
	Sustainability		**Sustainable development**
Means	Development of human capacities and organisation		Sustainable livelihoods and resource use
		Participatory learning and innovation	
Ends	Sustainable institutions		Security of livelihoods and resource use for future generations

Figure 2 Institutional sustainability as an influence diagram

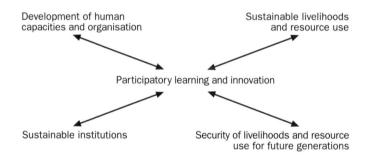

Once one starts looking at this matrix in terms of feedback loops, it becomes clear that the means and ends are fluid — there is a constantly changing and adapting process being socially constructed between stakeholders (who may also change) over time. Taking out the means and ends cells, the figure would then look like the influence diagram in Figure 2 with two-directional arrows between the outer cells and the central process of participatory learning and innovation.

While this model can conceptualise a way of negotiating meanings and areas of consensus or difference, and suggest a framework for ongoing dialogue, further steps are needed to give it substantive meaning, in particular to allow participants to have a say in how the involvement of different organisation s and individuals can be maintained over time.

This takes us to a second model, that of the familiar intervention spiral which we have presented in annotated form in Figure 3. Figure 3 interrogates the central core of Figure 2, that is, the process of learning and innovation, and the extent to which such a process can be empowering for participants. Discussion of the 'who?' questions posed in Figure 3 — which can be elaborated further than in this figure — is likely to show very quickly that stakeholders are embedded in a social dynamic, possibly hierarchical and possibly contentious, which is likely to affect the processes of planning, implementation and realisation of goals, as well as the extent to which learning is part of an organic process between participants.

The perspective behind these models is similar to — but also has some differences from — the process approach to sustainable development given by Carley and Christie (1992). Carley and Christie are concerned to develop an action-centred network approach to managing sustainable development. Their definition of management 'replaces control by a few people with that of negotiation and organisation al learning... *management is teamwork* based on a continually evolving consensus on the direction towards sustainable development. This more egalitarian, participative approach to management is fundamental to the idea of an action-centred network' (ibid.: 13, authors' emphasis). However, consensus-building, egalitarian, and participative approaches are neither straightforward nor

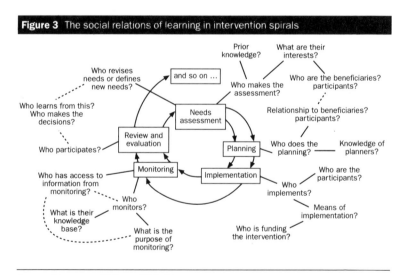

Figure 3 The social relations of learning in intervention spirals

Source: Johnson and Wilson, 1996: 18

always possible, given the probable social differences as well as those of values and interests in any given context. Nevertheless, we suggest that one of the functions of setting a negotiation framework and an *a priori* agenda for performance assessment is to help discover whether open processes of planning and managing the implementation of interventions are possible, even when stakeholders have different views and understandings over means and ends.

Operationalisation in practice: an approach to action-learning

Looking at Figures 2 and 3 thus suggests two further steps, one conceptual and one operational. The first is that the social dynamics of development interventions take place within existing institutional landscapes and help, intentionally or otherwise, to create new ones. However, the definition and realisation of 'collectively valued purposes' depends, as suggested, on the preparedness of stakeholders to negotiate agreed norms and behaviours, or, in other words, their commitment to building an institutional framework for action which has a broad legitimacy. The second step which links Figures 2 and 3 is to construct mechanisms or means of enabling learning and innovation. How can action-learning take place within and between groups and organisations during the course of development interventions or other forms of public action so as to contribute to sustainable development and build institutional sustainability? We focus on two issues:

- how to operate and steer towards the broad mission (sustainable development) in a 'turbulent' (Carley and Christie 1992: 165) context, characterised by uncertainty, inconsistent and ill-defined needs, unclear understanding of means and impacts of actions, and fluid participation from different actors (ibid.);

- how to supersede a goal-orientation rationale of management by an action-learning rationale based on teamwork and evolving consensus (ibid.: 13, 178) in order to build human capacity.

These two issues are of course interrelated, because in order to steer action we have to learn from it. This involves a process of continual examination and reflection of what we do which is used to construct modified or new action. In the management literature, this process is called performance assessment (PA).

To make PA effective in meeting the needs of different stakeholders, we suggest there should be a *conscious* social construction of it which involves negotiating three contested areas. For short-hand purposes, we label these the 'three As':

(i)   agreeing, investigating, and testing assumptions between stakeholders about sustainable development and sustainability, and about plans for intervention in the contexts in which it is intended to occur;

(ii) agreeing roles, responsibilities, and time-frames, and the means for making decisions — that is, negotiating an institutional framework for accountability;

(iii) establishing processes of monitoring and evaluation which allow discussion and understanding by stakeholders of what particular outputs and outcomes can be attributed to the intervention.

Box 2 Socially constructed performance assessment using the three As

Identifying and investigating **assumptions** is an important part of the ubiquitous development manager's tool — framework planning — where assumptions form the fourth column of the 4 X 4 matrix. Assumptions around interventions invariably relate to social contexts and power relations within which a given intervention takes place, the material, financial, and human resources available, and the social context of the implementation process itself. Failure to account for the latter especially has been identified as the cause of failure of many development programmes. In terms of the two major issues identified above, assumptions relate to both the turbulent or uncertain contexts of interventions and the substantive meaning that is given to sustainable development.

Attribution is an analytical process that interprets the observed impacts of interventions. At an operational level it turns the data of monitoring into the information of evaluation. To provide a hypothetical example: an irrigation project may have the goal of improving livelihoods of poor farmers in a drought-prone region. Over a period of, say, five years monitoring may show that livelihoods have improved. This may indeed have been due to the laying of irrigation channels, but it may also have been due to external factors: five years of good rains, improved markets and prices for the produce, or changes in a range of social conditions. Who can tell? Who can separate out cause and effect? This issue is recognised by major donors, such as the UK ODA (since May 1997 the Department for International Development [DFID]): 'A major difficulty in attempting to measure the benefits, is to determine the extent to which it is possible to attribute improvements to the project as opposed to factors external to the project such as economic growth, increasing demand for labour, investment in public services (health, education and training) and infrastructure, all of which have a positive impact on well-being' (Robinson and Thin 1993: 26).

Accountability is the most overtly political of the three As. Those to whom one is accountable exercise the power to regulate and guide interventions. They are the ultimate arbiters of the substantive meanings given to sustainable development and the two issues on which we are focusing: the process of steering towards sustainable development through a turbulent context or conditions of uncertainty, and the rationale (goal-oriented or action-learning-oriented) for interventions. Thus, a crucial issue in the construction of performance assessment is to whom an agency planning and implementing an activity is accountable. Is it to the donors (upwards accountability) or to the supposed beneficiaries (downwards accountability)? Or is it to all stakeholders, themselves defined by negotiation (multiple accountability)? (Edwards and Hulme 1995)

As indicated in Box 2, the three As share some important characteristics. None is easily divorced from social process and the social contexts in which learning takes place. They each direct learning away from the narrow confines of implementation to a consideration of wider context and a challenge of underlying goals. Also, because there is no question of any of them being settled in a technical sense, they each require the active engagement of the multiple stakeholders in an intervention. This process of negotiation between stakeholders becomes itself a learning experience that is transferable across a range of contexts — learning how to negotiate, and when to collaborate or challenge. Or, as Fowler (1995: 151) puts it, performance becomes '... defined as the — often contested — outcome of social judgements of the parties involved, using criteria which are important to them.'

Figure 4 Institutional sustainability as a learning cycle

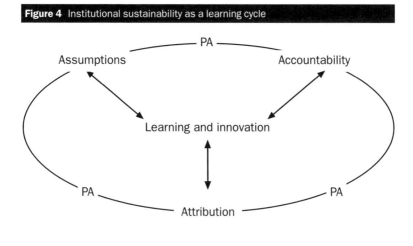

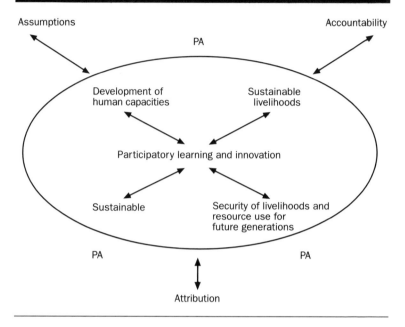

Figure 5 A provisional, 'working' model for the practice of action learning

Assumptions

Accountability

PA

Development of
human capacities

Sustainable
livelihoods

Participatory learning and innovation

Sustainable

Security of livelihoods and
resource use for
future generations

PA

PA

Attribution

Such a framework forms our next stage of model-building, represented by Figure 4. This portrays institutional sustainability as a learning cycle carried out through performance assessment. From Figure 4, it is a short step to incorporate the dynamics of action learning shown in Figure 2 which links learning and innovation and sustainability and sustainable development. This results in our provisional 'working model', which is shown in Figure 5.

The fluid action-learning dynamic leading to institutional sustainability portrayed in Figure 5 is given shape and meaning by performance assessment. The three As in turn provide an enabling agenda for performance assessment. It may seem a broad agenda, but its negotiation and resolution have direct implications for what is assessed, how it is assessed, and why. This is crucial because PA is typically represented (e.g. by the former ODA) as the measurement of effectiveness (performance in relation to targets set in the original plan) and efficiency (the rate and cost at which inputs result in outputs) (Robinson and Thin 1993: 6). However, measuring effectiveness and efficiency via monitoring and evaluation of performance in relation to previously defined goals can lead to a static view of what are essentially dynamic situations. It tends towards what has been described as the 'statistics of measurement' (Potter and Subrahmanian 1997) where the questions asked during monitoring and evaluation are of the 'what' or 'how many' variety: for example, how many poor farmers have been helped in an irrigation scheme; what impact has there been on their livelihoods? Negotiation of the three As moves beyond a statistics of measurement to a 'statistics of understanding' (ibid.) where 'why' and 'what if' questions are to the fore. For example, why have some farmers been helped by the irrigation scheme and not others? what if the irrigation scheme were implemented differently or even replaced by a different project? This in turn leads to fluid conceptualisations of effectiveness and efficiency and brings them into the process framework.

What kind of learning might we expect from our working model? Action-learning has been described as an iterative process that involves learning how to innovate, be adaptive, and deal with complexity and turbulence (Carley and Christie 1992). It takes place at several levels, for example:

- *learning in depth*, so that particular practices may be fully understood and then changed, adapted and/or improved; that is to say, virtuous circles of learning and practice are facilitated.

- *learning in breadth*, which places a special onus on performance assessment so that it is similarly broad. When sustainable development is the underlying aim it is not only the implementation of a practice that should be assessed, but also its underlying goals, assumptions, and the social context in which it takes place. In other words, the substantive meaning of sustainable development itself is continually re-assessed within the context of the intervention. Again, this puts a special onus on monitoring and evaluation to provide the statistics of understanding discussed above. In short, the PA practices of monitoring and evaluation become pro-active when learning in breadth is a goal, rather than reactive to particular and largely fixed conceptualisations of a given intervention's previously defined goals.

- *transferability of learning*, when the purpose of learning is not restricted to the improvement of implementation of a particular practice, but also about increasing the ability to weigh up options, to make decisions about all aspects of life — when to improve implementation of a particular practice, when to re-define the goals of a practice, when to do something else, how to identify opportunities and constraints. This is not just about personal, managerial life-skills, or even about organisational learning, but also the transferability of the learning process to new situations.

Finally, as we hope our model indicates, learning itself is a social process and therefore not neutral. What is learned (and who decides), how it is learned, who learns, and what they do with their learning, involves social power, negotiation, and conflict. This last cannot be overstated and it is the rock on which many a well-intended intervention has foundered.

Institutional sustainability and participation

Much current literature points to the key role that 'participation' can play in performance assessment. We agree with this view. However, there is a danger that some of the claims for participatory approaches are elevating them into a realm where expectations are far too high. Nevertheless, in our view, a framework that is based on the recognition of social process, power, conflict, and negotiation needs to be lubricated by participatory approaches. This is indicated in our final model (see Figure 5). Indeed, one can go further and claim that any negotiation requires participation of the negotiating parties, by definition.

Is participation a *sufficient* as well as a necessary condition for negotiation that takes different interests into account? The current elevation of 'participation' into a development paradigm is dangerous because not only does it raise expectations, but it also has the potential to provoke backlash when those expectations cannot be fulfilled, a backlash that might be aimed, moreover, at the basic tenets of the participatory approach. One of the easiest yet more questionable assumptions concerning participation is that, if one works hard enough at it, it leads eventually to consensus in relation to what needs to be done; and, having reached this consensus, reconciling accountability to different stakeholders is a simple matter because all have the same objectives. The main obstacles to achieving consensus in this view are the professionals and experts from the agencies and the solution is for them to 'up-end' and put themselves 'last' (Chambers 1995).

In this consensual view, the dominant mode of procedure is *inquiry* in order to find the common ground for consensus and then to use that common ground as a springboard for action. But development management is characterised by very deep value conflicts and takes place on an inherently conflictual social terrain (Thomas 1996). Is it not a self-delusion to believe that there are even grounds for consensus in such circumstances, and that inquiry then becomes little more than social engineering to reflect the wishes of the powerful?

An alternative, more conflictual, less 'nice', view of participation, but one that does not pretend to make grand claims, is to recognise that it often takes place in fundamentally adversarial settings where social power relations ultimately determine the outcomes. Here the trick is to strengthen the poor and powerless so that they are able to engage effectively and have a strong voice in these settings. A similar point is made by Munslow et al., when they introduce an author (Edwin Richken) who is writing about the South African Government's Reconstruction and Development Programme (RDP): '[L]ocal forums set up under the RDP to help communities decide upon their priorities are unlikely to be able to redress power disparities. For the author, the marginalised groups, such as rural women, need their own forums rather than being party to a multi-stakeholder forum where their concerns can be ignored' (Munslow, Fitzgerald and McLennan 1995: 20).

Interventions that seek to engage in this form of capacity-building are a far cry from more conventional interventions such as contributing to physical infrastructure, or public services in health and education, or creating micro-finance schemes to promote economic livelihoods. Nor can their efficiency and effectiveness be easily measured by conventional means. Because of this, interventions that seek to strengthen poor and marginalised groups appear modest, but they do attempt to recognise the realities of social power and enable the poor to have a substantive voice in defining sustainable development and operationalising it within their own local and social contexts.

Returning to our three As agenda, the requirement to negotiate accountabilities should at least make the power divisions between stakeholders explicit (which in itself can be a salutary learning experience for everybody!). This points to a way between consensus and conflict that seeks to create the 'win-win' ethos of the former, while recognising the importance of developing the capacities of the poor to negotiate their interests in adversarial settings. In this 'third' way, the negotiating parties do not pretend that consensus is achievable when clearly it is not, but they consciously try to achieve an accommodation of their different interests. Minimum requirements for this accommodation are firstly for all stakeholders to have the capacity to express and argue for their interests, and secondly, to find a common 'conceptual container' within which the interests can be accommodated, even if they are strongly conflicting (Isaacs, quoted in Thomas 1998). Operationalising the three As can form such a container.

Notes

1 Guba and Lincoln suggest that there has been a gradual evolution from evaluation as measurement (first generation) to the development of 'programme evaluation' (second generation) to evaluation as judgement (third generation) (Marsden et al. 1994: 16).

2 The concept of development management used in this paper is that defined by Thomas: 'The management of intervention aimed at external social goals in a context of value-based conflict' (Thomas 1996: 106). This is not to deny the importance of internal organisational goals and the management of organisations. However the main concern of development management is public action: that is, 'purposive collective action' (Mackintosh 1992: 5) in multi-actor fields from international organisations and governments to local voluntary associations, and in which actors only have partial control over processes and outcomes.

3 The authors have commented on some key aspects in Johnson and Wilson (1997).

4 '[A] simplification of the messy world that surrounds us'; 'relates to the real world and an imagined world' (Thomas 1998: 8).

References

Brown, D. (1997) 'Professionalism, participation, and the public good: issues of arbitration in development management and the critique of the neo-populist approach', paper presented at Public Sector Management for the Next Century Conference, IDPM and University of Manchester, 29 June–2 July 1997.

Carley, M. and L. Christie (1992) *Managing Sustainable Development*, London: Earthscan.

Chambers, R. (1995) 'Paradigm shifts and the practice of participatory research and development' in N. Nelson and S. Wright (eds.) *Power and Participatory Development*, London: IT Publications.

Edwards, M. and D. Hulme (1995) 'NGO Performance and accountability: introduction and overview' in M. Edwards and D. Hulme (eds.) 1995.

Edwards, M. and D. Hulme (eds.) (1995) Non-Governmental Organisations: Performance and Accountability, London: Earthscan.

Fowler, A. (1995) 'Assessing NGO performance: difficulties, dilemmas and a way ahead', in M. Edwards and D. Hulme (eds.) 1995: 143–156.

Guba, E. G. and Y. S. Lincoln (1989) *Fourth Generation Evaluation*, London: Sage.

Hulme, D. (1989) 'Learning and not learning from experience in rural project planning', *Public Administration and Development* 9: 1–16.

Johnson, H. and G. Wilson (1996) 'Capacities, performance and sustainability' in *Capacities for Managing Development*, Global Programme in Development Management, Milton Keynes: The Open University.

Johnson, H. and G. Wilson (1997) 'Performance, learning and sustaining: development management for sustainable development', DPP Working Paper No. 39, Milton Keynes: The Open University.

Lélé, S. M. (1991) 'Sustainable development: a critical review', *World Development* 19(6): 607–622.

Marsden, D., P. Oakley, B. Pratt (1994) Measuring the Process: Guidelines for Evaluating Social Development, Oxford: INTRAC.

Mitcham, C. (1995) 'The concept of sustainable development: its origins and ambivalence', *Technology and Society* 17(3):311–326.

Mosse, D. (1005) 'Social analysis in participatory rural development', *PLA Notes* 24: 27–33.

Munslow, B., P. Fitzgerald and A. McLennan (1995) 'Sustainable development: turning vision into reality', in B. Munslow, P. Fitzgerald, and A. McLennan, A. (eds.) *Managing Sustainable Development in South Africa*, Cape Town: OUP.

Murray, R. (1992) 'Towards a flexible state', *IDS Bulletin* 23(4): 78–88.

Potter, S. and R. Subrahmanian (1997) 'Information systems for policy change', in A. Thomas, J. Chataway, and M. Wuyts (eds.) *Finding out Fast*, Milton Keynes: The Open University.

Robinson, M. and N. Thin (1993) *Project Evaluation: A Guide for NGOs*, Glasgow: Overseas Development Administration Joint Funding Scheme, NGO Unit.

Thomas, A. (1996) 'What is development management?', *Journal of International Development* 8(1): 95–110.

Thomas, A. (1998) 'Making institutional development happen' in *Institutional Development: Conflicts, Values and Meanings*, Global Programme in Development Management, Milton Keynes: The Open University.

Uphoff, N. (1986) Local Institutional Development: An Analytical Sourcebook with Cases, West Hartford: Kumarian Press.

Managing institutional change: the science and technology systems of Eastern Europe and East Africa

Jo Chataway and Tom Hewitt

Introduction

The themes of this paper are institutional change, and efforts to create new networks and linkages in science and technology (S&T) systems in Poland and Tanzania. These are as much an aspect of managing social change as they are development programmes directed at socio-economic problems. Many similar concerns are raised, in particular in the need to integrate often dispersed actors. In looking at efforts to establish new types of integration, we are concerned with efforts to enhance domestic technology transfer between different national institutions such as universities, research institutes, industrial support organisations, and industry. The paper shows that the concept and practice of technology transfer is not straightforward and is closely linked to the management of the organisations and institutions involved.[1]

You may be wondering why we have compared Tanzania with Poland. At first sight they are very different. However, on closer inspection there are some remarkable similarities in the form of recent changes, despite differences in content and context. After introducing the context of institutional change based on notions of fragmentation and integration, we explain the nature of markets in a setting of institutional change. We then examine case material from Eastern Europe and East Africa. In particular we look at the breakdown of old state-led systems and recent attempts to encourage market-led institutional change. The conclusions draw out some of the institutional barriers to reforming S&T.

A primary aim of the restructuring efforts in East Europe and the structural adjustment programmes in East Africa is the dissolution of institutions based on state-led planning. In some instances disintegration of state-based institutions has led to high levels of fragmentation and periods of chaos. However, these changes also open up possibilities for new forms of integration and realignment of effort. In the area of reform of the science and technology infrastructure, reforms are constructed on the premise that market-led institutions, based on competition, will serve countries more effectively. In a sense, what these reforms are about is the destruction of old institutions and the promotion of new systems.

In both Poland and Tanzania there has been a breakdown of the idea of the state as the only institution involved in development, and the emergence of a more complex situation with a multiplicity of actors and agencies, often with competing interests and views. Whereas previously, the state played a highly centralised integration role, the emphasis is now more facilitative, on giving more autonomy to different institutions (industry, universities, and research institutes) to establish effective working relationships. While this has generated opportunities for greater and more diverse forms of coordinated public action, it has also led to a fragmentation in the development effort. It has highlighted uncertainty. The state, the market, NGOs, and civil society are now in a more complex relationship, exposing tensions between fragmentation and/or uncertainty on one side, and integration, cooperation, and coordination on the other. Later in this paper, we will look at some key factors which influence the ability to manage multi-actor relationships.

We suggest here that while much effort has been devoted to macro-level reform in the field of S&T, the emergence of new institutions does not happen as a natural consequence of macro-level liberalisation and privatisation. It requires policy efforts aimed at meso- and micro-levels. Thus, examples of efforts to reform the S&T systems in Poland and Tanzania illustrate how the ability to manage change is related to institutional capacity. The need to focus on targeted institutional building, rather than relying on the market mechanism invisibly to guide the emergence of appropriate new structures and skills, is often not appreciated. In a sense, this type of development planning is an effort to strike a new balance, which will always need constant re-jigging, between integration and fragmentation. This requires new types of management and dialogue between the different actors, organisations, and institutions involved.

Institutional change and stickiness

Unfortunately, changing organisational behaviour, still less, institutional behaviour, is not automatic. Old practices and mind-sets are deeply ingrained. In this way, making a transition to new practices can be described as 'sticky'.

One of the enduring legacies of the 1980s is the overwhelming rejection of state planning as an alternative to markets. The question that has confronted policy-makers in the 1990s, however, is what kind of institutions make markets function most effectively. This is not quite the same as coping with market failure. The term market failure indicates that some replacement of the market mechanism is necessary, whereas what many are now looking for are ways of supporting, moulding, and shaping markets so that they actually deliver.

Several things follow from this:

- first, recognition that markets are themselves institutions. This means that markets need to be considered in context.

- second, markets cannot be assumed themselves to give rise to appropriate institutions. If markets are themselves institutions and their effective functioning depends in part on the way in which they interact with other institutions, it follows that simply taking controls off economies and imposing free trade criteria will not deliver uniformly appropriate results.

- third, the desire to implement market reform needs in part, therefore, to create institutions which can make markets work. Figure 1, taken from a needs assessment exercise for small and medium enterprises (SMEs) in Poland, illustrates the type and variety of institutional structures needed to facilitate market-based development.

Figure 1 splits business needs into four categories: information, knowledge, capital, and environment. The second layer of boxes outlines broad categories which can facilitate business growth. The outer layer suggests programmes, initiatives, and infrastructure. Apart from anything else, the diagram shows the extraordinary complexity of private sector development.

There is still wide debate about how the institutional nature of markets should be reflected in policy. In some cases, policy initiatives ignore important institutional factors; in others, 'reformed' institutions still have their roots in old systems. Old habits die hard. The language of reform can be relatively easily adopted, but the reality of institutional change—adopting new practices, shifts in power relations, increased organisational agility—is much harder to achieve.

Figure 1 A framework for sustaining business growth

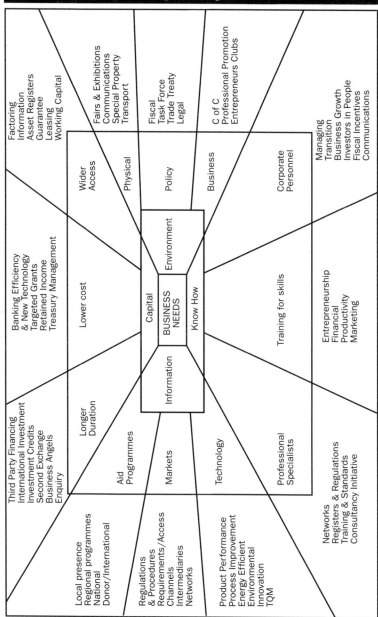

Source: Chattaway and Joffe 1998

The following sections look at two instances where structural economic reform has brought about limited institutional change despite huge pressures to rearrange the economies. Studies of efforts to promote market-oriented technology transfer practices in a number of Central and Eastern European (CEE) countries during 1995 and 1996 (Chataway 1999) and a study of technological networks in Tanzania in 1996 (Hewitt and Wield 1997), show that macro-level policy to introduce market mechanisms has not led automatically to the emergence of more efficient institutional structures.

Tracing the changes: linear approaches to innovation

Science and technology under central planning

Prior to the changes which began during the late 1980s and early 1990s, the basic framework for science and technology activity was the same throughout the former Soviet Union (FSU) and CEE. Work was located in three separate types of institutions: universities undertook training and some research work carried out by individual researchers; academy of science institutes undertook basic research; and applied institutes supposedly worked with industry on more practical applications. Universities were for the most part split into separate units along disciplinary lines, such as Chemistry or Philosophy.

This structure reflected a belief, widely held in both Western and Eastern Europe, in the linear theory of innovation which envisions science leading to technology leading to innovation. Critiques of this linear approach to innovation have been widely discussed and the limitations of the approach broadly accepted (Dosi et al. 1988). However, even given the limitations of the approach, the linkages which might have facilitated some productive activity were not strong. On a formal basis, these institutes worked largely independently of one another. Linkages which, in theory, were meant to exist in Eastern Europe often did not in practice. Applied or industrial research institutes were meant to feed their findings into industry. Indeed, rhetorically, services provided by scientists and technologists to industry were often used to justify spending in these sectors. In reality, links were often weak. Industry, which was meant to handle all technology transfer activities internally (there were no intermediary or facilitating organisations), often did not have the expertise to identify the type of technology needed. Radosevic comments:

Although R&D [research and development] systems in socialist economies were very much oriented towards the needs of industry they were not organisations in industry but for industry... R&D was externalised and treated as a separate activity with enterprises seen as passive recipients of R&D achievements ready for implementation' previously developed by the R&D institutes. The neglect of the role of enterprises as a source of technology and emphasis on extramural R&D were at the root of the problems of R&D in the socialist system. (Radosevic 1996: 10)

Product development in itself is not necessarily the problem. Indeed, the product development approach is one way of becoming more market-oriented. Sony is a classic example of this. However, there is a need for robustness of design and constant innovation to avoid the need for major redesign effort for each new product.

The lack of capacity in firms left them unable to specify technological needs or appropriate uses. According to Webster,

...industrial production enterprises never developed a genuinely internal R&D capacity that could have established a basis on which a firm could develop a 'business' (and not merely a production) strategy, shaped by an understanding of its technical competencies, an awareness of how its needs might be satisfied from external sources and an ability to evaluate and assimilate externally supplied inputs. (Webster 1996: 3).

Webster goes on to point out that research in innovation economics has stressed the importance of this internal capacity to absorb R&D, 'even more so, paradoxically, as firms outsource some of their research needs: only by having a genuine grasp of research requirements can external suppliers be properly judged on their ability to meet those needs' (ibid.).

Additionally, effective linkages were made even more rare because institutes were often reluctant to adopt the agendas of others, preferring to work on their areas of interest. In any case, in the context of centrally planned economies, with the emphasis on mass production of standard products and without competitive pressure, there was no need to design systems around constant innovation. Where linkages did operate, product development was the predominate focus rather than R&D or chnological effort focusing on process technologies, cost reduction, and increased efficiency (Radosevic 1996: 10).

While scientific and technological achievement had an important place in ideological and sociological terms under the old system, it was not integrated into economic structures. Given the relatively static nature of the socialist innovation system, even when significant results were achieved, they were seldom incorporated into production of civilian goods. Much of industry outside the military and space spheres was technically stagnant. There was no need to innovate; only to produce large quantities of goods. Despite talk of ongoing 'scientific-technological revolution', neither applied nor basic research institutes were able to make a significant contribution to economic development during the socialist period.

Science and technology under the development state

Although it remains predominantly an agricultural economy, Tanzania has a small but significant industrial base, with quite rapid industrialisation in the 1960s to mid-1970s (Barker et al. 1986). Accompanying industrial expansion was the installation of a range of industrial support organisations whose main function was to service the R&D needs of industry and, to a lesser extent agriculture. Ironically, it was this integrated effort at industrialisation — based on state-owned enterprise — that appears to have led to the fragmentation of S&T effort in Tanzania.

To this extent, Tanzania has a quite different industrial history to Eastern Europe: there was very little industry until the 1960s whereas Poland, for example, had industrial growth from the late 19th century and then, under communist rule, mass higher and secondary education. Tanzania, by contrast, had a tiny proportion of its population in secondary education, and only one university, until the mid-1990s. Nevertheless, there is a strikingly similar story to that of Eastern Europe. The Tanzanian state has been a key player in the development of its S&T infrastructure, funding R&D institutions, university research and other forms of 'support'. However, the extent to which this support was ever effective is questionable, at least in the case of R&D organisations. The similarity lies in the model of internal technology transfer. In both cases there was an assumption that there would be a linear transfer from 'laboratory' to factory. In both cases this model was flawed.

The S&T infrastructure was set up by the Tanzanian state to support industry and agriculture. The example of eight such institutions is sufficient to paint a picture of their situation.

Figure 2 Industrial support organisations in Tanzania

Name		Function
TISCO	Tanzania Industrial Studies and Consulting Organisation	Government-owned consultancy to industry.
TIRDO	Tanzania Industrial Research and Development Organisation	Government-owned and funded R&D services to industry.
TBS	Tanzania Bureau of Standards	Government-owned. Prepares and establishes standards; testing, certification and training in quality assurance.
TEMDO	Tanzania Engineering and Manufacturing Design Organisation	Government-owned. Designs industrial products/processes; technical consultancy for spare parts and component design; engineering training.
CAMARTEC	Centre of Agricultural Mechanisation and Rural Technology	Government-owned. Supports low-price technology development of farming implements (water tanks, solar cookers, sunflower oil press, wood carts, bricks).
SIDO	Small Industries Development Organisation	Government-funded promotion of small and micro enterprises, regional representatives, offers range of services (loans, hire purchase, consultancy, training, workshop premises).
MEIDA	Metal Engineering Industries Development Association	Self-financing organisation (at least non-state but attracted donor funding), from membership fees. Administers Import Support Fund for members (donor funded). Provides training for members. Association membership has dropped rapidly.

The other organisation worthy of mention is the Faculty of Engineering at the University of Dar Es Salaam. Apart from the provision of trained engineers, many of whom work in the above organisations, the Faculty has run its own R&D unit (Materu 1996).

As in Eastern Europe, these organisations were set up to provide for industry and agriculture with strong links to the government coordinating bodies such as the National Development Corporation, the Commission for Science and Technology, and the Ministry of Science,

Technology and Higher Education. In theory, these were part of a web of development organisations which were to feed off each other and generate mutual and national benefits. As in Eastern Europe, there was a linear 'technology-push' view of how the R&D organisations would function. It was assumed in many quarters that by their mere existence, industry would call on the services offered and that this same industry would take up the 'innovations' produced by them.

This did not happen on any meaningful scale. On the one hand, staff of the research organisations appear baffled when trying to explain why industry does not make contact with them or buy their prototypes. On the other hand, industrialists feign ignorance of the organisations' very existence (or, at best, dismiss them as irrelevant to their concerns). As a result, the support organisations went into financial decline and turned to other activities for financial survival (selling off land, renting out premises, and carrying out individual consultancies out of hours) (Aguirre-Bastos and Materu 1993; SIDA 1996; TIRDO various).

International donors stepped in to support several organisations, particularly Scandinavian aid (SIDA 1996). Donors, however, are losing patience with the continued ineffectiveness of research institutions. The medium-term prospect for this network of organisations looks bleak. Since most of their clients are para-statal firms in the process of being, or already, privatised, there is some doubt about their sustainability. Fragmentation of effort is compounded by isolation and scarce resources. There is now considerable pressure for these organisations to restructure in an attempt to survive in the post-adjustment era. This pressure comes from inside the organisations as well as from the government and from donors.

Managing technology transfer with multiple actors: a non-linear approach

One of the important characteristics of the reforming S&T systems in Eastern Europe and to some extent in Tanzania is that there are multiple actors involved. No longer are the S&T systems controlled by the state. Multiple actors can imply fragmentation of effort. Johnson (in Chataway et al. 1996) identified three factors which will have a strong influence on the ability to coordinate action in multi actor fields:

1 *Negotiating new organisational goals or agendas:* if these differ greatly between organisations and institutions involved in a particular field – for example, science and technology – it may be difficult to establish agreement on an overall policy or action framework.

2 *Recognising the resource base of different organisations:* the capacity of different organisations to mobilise resources to meet their goals and agendas is likely to affect their role in any process of negotiation. For low-resource organisations, integration with others could be an enabling process allowing them to be part of a wider and more influential arena. However, it could also limit the effect of their particular 'niche' or competencies if they are part of a wider process in which high-resource organisations such as multi-lateral agencies dominate and seek to impose a particular agenda.

3 *Promoting organisational capacities to learn, adapt and change:* given that each organisation will (in principle) be working towards its given goals and agenda, the process of working with others may involve new practices, forms of negotiation, and compromise, as well as potential areas of struggle and conflict. Thus an organisation's capacity to overcome barriers to changing its 'organisational culture' and its ability to learn from different approaches, or to work together with organisations and institutions which have different approaches, might well be key.

These three factors have a direct bearing on managing tensions between fragmentation and integration, and in the directions that institutional changes may take.

Eastern Europe

Models of economic reform have differed in Central and Eastern Europe, with some countries — Poland, for example — moving very quickly to adopt the market, and others such as Slovakia displaying a much more ambiguous approach to liberalisation and privatisation. In terms of corresponding reform in S&T systems, there has also been a wide variety of approaches.

In this section, we explore some of the features of reform of the S&T system in Poland and some features of the reform process in other countries. The main point is that macro-level economic reform does not automatically lead to the emergence of 'market friendly' institutions. In the area of S&T, and efforts to promote technology transfer in particular, a great many linkages and relationships between market-based institutions and organisations, and between market-based and non-market-based institutions and organisations, create effective systems. These linkages and relationships are fostered by conscious nurturing and shaping, and depend on institutions' capacity to manage them.

One of the first elements of reform in the S&T system in Poland was to change the institutional structure for funding and S&T policy. The funding of all science and technology research, without regard to the institutional base, is now channeled through one body, The Committee for Scientific Research (KBN). One of the main reasons for establishing KBN was to try and create a level playing field among different kinds of institutes. The new structure was also designed to increase administrative efficiency and introduce a level of autonomy; the KBN as an autonomous institution is less subject to the political whims of other ministries. Scientists and academics, bruised from the high level of centralised control experienced under the previous regime, were keen that autonomy be protected. While autonomy has allowed the new institution to move relatively quickly and to break out of the previous structure, it has meant that integration with other government and non-government bodies has sometimes been difficult.

Negotiating new organisational goals or agendas: balancing S&T in the new Polish system

The fact that S&T has its own policy-making and administrative unit has meant that it has been able to protect itself more than might have been so otherwise. The funding system that emerged out of the new set-up was based on principles of participation and equal opportunity. However, it worked in favour of more scientific activity rather than technological development and transfer.

Additionally, while peer-review is in many ways desirable, members of the sub-committee tend to be respected academics. An OECD report noted, 'It should be noted that virtually all the members of ... [the KBN funding commissions] are elected by a voting population which is heavily dominated by university teachers (80 per cent). As a result a large majority of seats is filled by the latter (70 per cent)' (OECD 1995). In the Polish context, where little credit was given for more applied work and where 'commercialisation' was still viewed with great suspicion, interesting basic or more fundamental work tended to be favoured. Some of the other funding streams which related to commissioned projects, and which could have favoured more applied work, were too small to compensate for the cuts in these two principle mechanisms.

The KBN developed a targeted R&D funding mechanism, as did other CEE bodies allocating S&T funding. These are co-financing mechanisms. Public or private business are eligible and KBN will cover up to 50 per cent of costs. KBN funds can only be used to support pre-competitive aspects of the project. Co-financing mechanisms are in principle important, but in many contexts have not yet worked well.[2] The problem was that these budgets tend to be small and the lack of money in the private sector meant that the available funds were in many cases not disbursed.

Efforts were being made in 1995 to examine state funding of S&T and may well have gone some way to introducing a new balance in the system. The point here is that even in a situation where a new institution was created with explicit remit of creating systems conducive with the need to foster new linkages and create a S&T system relevant to the new market-based environment, a variety of problems related to institutional stickiness and lack of capacity were experienced.

There have been problems in agreeing action frameworks, with non-academic components of the system frustrated at not being able to find a voice in the new set-up. KBN is, in part, a reaction to the very highly centralised forms of control that went before. Scientists' determination to operate in a very autonomous manner, the lack of effective linkages which would foster technology transfer (with industry and the ministry of industry for example), and the lack of support for applied projects which would require the involvement of others, have to be understood in this context.

Recognising the resource-base of different organisations: change at the micro level

A variety of structures and experiments are taking place at the level of research institutes, small companies, and individual researchers. In many contexts, individuals from applied institutes, academy institutes, and universities are setting up small technology-oriented firms. They are often driven to do so by low salaries or redundancy. In many cases, the firms are set up within the walls of their parent organisations, sometimes with no legitimate rights and usually with no official recognition or assistance. Lack of knowledge in managing a business, patenting, licensing, and forming useful partnerships, not to mention lack of finance, often makes life very difficult for these firms.

Institutes' ability to adapt to the new economic situation depends on a number of factors: the sector in which the institute operates, the strength of that economic sector in the country; decisions made within the institute; reforms at the macro level; access to foreign expertise and finance. In Poland, while many institutes have been supported by statutory funds, the level of funding has been very low in many instances. Some institutes, even when a clear need for their output has been identified, have found it difficult to adapt and fit into the new environment.

The Packaging Institute is an example of an institute which provides a much-needed service for many Polish firms, including emerging SMEs, but which has suffered from a lack of effective demand from firms. Several consultancy studies and needs assessment exercises have concluded that packaging is an essential element if Polish firms are going to be able to compete in increasingly competitive national and international markets. The Institute has worked hard to form links with industry and has had some success in reorienting itself to new conditions, providing testing, consultancy, and information services. Nevertheless, new small firms are not in a position to pay the full cost of services and development of new projects. The Institute is also classified as a 'B' category institute and 80 per cent of its funding comes from non-statutory sources. KBN has additionally funded a 'special project' relating to recyclable packaging. However, there is still a serious shortfall in funds to work on a wider range of projects.

The Packaging Institute is beginning to provide key services to a number of firms, but is operating in a difficult context. Its success depends of firms identifying packing and marketing as important areas for them to improve — and having funds with which to invest in improvements in this area. The 'push' factor of cuts in statutory funding has indeed provided an impetus for the Institute to change direction, but private sector lack of funds and low levels or project funding and co-financing mechanisms have been major constraints. Efforts to stimulate demand and to educate and inform about packaging have been limited. Attempts to integrate the perspectives of firms and needs of new entrepreneurs into the work of the institute have also been very limited. This type of networking and learning between different actors involved in technology transfer is rare.

The very different levels of resources available to organisations means that their ability to engage in effective technology transfer will also differ. The Packaging Institute which potentially has a key role in improving the competitiveness of Polish firms, is effectively constrained by very limited resources.

Promoting organisational capacities to learn: reforming the old and responding to the new

Technical consultancy firms are emerging in some CEE countries, but these firms often need a significant amount of non-technology business, usually trading, in order to survive. A variety of 'science and technology parks' and incubator-type institutions are being created. These terms are used to describe a wide range of outfits. Sometimes all they amount to are attempts by a research institute to rent out unused space. As noted above, often the extent to which these new organisations network with others is limited, although in many cases they would benefit from doing so more. Benefits could well be felt both in terms of the substantive gains to be had from creating links with other S&T-based outfits, but also in terms of marketing themselves.

The rather insular way in which both old and new organisations tend to work constrains their capacity to respond to a constantly changing external environment. In part, at least, this limited openness can be explained by the way in which organisations operated in the past. There is a tendency to try and maximise the range of activities within an organisation rather than creating relationships with others (Jasinski 1996).

Another way in which the past still influences current modes of operation is in the belief that technology alone will create successful products and demand. The 'logic of technology push' which so dominated the past often re-emerges. In some cases it can it reinforces a desire to create new institutions, rather than to learn from, work with, and reform existing ones. Work in Romania in 1996 showed that there is a tendency, among research institute directors and national policy-makers, to think that if there is a lack of demand it is not because the technology being offered is inappropriate; it is because companies do not realise the potential. Therefore, the answer is to encourage the growth of state-owned new companies. This is perhaps an unlikely outcome to a set of reforms meant to promote market institutions! It also ignores the needs and problems of existing companies.

The extent to which technology transfer can be made more effective then is hampered by the limited learning between organisations. Firms, research institutes, and universities tend to work in relative isolation. New organisations, which have emerged in part, at least, with the remit of facilitating new linkages and promoting transfer, tend, themselves, to be inward-looking.

Restructuring S&T in Tanzania

There is little question that restructuring of Tanzanian industry and S&T is long overdue. Our interest here is how this restructuring is taking place. The short answer is that it is piecemeal, slow, and entrenched in previous practices. Through the 1990s there has been considerable fragmentation as a result. But there are also (potentially) new forms of integration.

The fragmentation is partly an outcome of the operation of the 'old' system. Industrial output from state-owned firms was well under capacity. Research institutes such as those identified above, were not working in areas relevant to industry, and a cumbersome bureaucracy was left with little or nothing to coordinate, in particular in the National Development Corporation (NDC). In short, the fledgling industrial structure of the economy as well as its component parts were crumbling before everyone's eyes.

The research organisations were, with one exception:

- running operational and market share losses;
- losing their market share to private companies (particularly in consultancy work);
- suffering from declining staff productivity and morale;
- selling fixed assets to finance recurrent costs.

The exception is the Tanzanian Bureau of Standards (TBS). TBS has a clear role to play in providing a service that is in demand to Tanzanian business. The singular success of TBS compared with the failure of other industrial support organisations raises an important point: while the state has concentrated on organisations – maintaining them because they are there, not because of what they do – there is a need to focus on function: what kind of support does business need in order to flourish? TBS is thriving because its function is required by business.

The quandary for development management is how to reverse or halt this decline. Perhaps more crucial still is the answer to the question asked by one weary-sounding donor's report: 'who can do what?' (SIDA 1996).

Success (actual or likely) in turning these organisations around is, we would argue, largely dependent on the three factors we introduced at the beginning of this section. S&T is a multi-actor field and, in Tanzania, the relevant actors are not able to talk to each other. It is questionable whether they have ever been able to work together.

Negotiation of organisational goals or agendas

Despite the despondency, there have been some attempts to realign goals and agendas. Organisations have made business plans and survival strategy documents in recognition that the situation is dire, but government response is minimal. There appears to be an expectation that government will (or should) continue to support R&D as in the past. Government, whether it wants to or not, is disinclined to supply this. The view is that R&D organisations should begin to stand in its own feet without subsidy (the irony is that these continue to be state-owned). This is the first difference in goals hampering restructuring. The second is that already mentioned: R&D organisations' potential customers (and, therefore, source of financial support in the absence of government funds) is industry, which also has differing agendas. Industry is either not interested in R&D, or it sources technology elsewhere. Donors, finally, have developed a certain fatigue in supporting R&D organisations.

Recognising the resource-base of different organisations

The resource-base of R&D organisations went into steep decline in the 1980s and continued into the 1990s. The capacity to mobilise resources had depended primarily on the state and, in a small number of cases, on subscription. As a result, other forms of resourcing had to be found. At first, the organisations turned towards international donors. Of late, even this source is drying up. This fragmentation (every organisation for itself) has reduced the chances for meaningful industrial support activity.

As a result, these industrial support organisations have moved towards 'soft' consultancy activities as a means of survival. This has brought with it its own problems and is the source of human resource fragmentation in Tanzania. Donors and NGOs are in the practice of using consultancy as a route to 'nabbing' the best Tanzanian experts (invariably with individualised payment well above the going rate in Tanzanian institutions). In theory, such a strategy could be seen as a source of learning. In practice, however, it has heightened the sense of fragmentation.

Promoting organisational capacity to learn, adapt, and change

As we have said, the ability to learn from other approaches, and to work with organisations which have different approaches, may be key to getting out of the impasse. The key players in any process of institutional change intended to achieve greater integration with the Tanzanian economy are:

- the government, particularly relevant ministries;
- the Boards of Directors of industrial support organisations (ISOs);
- the Management of ISOs;
- the staff of ISOs;
- the clients of ISOs.

All have a part to play in the management of the tensions around the fragmentation and integration of S&T. For example, the government needs to decide on whether it continues to want the ISOs and, if it does, to resource them appropriately. Resources, however are only the start. Relevant ministries need to set measurable objectives and ensure that they are monitored by a competent board. Managers require the confidence, wherewithal, and tools to put in place plans for action; and ISO staff need a purpose for turning up for work. This action needs to be focused on the production of things of value to clients. Clients in turn need to make demands on R&D organisations to be a part of the decision making over which products are of value. It is the dialogue between these last two which is perhaps the most crucial, and yet it is the one which has never taken place (SIDA 1996).

Conclusions

A primary aim of the restructuring efforts in Poland and — though less advanced — in Tanzania is the dissolution of institutions based on state-led planning. In some instances, disintegration of state institutions has led to high levels of fragmentation and periods of chaos. However, these changes also open up possibilities for new forms of integration and realignment of effort. In the area of reform of the S&T infrastructure, reforms are constructed on the premise that market-led institutions, based on competition and the profit motive, will serve economies more effectively. Thus, these reforms are about the destruction of old institutions and the promotion of new systems.

Enhanced internal technology transfer depends on new funding systems for S&T and new networks and forms of integration and cooperation between different actors. Yet, macro-reform packages based on privatisation and liberalisation have had very limited success in promoting these new interactions. As stated at the start of this paper, market-based reforms in themselves are no guarantee of useful outcomes. Institutional reform has tended not to address the need for integration with other actors. Lack of resources and resistance to change in funding bodies, research institutes, and industry are all barriers to change

In relation to Poland and Tanzania a number of specific issues arise:

- Government funding and policy is not oriented toward internal technology transfer (that is, the useful transfer of products and processes from research organisations to firms), whether the focus is on basic science as in Eastern Europe or fosters R&D in a vacuum as in the case of Tanzania. Cultural legacies mean that disjointed scientific and R&D efforts tend to be thought of as more important than technological development. It is also in some important respects easier to classify the quality of scientific achievement, and there are very well established mechanisms for evaluating research. The mechanisms in both Western and Eastern Europe for evaluating projects oriented more towards development tend to be more difficult to implement. The difficulties in constructing policy with regard to applied institutes, and adopting a framework for promoting technology transfer, have meant that change in this area is slow.

- There is a lack of knowledge and experience of the technology transfer process. This manifests itself in a number of ways. For example, many research institutes see technology transfer principally as an attempt to market the results of their research and their technology artifacts. Strategy is based on technology push. For most companies, however, output from research institutes in artifact and prototype form is unlikely to be of any use. Companies need forms of technology and technological assistance which relate much more closely to their business and their existing operations. It is the process of communication over the longer term, which could lead to jointly conceived projects, that is lacking. The experience of this type of partnership and way of working is often absent both in research institutes and in companies. There is also an absence of experience in managing patent portfolios, licensing technology, or evaluating technology in terms of market need.

- A great deal of faith is often put in establishing databases which detail research projects. It is thought that these databases will facilitate a 'supply and demand' match. In practice this is rarely the case. While information about where institutional and individual expertise might be located is useful, very detailed accounts of particular research projects are less so, for the same reasons as mentioned above.

In sum, the concept of technology transfer among policy makers in the two cases examined is still linear. The idea of science leading to technology leading to innovation, which prevailed under the old system, is very much predominant in policy thinking today. If the creation of a centralised integration or coordination system has failed to work in the two cases, what should be the overall aim of S&T restructuring? From the above evidence, our view is that it should be the creation of a system which allows multi-agency action, not top-down, hierarchical coordination or market 'free for alls'. This at least opens up the possibility of adopting non-linear approaches to technology transfer. We have argued that a good starting point for this is a consideration of organisational goals and agendas, the resource-base of different organisations, and fostering organisational capacities to learn, adapt, and change.

Notes

1 This paper combines two elements. The first is research carried out by the authors in Eastern Europe and Tanzania in 1995, 1996, and 1998. The second is a reflection on The Open University's teaching on development management in which we have been involved over the last three years. We are grateful to Hazel Johnson and David Wield for comments on earlier drafts.

2 In Romania the co-financing mechanism has been slow to become operational and only covers 20 per cent of the overall costs of the project, further limiting the uptake of available funds.

References

Aguirre-Bastos, C. and P. Materu (1993) Establishment of a National System of Technology Acquisition, Internalisation and Monitoring in Tanzania, Vienna: UNIDO.

Barker, C. E., M. R. Bhagavan, P. V. Mitschke-Collande and D. Wield (1986) *African Industrialisation: Technology and Change in Tanzania,* Aldershot: Gower.

Chataway J. (1999) 'Technology transfer and the restructuring of science technology in Eastern Europe', *Technovation,* forthcoming.

Chataway J. and A. Joffe (1998) 'Communicating results' in A. Thomas , J. Chataway and M. Wuyts (eds.) *Finding out Fast,* London: Sage Publications.

Chataway J., T. Hewitt, H. Johnson and A. Thomas (1996) 'From public sector to public action', *TU872 Capacities for Managing Development* Part 4, Milton Keynes: The Open University.

Dosi G., C. Freeman, R. Nelson, G. Silverberg and L. Soete (eds.) (1988) *Technical Change and Economic Theory,* London: Pinter Publishers.

Hewitt T. and D. Wield (1997) 'Formal and informal networks in Tanzanian industrialisation', *Science and Public Policy* (24)5: 395–404

Jasinski, A. (1994) 'Science and technology policy and changes in Polish industry in the transition period', *Science and Public Policy* (21)3: 188–192.

Jasinski, A. (1996) 'Academic-industry relations and transition in Poland', in A. Webster (ed.) *Building New Bases for Innovation,* Cambridge: Anglia Polytechnic University.

Materu, P. (1996) 'The Faculty of Engineering and the building of an engineering (academic-based) network in Tanzania', Draft Working Paper, Dar es Salaam: University of Dar es Salaam.

OECD (1995) *Examiners Report,* Paris: OECD.

Radosevic S. (1996) 'Restructuring of R&D institutes in post-socialist economies: emerging patterns and issues, in A. Webster (ed.) *Building New Bases for Innovation,* Cambridge: Anglia Polytechnic University.

SIDA (1996) Restructuring Tanzania's Industrial Support Organisations, Dar es Salaam: SIDA.

Tidd J., J. Bessant and K. Pavitt (1997) Managing Innovation: Integrating Technological, Market and Organisational Change, Chichester: John Wiley.

TIRDO, Various Annual Reports 1988–92, Dar es Salaam: Tanzania Industrial Research and Development Organisation.

Webster A. (ed.) (1996) *Building New Bases for Innovation*, Cambridge: Anglia Polytechnic University

Inclusive planning and allocation for rural services

Doug Porter and Martin Onyach-Olaa

Introduction

Sloganeering about 'participation in development' no longer goes without challenge. Tallying up the once-hidden vices of participation alongside its known virtues, a recent review concluded that participatory development is an 'essentially contested concept'.[1] Yet it is clear that delivery of sustainable, equitable, and affordable rural services is helped if users are involved in choices about priorities and delivery options. They tend to be more prepared to invest their own resources and sometimes, though not as often as hoped, this involvement makes those services more accessible to vulnerable sections of the population (Cernea 1985).

In developing countries, it is often argued that this kind of participation is constrained by the representative political process. The 'distance' — political, economic, and social — between elected leaders and their constituency is simply too great for voices to be heard and participation to be effective. Special measures are necessary. In response, it has been agreed that intensive community consultation techniques (such as found in the 'PRA toolbox' much popularised by Robert Chambers and associates) can greatly improve the quality of local service planning decisions. Most donors now insist that these techniques are adopted and many are supporting networks, training programmes, manuals, and guides to help to install them in routine planning practices in developing countries.

Two issues are being debated in countries like Uganda, where participatory practice is promoted by a host of NGO and government agencies. One is about 'cost effectiveness'. Given limited resources, pragmatic local leaders ask whether the return on intensive participatory planning justifies the investment? Advocates of participation answer with a resounding 'Yes'. But the evidence is less tidy and unequivocal. It is not clear where it is best to invest scarce resources in the many decisions that need to be made in identifying and responding to service delivery needs. Where should participatory 'entry points' and 'veto points' be created in the planning and delivery process? Advocates of participation seldom give clear advice. A second issue now arising is whether current approaches to participation in planning actually divert attention from other, more pressing, problems in ensuring services are not just well planned but that resources are sensibly allocated, and that delivery is appropriately regulated and sustained.

We try to put this debate into a broader context. When asked to define 'participation' priorities, advocates tend to focus narrowly on the technicalities of a planning process. Their concern is to maximise participation when 'community-service users' identify 'needs', then prioritise investment options amongst competing possibilities and assemble these in the form of 'community plans' for action by higher authorities. In contrast, we illustrate the many other points in the process, possibly more significant, where things go wrong and, ultimately, where the actual delivery of services is determined.

Our second concern is more fundamental. In many cases, the techniques of participatory planning are becoming absorbed in the routine administrative process of planning. While some advocates of these techniques applaud this, we think this both sells short the potential contribution of these techniques and, more importantly, can have adverse, negative impacts on the quality of the process of allocating resources wisely to competing priorities. This approach can weaken the political relationship between leaders and their constituency. Increasingly, the administrative apparatus of planning comes to stand between leaders and constituencies. Constituents' political demands become administratively disciplined at the same time that the administrative and technical organs of local government become politicised. We argue that the key is not participation in planning, but rather creating an accountable, inclusive process within the broader frame of political representation at all levels and stages in the service planning and delivery cycle.

We suggest that participation be regarded as part of a broader process of 'inclusive planning and allocation'. Accountability is the key to this. Accountability of politicians to their constituency is the main rationale for popular participation. Accountability of technicians is also essential to ensure the range of design, engineering, fiscal, environmental, and other 'technical' factors are competently brought to the attention of politicians. And finally, inclusive planning and allocation requires accountability between different levels of local and central authorities responsible, to set the policy framework, regulate, and enforce compliance.

Background

These observations draw on experience gained through the District Development Project (DDP) in Uganda since 1996. Uganda's turbulent history since independence in 1963 is well known — coups in 1966 and 1971, the war with Tanzania in 1979, the protracted guerrilla struggle 1981–85 and victory of the National Resistance Movement (NRM) in January 1986. Less well known is Uganda's radical experiment with democratic decentralisation since 1992, one of the few instances of classic devolution on sub-Saharan Africa.[2] The DDP is part of the far-reaching changes occurring in the way development services are planned and financed as a result of decentralisation (see Villadsen and Lubanga 1996).

The project aims to test participatory planning and decentralised financing procedures under the 1997 Local Government Act. The Act empowers local governments with responsibility for a wide range of services — in fact, central government ministries, by and large, are left with responsibility for policy development and for regulating and providing technical guidance to local governments. Although still under-resourced, there is a commitment to devolve a major share of the national budget to fiscally, administratively, and politically autonomous local governments. There are problems as well: the new 'rules of the game' are unfamiliar, some central ministries resist devolution of their powers, there is conflict, corruption and mistrust amongst different levels of local government and their constituents. But there is also a surprising amount of innovation and creativity.

To take decentralisation further, government has defined two key tasks for the DDP. First, the need to improve the capacity of local councils to plan, finance, and manage the delivery of services to their constituencies. Second, there is a pressing need to develop a system of incentives and sanctions to promote accountability and establish a clear link between taxes and transfers received and services delivered. DDP is therefore piloting different approaches to decentralised planning and financing for rural services.

Formulation of the DDP began with an analysis of how services were currently planned and produced. Communities, Local Councillors, contractors, NGOs, and community-based organisations (CBOs) were therefore asked to help construct 'service decision trees' by talking through, in a structured way, each step in the process. Lively debates ensued about the rules of the game and how it was played. This led to talks about how it could be improved before significantly greater amounts of funds became available through decentralisation. For three months across five districts, we moved back and forth over the following kinds of questions:

- how were investment projects identified and prioritised, who was involved, with what effect?
- how were priorities designed, costed, and appraised?
- how were decisions made about who would be the 'owner' of the investment if many different agencies were contributing to creating and maintaining the service?
- how were designs and bills of quantity produced and checked when facilities needed to be constructed or rehabilitated?
- what were the different arrangements for involving contractors or local *fundis*; who hired them, who decided to hire them, who monitored and supervised their work, etc.?
- how were arrangements made to ensure the ancillary services were made available (such as the drugs for a health clinic, the health workers were trained and assigned to work in the facility, etc.)?

Service decision trees

The rough and ready 'service decision trees' revealed interesting, sometimes surprising insights into how business is done at the local level. We learnt the following:

1 *The 'formal' versus the 'actual' way of doing business.* While the formal rules of the game (for planning, appraising, budgeting, delivering services) are the same across the country, there is an extraordinary range of local practices. At various times, in the same locality and for the same sector of service, rules were observed for part of the process, at times they appeared to be flouted, at times a mixture of rule and local arrangement was applied. Practices were not often just 'changed at will', but it was clear the mix of local history, politics, skills, and traditions were crucially important in how local governments, community organisations, informal leaders, contractors, and so on actually worked to plan and produce services.

2   *Linear versus iterative planning and allocation.* Although planning and production of services is typically described in terms of a series of linear steps, actual practice is more typically iterative where steps are often 'leapt over' and missed, earlier decisions are constantly revisited and changed. For instance, 'appraisal' of proposals or designs rarely occurred as a single event, but was often continuous — once the cost implications of a prior choice became known, for instance, people often moved back to change the early choice. Sometimes design standards were altered, the scale of investment was increased or decreased, and 'burning priorities' constantly changed. The volatile and itinerant political process of planning and investing in services was in constant tension with the administratively defined, linear, and forward-moving process defined in statutes and regulations.

3   *Community service provision and 'transfer funding'.* A large share of the resources needed to establish and maintain local services came from outside the local government sector, from community contributions, external donors, local politicians and other elites. We learnt that the bulk of services was created and sustained by communities, with next to no involvement of local councils. We also learnt that in addition to taxes, community contributions sometimes funded significant parts of the local authority mandated to deliver the service. School fees, for instance, were often 'trapped' at the district level, to cover the gaps in funds available for keeping the district education office functioning.

4   *More exclusive decisions once the need had been prioritised.* Not surprising was that many people were excluded from decisions, and often the 'wrong priority' was funded. Less expected was realisation that as the process progressed from establishing priorities to appraisal, budgeting, and delivery of services, decisions were made by increasingly fewer people and according to more exclusive criteria. Consequently, local priorities were often radically reshaped as they moved through the hands of councillors and technicians toward final delivery. Decisions tended, therefore, to become increasingly parochial, ignoring wider ramifications and consequences, and less accountable.

5   *Participation and priorities for improvement.* Most people wanted greater say in how investment priorities were decided. But *more* were concerned with what happened once the list of priorities had been decided, regardless of whether they had been directly involved. In other words, more people were concerned about the fact that the technical quality of decisions was often poor.[3] They were annoyed that

what was often defined as a 'technical' issue was often a 'political' judgement. And irrespective of whether their priorities had been accepted, local people were often more concerned that leaders and technical staff (of local governments, NGOs, and CBOs alike) tended not to be accountable for their conduct once decisions had been made.

All this varied by sector. Some investments were easier to handle than others; some kinds of investment were more 'accessible' to scrutiny by the community, and tended to go off the rails less often than others; under some arrangements, complaints were fewer, satisfaction was higher.

Yet in all this diversity, we began to question four key aspects of the approach that lies behind the push for more participatory practices in service planning and delivery. First, like many similar programmes, we had assumed it would be most important to ensure community access to the 'front end' of the planning process, when needs were assessed and priorities decided. This was clearly misplaced. As one market vendor said to us, 'It doesn't really matter whether it's the roof that's improved this time, or that drains on the edges of the market are given priority. The priority is less important than what they actually do on the ground'.

Second, the planning and production of services is conventionally understood as a linear, step-wise, and uni-directional process. This is clearly at odds with the procedures employed by local people in most situations to meet their service requirements. By implication, if the intention was to support local capacities for delivery of services, it took little foresight to realise that much of what was currently offered in planning manuals, training and 're-tooling' exercises would have little value. And neither, perhaps, did it make sense to focus scarce resources on instilling this technical, rational approach in the minds of the administrative organs of local councils or NGOs. This has been a major focus of capacity building efforts for more than two decades. In few cases did we find that the administrative cadres of local councils or NGOs were not reasonably well versed in the rudiments of planning discourse. In fact, in Uganda, as throughout east and southern Africa, there is a marked contrast between the administrative staff and political leadership. On one side is a reasonably well-trained administrative cadre able to rehearse (but seldom apply) the litany of 'good planning practice'. They sit at some distance from a local leadership often alienated, completely at sea with the administrative process, and frequently determined to free themselves from the restrictions they feel it unreasonably imposes. Our third realisation, therefore, was that pushing for a PRA-type process to be installed in the local government planning process would probably backfire. It could further politicise the administrative organ of councils and place technicians as interlocutors between local communities and their leadership.

It seemed, therefore, that large parts of the kind of 'capacity building' delivered in decentralised or participatory planning and financing programmes was ill suited to needs. Undeniably, technical skills could usefully be enhanced. But of more significance were the political skills of bargaining, compromise, and assembling the many social, technical, financial and other factors necessary for leaders to make wise decisions throughout the service planning and delivery process. Quite clearly, decentralisation has heightened political contest at the local level, and the devolution of development funds under a programme like the DDP quickly over-stretches the political skills of elected leaders. This realisation underpins the emphasis here on 'inclusive planning and allocation procedures'. However, while new skills are needed, the keystone to this approach is not 'capacity', but 'accountability'. This requires sorting through the nests of sanctions and incentives that bear on the performance of political leaders and technicians both at local and higher levels. Accountability is evidently many-sided, but the fourth thing we realised from these consultations was that accountability among different levels of local and central government was at least as important, if not more so, as the accountability of leaders to constituents, the concern that pre-occupies the contemporary clamour for 'participatory planning'. We say more about these points below.

The limits of front end participation

During our consultations, most communities were able to articulate a 'long list' of many and varied needs. People *were* concerned that priorities were often determined by the boys in the backroom, and then given a rousing beat up by politicians and leaders when presented to the expectant mass as their 'real priorities'. They wanted a wider range of priorities to be considered. But in the main, people seemed less concerned with the actual 'need' that was finally decided on, than they were with the problems that arose following this decision. This led us to wonder whether the 'opportunity cost' of one priority over another was lower than we assumed? Perhaps higher was the 'opportunity cost' of the litany of problems that occurred following the decision on what was to be the immediate priority for action? Certainly more anger was expressed about mismanagement of resources, failure to honour commitments, poor coordination and so on, than ever arose about whether one priority or another was agreed.

This contrasts with conventional thinking about participation, which focuses on planning, and, within this, narrows to discussion of the best approaches to encourage direct community participation in the early steps in the process. Why is this? One reason is perhaps a legacy of the 1970s tradition of development where special prominence was given to the production of plans (national, regional, community, project) and to the central role of technicians, particularly planners.[4] In rural service planning, the approach is a linear process. First, baseline studies establish the 'local situation'. Typically this is understood in terms of how many people have access to what services: ratios of doctors to population, ratios to school-aged children to enrolled school pupils, the density of roads in relation to agricultural potential, and so on. Service deficits are then identified by comparing the 'local actual' against the nationally (or internationally) prescribed standard. It is then a simple matter to identify requirements and produce the plan.

Many volumes of reflection on the unhappy 1970s and 1980s experience (when plan-based approaches to rural development reached their peak) have shown how elaborate district plans, comprehensive databases, land-use potentiality studies, resource endowment studies, etc., all produced at great cost, were consigned to a dusty neglect (e.g. Porter et al. 1991; de Valk and Wekwete 1990). Decisions by local leaders avoided priorities established in this way because they had other ideas about what needed to be done, about what were 'pressing priorities', and how the resources should be used.

In today's jargon, there was a 'disconnect', of three kinds: between the plan and the allocation process; between administratively calculated needs and politically articulated demands; and between modernist ideas about what planning should involve and how matters have tended to be decided locally. Local leaders routinely judged that the plan was wrong, technically confusing, or outdated and that it tended to take decisions away from them, decisions they appropriately judged to be theirs to make. As local leaders, as they said then and repeat today, they had the 'pulse' of local priorities. Needs and demands were often not the same thing.

Much, of course, has changed since development practice was gripped by the monetarist-inspired policies of the 1980s. The issue is not the 'plan' but the 'allocation' process. Private market forces are believed to be the most efficient allocators of scarce resources according to demands.

Administratively defined and plan-centred definitions of how development should be organised have been set aside. But not quite. Since the initial rush of enthusiasm, it has been realised that implementing market-friendly policies requires a State that is capable of creating inclusive and politically durable arrangements with a host of non-government interests — consumers, community organisations, NGOs, contractors, and other private sector groups — to deal with market externalities and promote equitable service delivery. Termed 'good governance', this nesting of private-public, state-civil society relations is said to be best achieved through decentralisation.

Ironically, the contemporary emphasis on decentralisation and participation shows how development policies travel along many paths in many directions. Both concepts have visited development previously, but then, in a kind of elliptical orbit, they shifted away from popular attention in the 1980s. Now they have returned, bending back, not to where they had been before, but nevertheless pulled in part by lingering influences from the past. In the remainder of this article we illustrate how this is occurring in recent attempts to improve decentralised, participatory planning in service provision, the unintended and negative consequences of this, and how it might be averted in future practice.

We earlier noted that our view of inclusive planning and allocation was under-written by a three-sided concept of accountability. Our comments about participation and decentralised service delivery are organised around this concept. First are relations of accountability between political leaders and their constituency. Sometimes local leaders are popularly elected: most often they are not, and in all cases and for many reasons their relationship with the citizenry is highly contested.[5] Second are relations of accountability between political leaders and their staff, including a administrators and technicians responsible for reliably advising decision-makers to promote what we've called inclusive planning and allocation. These relations are also vexed, due to historical biases in favour of administrative and technical 'fixes', as well as more enduring tensions found world-wide. Third are relations that are often not discussed in terms of accountability, but increasingly are understood as the key to successful decentralisation and local democracy. Rather than understanding decentralisation purely as the devolution of power to lower levels of public-private decision-makers, it is clear that a strong centre is as important as an empowered local level organisation bound to its constituency.[6]

Local accountability: representative and direct participation

How to get leaders to listen to the voices of their constituents, to make decisions which balance both parochial and general interests and then to stick with the decision once made, all this has been a major concern of public administration and popular democracy. It has evidently surprised many development agencies that bringing local leaders 'to account' has become even more problematic with the devolution of key powers and responsibilities to local governments. Perhaps this surprise reflects the mistaken tendency to see the local space of politics (in contrast with the national scene) as tending toward harmony, common interest, and relatively easy compromise. It may also be the result of a long running hostility to local representative government, and to local political leaders. This hostility supported the dismembering of local governments during the 1960s, when development policy favoured strong central states as the engines of change, and condoned almost three decades of neglect and incapacitation of local government.

For these and many other reasons, the tendency in rural development practice has been to devise techniques to achieve *administratively* what is judged to be difficult through local official *political* processes. Planning procedures, in this light, are often seen as a way of putting fetters on local political leaders, to discipline them, to make them accountable through administrative means. The central difficulty of this approach has been how to establish the legitimacy of a planning and allocation process that effectively sidelines and limits the involvement of political leadership in the re-presentation of local needs and priorities. The special privilege given to administrative practices in decentralised planning and financing has, as a result, faced three problems: how to tune administratively defined needs and priorities to local preferences; how to provide a measure of legitimacy to the list of priorities and plans for action that eventually must be served up to officials for endorsement; and, how to make sure the leadership is accountable to the subsequent recommendations of the technical/administrative professionals.

The increasing popularity of PRA among all shades of development professionals is in large measure explained by these problems. First, PRA promises direct access to 'needs' (within the limits of what is judged administratively reasonable by the agency directing the process). Second, it offers the authority of having 'spoken to the people', and is in practice becoming an essential support to the administrative cadre in their contest with political leaders. And, third, in the 'best case' PRAs, it offers the veiled threat of direct action by a newly empowered community in the event that leaders choose not to adopt the results of direct participation. In short, techniques of direct participation (and PRA is only one of a range on offer) provide political legitimacy to the first steps of an administratively dominated process.

However, these 'strengths' of direct participation are also problematic. As we learnt during the 'service decision tree' consultations, the more acute problems of performance and accountability arise later in the delivery process — in appraisal, contracting, supervision, not to mention sustaining the service over time. Second and far more importantly, this understanding of participation confuses the question of accountability. It intends to politicise the administrative cadre (be it employed by NGOs, or the local government, or departments of the central state) in the mistaken belief that it is they that should be directly accountable to the citizenry. Not only does this ensure the continued contest between administrators/technicians and elected local leaders, it also locates the former between the leadership and their constituency and thereby dilutes the most important relationship of accountability intended by decentralised governance.

Leaders, technicians and more inclusive decisions

Relations of accountability between professionals and elected leaders have received little attention in discussions about improving the quality of rural service delivery. Not surprisingly, if quality is understood to be primarily dependent on the degree of match between social preferences and planned priorities, it makes sense to focus attention and resources on what we have termed the 'front end' of the planning process. But local experiences show time and again that social preferences are only one aspect of producing a quality decision — technical and financial considerations are often deservedly paramount. At other times the managerial feasibility and risk of different options must hold sway.

The devolution to local governments of responsibility to balance these factors, and to negotiate amongst the interests these factors reflect, has been considered a panacea. Unfortunately, the focus on the administrative resolution of the problems that arise in 'balancing and bargaining' has tended to misconstrue the direction of accountability between professionals and official leaders. We argue that the techniques developed over the past decade to support direct participation have much to offer in redirecting this relationship and realigning the administrative cadre to become more accountable to elected leaders. This however, requires that we understand these techniques, such as in the PRA toolbox, in a different way. Their relevance is not in providing the stamp of an unassailable, once-for-all 'truth' to local needs and priorities, as tends to occur when the results of PRA exercises are incorporated into local plans. Rather, their potential lies in their use as an aid to thinking, to transparency, and to inclusiveness in the many decisions that need to be made by political leaders as a proposal moves from early prioritisation through to delivery of the service.

The crucial need for inclusive planning and allocation is to introduce more creative ways of ensuring that the technical, administrative and financial dimensions of decisions are included alongside social demands and political priorities. Much attention has been given to 'opening up' local-local dialogue. This is the focus of PRA practice. We suggest the political process of formal, institutional politics needs also to be opened up and made, as defined earlier in this article, more inclusive and accountable. Many local leaders will agree their meetings need to be opened up. Others, of course, are keen to ensure that curtains are pulled around official meetings. But, by opening up, some local leaders suggest a different twist to 'accountability' by agreeing that decisions need to *account for* the many social, technical and other factors necessary for quality service outcomes. In this view, professional staff, the employees of the leadership, are accountable to politicians in both old and new ways. Well established, though often neglected, is their responsibility to ensure timely, appropriate and accurate information is brought to the table for consideration. New, is a broader understanding of their responsibility to introduce skills and techniques through which a range of possibilities, other interests, other implications are included in decisions that tend, under normal procedures, just to 'be taken'. Rather than mistakenly seeing themselves as torchbearers for the community in a contest with political leaders, administrative cadres become accountable to facilitate an inclusive planning and allocation process and accountability between leaders and their constituency.

For observers of local political meetings, the needs are obvious. Most leaders tend to 'go to sleep' as the Chairperson moves, item by item, through an over-packed agenda. Their attention may come alive, in the manner of a late night game of cards, when it is their turn to deal, when their particular interests are at stake. On the positive side, meetings are energised when the pro-forma process is disrupted by an unusual turn of events, by an unexpected or novel way of approaching a decision. In this sense, the quality of the technique used to engender 'novelty' is of little importance — introducing a SWOT analysis, a pair-wise ranking, or a GAP assessment is energising the first, second, and maybe the third time, but once it becomes routine, any technique becomes just another box to be ticked and ... well, let's move onto the next agenda item, and '...What time do we break for lunch?'

The impressive tool box of participatory techniques developed for local dialogue about needs and priorities could easily be adapted for use in the political process where appraisal occurs, budgets are allocated, and arrangements are made to contract and deliver services. In best practice, PRA techniques are more useful as instruments for enhancing dialogue. By simply introducing a novel approach, humour, or the different angle to a problem they can help achieve a profoundly different outcome to proceedings. Sometimes this includes introducing the 'Ah, ha' element into decisions, where the obvious question can be asked about who is to benefit from a decision, who will lose out, and decisions are made more transparent. It can also mean awareness about the long-term implications — financial, social, environmental — of a decision about to be made that would otherwise be neglected, not for any malign reason, but because issues may 'not have been thought about that way'.

We noted that this article was in part prompted by a concern about how the participatory approach of the conventional PRA-style methods could be 'scaled up'. It is often imagined that with greater institutional capacity, with more resources, and time, that the intensive planning dialogue at community level will become routine. In Uganda, there are 847 sub-county governments, many times more village level councils — the smallest mandated planning unit. Inside each is a wide array of associations of interests by virtue of gender or class, proximity to a watercourse, an access track, a field or valley. All have particular attributes deserving special planning consideration. The imagination of 10,000 village PRAs is a fiction. It wrongly perceives priority issues in service delivery. It works to undermine key relations of accountability that must be strengthened in rural politics. It is also profoundly wasteful of resources at the same time as discrediting the potential contribution such techniques could make to inclusive planning and allocation for rural service delivery.

Capacity versus performance in inclusive planning and allocation

The case studies of how particular services were planned and delivered in rural Uganda clearly affirmed the importance of 'vertical' accountability in producing quality outcomes. The responsiveness of leaders to constituents is undeniably important, as is the contract of accountability between professionals and elected leaders. But these relationships seldom in themselves determine whether enduring arrangements are made for equity, quality, and sustainability in service delivery. The quality of local planning processes, the observance of service design standards, the thoroughness of appraisal, financial management, compliance with audit, contracting, and other procedures all depend crucially on the relationships between higher and lower authorities charged to set standards, to regulate and enforce compliance, and to encourage good performance. As one astute local official remarked, 'Decentralisation and centralisation are two sides of the same coin'.

Ugandan government officials acknowledge that decentralisation and local democracy implies a fundamental reorientation to central government. It must move from a 'command and direct' relation with local governments and develop a 'monitoring, mentoring and regulatory' function. But how to achieve this has been elusive. Clearly, under decentralisation, new skills and capacities are required in central and local authorities to apply standards, to follow procedures, to ensure more participatory or technically competent decisions. But the results of the popular focus on 'capacity building' often fall short of expectations. In part, this is because capacity building efforts frequently emphasise 'inputs' at the expense of 'outcomes', and judgements about required inputs tend to reflect externally driven perceptions of needs. The earlier mentioned example of linear, step-wise planning is a case in point. It is fair to say that all planning implies elements of a step-wise rationality: it makes good sense to have adequately appraised a project before resources are committed to detailed design work. But capacity-building programmes have ambitions that seldom stop at this point. Rather, they often aim at the wholesale replacement of existing ways of doing business locally. Many local governments and central ministries have bookshelves crowded with comprehensive planning and other manuals untouched since the day capacity building courses ended.

Unless there is a change in approach, these problems are likely to be exacerbated under decentralisation. Central government no longer has control over the kinds of levers previously used to command the performance of lower level authorities, even if this was a rather pro-forma compliance. Under conditions of decentralised governance, central government must find ways to encourage adoption of its priorities — such as observance by local authorities of national policy on poverty or issues such as HIV/AIDS — just as local governments (and lower level communities) must find new ways to attract transfers of additional resources from the centre. In many, if not most instances, capacity is not the issue here. Rather, it is devising a compact of association between the centre and local governments through which vertical accountability is encouraged by sanctions and incentives.

How to achieve this was discussed extensively with local governments, NGOs and community organisations during design of the DDP, resulting in a number of innovative measures. A central point is that clarity about rules and procedures for decentralised planning and financing is important. However it is not sufficient. Transparency must be linked with incentives that promote the good performance of the wide range of actors included in the process, and sanctions when the various actors do not comply with agreements. To support vertical accountability, sanctions and incentives are agreed between central and local government whereby each regularly assesses the other's performance, and villagers and community organisations are involved in judging the performance of lower level local governments. Performance is measured by questions such as: were local plans honoured in practice? Do plans and budget decisions recognise the needs of different groups in the community? Was there adequate awareness about the rules, the amounts of funds transferred, about the responsibilities of local officials, about the rights of citizens? Were audit requirements met?

Making this system workable will, of course, take time, and may depend on many events beyond the ability of communities or governments to influence. But the crucial point is that there is less concern with the inputs — that is, the procedures adopted, say, to prepare a plan or budget — than in the quality of the outcomes achieved. Also important is that the results of these accountability assessments are immediately translated into incentives and sanctions, in short, the availability of development funds to local governments and community. By specifying the terms of the relationship between the centre and local government, between local governments and constituencies, a multi-sided basis has been created for accountability. If central government fails to deliver on its obligations — for instance, to prepare cost-effective service standards in primary health care, or to ensure audit services are provided on time — it is poorly placed to insist that local governments should be accountable for their performance. Similarly, unless local governments demonstrate performance, both upwards to the centre, and downwards to their constituencies they are aware there is little prospect of attracting transfers of funds from the centre or encouraging payment of taxes or fees for services delivered.

Summary

Participation is obviously an essential requirement in improving the quality of rural service delivery. But where quality is understood to imply judgements about technical feasibility, financial viability, assessments of risk, and managerial complexity, in addition to social preferences, the focus on direct, intensive community level participation in the planning process is clearly limiting. Competent decisions and accountable performance is required from a range of actors, some of who have been systematically sidelined, and often alienated, by conventional approaches to participatory planning.

In some respects, Uganda stands apart from many countries. Its courageous commitment to political, administrative, and fiscal decentralisation in many ways matches the extraordinary strength with which everyday Ugandans survived 20 years of coups, war, and lawlessness. But issues raised here about participation, accountability, and performance are not unique to Uganda. Here, as elsewhere, it is true that special arrangements often do need to be made to ensure the voices of marginal sections of the community are heard. But frequently, the techniques used to stimulate participatory 'events' have the effect of distorting the relationships of accountability between leaders and the public, and between leaders and their technical advisers, that is essential for long term local democratisation.

We need to think more like the fox (darting around, seizing opportunities, looping back) than the tortoise (plodding along a straight path) in rural service provision. What is characteristic of successful cases where rural services are provided, or where technicians finally learned to apply sophisticated techniques of identifying needs, is not that the planning cycle is slavishly followed. Rather, successful experiences are found where local leaders and people are able to cope with the unpredictable, the unexpected, and are able to turn back, review and change what they previously thought to be the 'obvious answer'. This requires skills for a flexible, non-linear and essentially political process, in which, as Vietnamese say, 'fences are broken' and the rules are nudged a bit in the interests of representative local governance.

Notes

1   Day (1997). Various critical commentaries on the participatory ideology are well illustrated in contributions to Sachs (1992) and Crush (1995).

2   Uganda's decentralisation corresponds to Mawhood and Davey's (1980: 405) five principles of 'classic' decentralisation.

3   This included a host of problems — poor assessment of options and risks, poor quality technical appraisal and design, poor costing, etc.

4   Leonie Sandercock (1998) provides a helpful, and critical, review of this legacy.

5   A recent article by Robert Kaplan develops this point particularly well (Kaplan 1998).

6   This is the main contribution of Judith Tendler's (1997) book on decentralised governance in Brazil.

References

Cernea, M. (ed.) (1985) *Putting People First: Sociological Variables in Rural Development*, New York: Oxford University Press.

Crush, J. (ed.) (1995) *The Power of Development*, London: Routledge.

Day, D. (1997) 'Citizen participation in the planning process: an essentially contested concept?', *Journal of Planning Literature* 11(3): 421–434.

Kaplan, R. (1998) 'Was democracy just a moment?', *The Atlantic Monthly* 280(6): 55.

Kullenberg, L. and D. Porter (1998) 'Accountability in decentralised planning and financing for rural services in Uganda', *Entwicklung und Ländlicher Raum* 32(3): 11–15.

Mahwood, P. and K. Davey (1980) 'Anglophone Africa', in D. Rowat (ed.) *International Handbook on Local Government Reorganisation*, Westport: Greenwood Press.

Porter, D., B. Allen and G. Thompson (1991) *Development in Practice: Paved with Good Intentions*, London: Routledge.

Sachs, W. (ed.) (1992) *The Development Dictionary: A Guide to Knowledge as Power*, London: Zed Books.

Sandercock, L. (1998) *Towards Cosmopolis*, Chichester: John Wiley and Sons.

Tendler, J. (1997) *Good Government in the Tropics*, Baltimore: Johns Hopkins University Press.

Valk, P. de and K. Wekwete (eds.) (1990) *Decentralising for Participatory Planning?* Aldershot: Avebury.

Villadsen, S. and F. Lubanga (eds.) (1996) *Democratic Decentralisation in Uganda: A New Approach to Local Governance*, Kampala: Fountain Publishers.

Finding out rapidly: a soft systems approach to training needs analysis in Thailand

Simon Bell

Background and context

This paper is written from the perspective of a researcher and problem-solver approaching a rich economic, cultural, and methodological context — one in which change is happening rapidly and in which there is little time to prepare and plan for responses to it. The paper describes a project in Training Needs Analysis (TNA) in Thailand. I will open by briefly describing the background to the project and the thinking which informed the TNA intervention itself. Throughout, I use the first person because I wish to convey this as a human, personal intervention and not as a remote academic discussion. This approach becomes particularly relevant in describing the learning involved in the exercise presented in the final part of the paper.

Economic and cultural background

Historically and culturally Thailand (formerly the Kingdom of Siam) has been independent and unique as a sovereign Buddhist state for several centuries, unlike other kingdoms in South Asia that fell victim to the imperial and colonial European powers from the sixteenth century.

Although Thailand has not enjoyed consistent political stability in recent years, economic growth seemed to be assured and in the last decade opinion has focused more on the international confidence produced by strong economic performance. For instance, articles (e.g. on derivatives and investment policies) have been published in specialist financial journals indicating Thailand's association with the ranks of the 'Asian Tigers' and a keystone of the 'Asian economic miracle'.

However, since August 1997 other news has predominated. The headlines themselves are instructive: 'Danger Ahead', 'Just a Technicality', 'Few Takers at Asia's Great Firesale', 'Hard Times Roll', 'Rudderless', 'Bailout Blues', 'Austerity Overdose' (from *Far Eastern Economic Review* 1997–98). From a dynamic, growth-driven economy Thailand has succumbed to the regional recession, with growth down to three per cent and interest rates pegged at 15–20 per cent. From being a country with a sound balance of payments surplus, Thailand must now borrow money in order to stay afloat.

This is a major element of the context in which the project described in this article was undertaken. Thailand's economic position requires international aid in the form of projects. The education sector is regarded by Thai and multilateral agencies as being of specific importance in this regard. What was not known was the local capacity to manage such projects. My position as a researcher was that of an interested and reasonably informed outsider seeking to undertake an analysis task, which had been highlighted as necessary for the further adoption of internationally funded projects in the Thai education sector.

Methodological background

Two elements combined to form the major content in terms of methodology:

- The popular understanding of Training Needs Analysis (TNA)
- The projectisation process in development

Understanding TNA

If the analysis of training needs is a complex area, training in the development context could be said to have an 'image problem'. Training has been an integral part of technical assistance policies for many years, with numerous attempts to adapt and adopt training policies and practices which are relevant to developing and transitional economies. In their study of training adoption, Jacob and McLaughlin (1996) indicate that it can have positive impacts upon 'the individual, the work group and their organisation' but the process of evaluating technical training impact is still in its infancy. Chambers (1997: 72) describes the largely failed Training and Visit (T&V) systems instituted by the World Bank as 'a mechanistic management blueprint for the transfer of technology'. TNA can be seen as being similarly mechanistic as we shall see shortly.

Training has many sponsors, most notably the World Bank, whose policy paper on vocational education and training has been implemented throughout Sub-Saharan Africa. Bennell (1996) indicates that such initiatives are not proving to be as 'demand led' as donors might wish and the up-take of vocational educational training in Africa is disappointing.

The overall picture is one of well-intended donor-driven policies on training, but a less than enthusiastic response from the potential recipients of training and mixed results of previous initiatives. The terms 'top-down' and 'mechanistic' might apply to much of the training provision.

But what of TNA itself? Boydell (1983) has been influential in establishing TNA as a vital aspect of systematic organisational strategy, and others provided insights into defining areas of performance deficiency within organisations where training can occur. Recent literature has attempted to provide a definitive guide to the procedures for TNA and some authors have argued that the focus of TNA needs to be expanded from a narrow emphasis on the effectiveness of personnel, to a wider analysis of a range of levels within organisations. Denning and Verschelden (1993) have indicated the potential for the use of 'softer' tools in TNA and others have indicated that developmental issues has impacts upon the form and content of training. TNA is a developing field of involvement and there is no single approach to it. The literature indicates considerable awareness of the complexity of the task of any needs analysis. In an attempt to gain an overview I looked at the British government agency for information systems, the CCTA guide to quality management. This provides the following overall guidance. The TNA should take into account:

- business and IS (information systems) strategies;
- current and future customer needs.

The scope of the TNA includes:

- identifying existing training and education, including core competencies and methods;
- comparisons of findings against customer and business needs;
- identifying the gap in skills, training and development;
- producing a plan to meet these needs.

When identifying existing training, the TNA should evaluate the effectiveness of training in terms of:

- meeting present and future business and customer needs;
- delivering the required quality in products and services
- improvements in business practice
- improvements in customer satisfaction
- return on investment. (CCTA 1992:22)

Many of these features are common to other TNA approaches and I interpret the CCTA approach to TNA to include:

- a top-down approach — the language used by the CCTA does not sound like the type of approach undertaken in consultation and partnership with employees;
- a managerialist tone (e.g. 'core competencies and methods', 'return on investment');
- a lack of explicit emphasis on mutual learning processes and learning objectives and outcomes;
- a 'one-stop-training' feel (a sense that the training is 'complete' at some point — little evidence of feedback);
- a lack of emphasis on trainee ownership of the outcomes of training;
- a business-centred rather than trainee-centred approach.

Other have focused their training initiative on learning rather than on training (e.g Craig 1994), while Denning and Verschelden (1993) indicate the need to consider a wide range of issues in undertaking TNA. However, I considered that generalised approaches such as that outlined by the CCTA would present a range of problems if adopted in the Thai context — which is complex, sophisticated, and quite unlike that which one might find in a UK business environment. Although I accepted the essential need to link TNA to both local core competencies and organisational vision, I was more concerned with understanding and learning from the actual context in the TNA process. The CCTA guidelines did not enable me to select an approach for the TNA, and so I referred to the wider literature on projects in developing countries to seek potential guidelines there.

The projectisation process

Projects are now a major element of development work and have become the focus for almost all development intervention. Projects are the major vehicle for providing training in the development context. Generally, training is provided under the remit of a project and therefore it is expected that it will be highly focused on the needs of that project itself. The projectisation process has partly been an attempt to control expenditure on development to narrow, well-defined goals and purposes. Taylor (1995) illustrates the change in development procedure and draws out some major lessons for trainers, sponsors, and client organisations in project contexts. In contrast to the stark CCTA guidelines, he indicates the need for flexibility in training provision. In summary his main points (op. cit.: 491) are:

- operational and learning objectives can be too tightly prescribed. There are many different means to arrive at the operational objectives.
- creativity should not be strangled out of the training process by the application of unnecessary pressure.
- time should be allowed for unanticipated learning.
- rather than feeling that everyone on a training programme should come away with the same outcome, it must be recognised that people will learn and contribute according to their own talents and interests.
- understanding the context and the relationships among trainers is vital.
- achieving links and trust is as important as the assimilation of subject material.
- training cannot overcome long-standing structural difficulties.

These recommendations for improving the chances of success in project training were taken as guidelines for the approach to TNA described here. Thus, my rubrics were:

- don't predetermine objectives;
- try to be open to assessing local capacities with which you are as yet unfamiliar;
- listen;
- continue to learn about the context;
- develop trust;
- don't develop training to address issues at a more structural level.

Although I had some prior experience of empathetic forms of research, these points indicate the mindset which I adopted for my TNA and which also informed my thinking as I decided upon methods and approach.

Terms of reference for the TNA

My task was to undertake a TNA in Thailand across the educational sector but with specific focus on projects and management. I had one week to carry out this work, though the British Council in-country had arranged my itinerary prior to arrival. I was to:

- document the context of the TNA and provide a brief overview of the Thai Education and Training Sector;
- identify and document training already delivered or planned in this sector; and
- document key weakness in educational project management (e.g. planning projects or dissemination).

Following this, I was to design an initial Educational Project Management course to address priority training needs, identify a training delivery team, and document the level and quantity of trainees. Finally, I was to draft a training schedule.

Prior to departure, I imagined that my main task would be to identify the major problems in project management at present and provide training in these areas. However, I was mindful that TNA can appear to pre-judge that there will be a training issue at the root of the problem. In the Thai case this might not be so, and I was wary because of Taylor's comments on the nature of project-based training. Whatever I came up with should be produced in partnership and collaboration with the Thais and address issues of key relevance to them; and not assume that any amount of training can, of itself, reverse long-term and structural development problems.

By the time I set off, I had decided that I had to find out rapidly what the situation was and that I needed to do this in an empathetic and participatory fashion, listening and not lecturing. However, I would need a framework in which to construct such a review. I was considering this and drafting outlines of potential means as I travelled.

Reflective practice on the ground

By the time I arrived, I had decided to adopt two approaches to the TNA. I wanted to be able to assess the current state of project planning, management, and delivery; and at the same time to describe areas of potential for directed project training (workshops and other training events). So, I would need a tool for *comparison* (of what is happening at present with what is needed in project work) and a tool of *analysis* and *agenda-setting* for training development. Given the need for participation and listening, neither tool could be too prescriptive, or expert-driven. I therefore decided to make use of the Kolb learning cycle for the comparison (Kolb 1984) and the soft systems methodology (SSM) for the analysis and agenda-setting (Chambers 1981; Checkland and Holwell 1998). I used Kolb as an ideal type or paradigm for what should be happening in any learning context. My use of SSM would be to develop potential action plans from the earlier use of Kolb. The seven major aspects of SSM as developed and taught by The Open University (Open University 1987) in the UK are shown in Figure 1. To my knowledge, no-one had previously applied these approaches together in undertaking a TNA in developing or transitional economies.

Figure 1 SSM approach to problem-solving

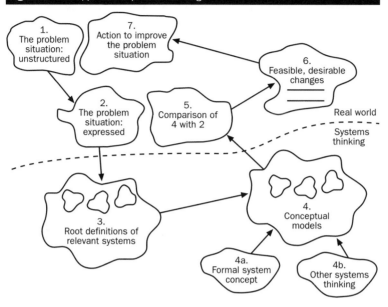

Source: Open University 1987, building on Checkland 1981:163

Over my one-week stay in Thailand, I intended to make use of the comparative and analytical methods in harness, allowing the comparison to develop and change over the week and trusting the analysis to keep pace. The inherent risk was that comparison could vary considerably in different areas of the education sector and that the resulting agenda-setting would be messy and inconsistent. This potential weakness was recognised at the outset but, as the alternative appeared to be to pre-judge the context and go in with a set of pre-selected training products, I continued with the original approach.

Comparison

The 'Kolb' learning cycle as adapted and interpreted in this paper comprises four stages — connection, decision, action, and reflection — that might be expected to underpin any specific learning process. In the Thai context, these stages were considered as follows:

- *Connection*: in what ways does the Sector at present learn from experience elsewhere in education and training (and outside the Sector), within and outside the region — in all aspects of project design and management?

- *Decision*: in what ways are decisions made about what types of project to do and what form of approach to take to these (questions of methodology and the process for the selection of methodology)?

- *Action*: how are projects actually undertaken and how are they learned from (questions of monitoring and evaluation — M&E). Are the successful? What sort are more or less so?

- *Reflection*: (the end of the cycle and the beginning of a new one). What active procedures for learning from the project experience are engaged in and how is this learning taken forward from one project to the next?

The four come together in what is described as a learning cycle (Figure 2).

The comparison stage of my overall TNA (not be confused with the comparison stage of the soft system approach) occurred at the same time as the analysis and agenda-setting that the soft system approach required. All information was derived from interviews. The brief comparative analysis resulted in the observations set out in Table 1, and these themes are also shown in Figure 3 as a 'spray' diagram.

At this comparison stage in the TNA, I was concerned to identify potential trainers already active in the field. There appeared to be two main providers of training in the education sector at present: both were quite narrowly focused — one in the higher education/science and engineering sector, the other in vocational training — and both produced highly generic training products not specifically focused on broad-based Thai issues.

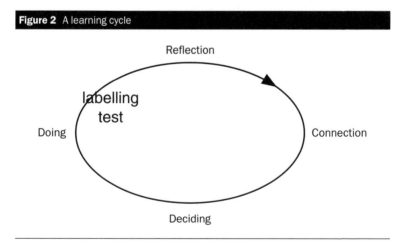

Figure 2 A learning cycle

Reflection

labelling test

Doing

Connection

Deciding

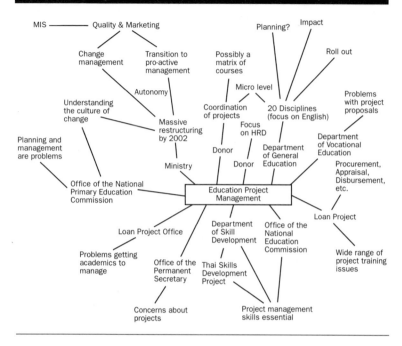

Figure 3 Spray diagram of themes

This made it possible to set out some reflections on the current state of project planning in the Thai education sector and place these in terms of a learning cycle. In a generalised sense we can consider the four elements as follows:

- *Connection*: apart from specific cases (e.g. 'The Skills Development Project') there appeared to be little existing connection and learning in-sector about project management experience.

- *Decision*: project methodology was not an expression used widely, and the decision to develop projects appeared to originate from outside 'push' not internal 'pull' initiatives.

- *Action*: questions relating to project result seemed a little previous. There was little information about how projects were managed and handled, but the widespread interest in techniques maybe told its own story.

- *Reflection*: (the end of the cycle and the beginning of a new one). There was little information which would indicate that learning was taken forward in a planned manner from one project to others.

Table 1 Observations arising

Higher Education	Massive restructuring of the Higher Education (HE) Sector by 2002, a transition to more autonomous proactive management, improved HE marketing of skills within and outside region, collaborative programmes, all aspects of management but most especially culture change, issues of autonomy, Total Quality Management, transition from administration to proactive management.
Donors	Concerned with overall coordination of projects, focus on the micro level in the first instance, need for the output of the project to be well documented (leading to documented impact), could be room for a matrix of courses elements (different levels and combinations for different groups) need for focus on Human Resource Development.
Ministry of Education	Many projects running — issues of quality, impact, rolling out of the national programme, planning and management issues.
Ministry of Labour	Problems in assessing the relevance of supply and demand of training (TNA). Thai Skills Development Project indicated the value of project training (in all forms).
Office of National Education Commission	Need for project training, MIS training and a focus on local 'Thai' issues.
Specific Projects	Identification of severe problems with the recruitment and training of staff in the projects. Specific areas of concern include project management, procurement, disbursement, and appraisal.

My perception of the situation in a learning cycle sense is set out in diagrammatic form in Figure 4.

This comparison stage revealed a general lack of awareness and understanding of project approaches in the education sector. But I also gained the insight that a focus on providing project approaches, tools, and techniques was also not the central issue. Rather, there appeared to be a need to take a step back from any prescription and to think about the prior learning that needed to occur in order to allow Thai managers to decide what they needed. This dawning reflection was to grow, and informed the analysis which was facilitated by the use of my adapted version of SSM.

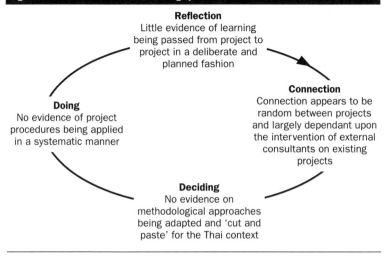

Figure 4 A second view of the learning cycle

Reflection
Little evidence of learning
being passed from project to
project in a deliberate and
planned fashion

Connection
Connection appears to be
random between projects
and largely dependant upon
the intervention of external
consultants on existing
projects

Doing
No evidence of project
procedures being applied
in a systematic manner

Deciding
No evidence on
methodological approaches
being adapted and 'cut and
paste' for the Thai context

Analysis: the root definition or mission for the project

During the week, I took part in over 30 interviews with those representing the education sector. The reflections on the outcome of these meetings focuses the remainder of this article upon systems to develop training potential and sound project delivery. From the comparison set out above, I developed the SSM analysis of the TNA. SSM usually comprises seven stages (as shown in Figure 1) which in turn are comprised of three major tools — these are the rich picture (RP) for assembling the conception of the problem context (gaining an understanding of the soft and hard or informal and formal, processes and structures of the context), a root definition (RD) of the change process which will deal with some selected task or issue evident in the RP, and a conceptual model (CM) of the change process (which can also be seen as an agenda for action). In the following description, the reader will realise that I have adapted SSM for the purposes of the TNA. In the previous Kolb-related comparison stage I believed that I was developing my own conception of the context, as primarily demonstrated in Figure 3. For my purposes this fulfilled the usual role of the RP. Having assembled my understanding of the context I set about developing, through meetings with the various stakeholders, an RD and a CM. These stages are described below.

For my purposes, the RD was required to set out the 'transformation' of the context (a transformation is usually included in a RD). I initially asked stakeholders and myself: What would you like to see changed in the project context in the education sector in Thailand?

However, as indicated above, I found that in practice this question presumed that the stakeholders already had a sound understanding of this context, and this was not an assumption which held up to close scrutiny. In stepping back, a new question was formulated: What do you need to understand about projects to be able to make useful decisions about further training requirements?

This second question — arising from the Kolb learning cycle review, implicit in Figure 3, and now forming the basis of a SSM 'primary task' — proved more answerable and more catalytic in taking thinking forward. As I developed it from the primary task with the stakeholders, the RD was intended to show that it is possible to set out a potential RD or 'mission' for a training initiative which would become the next phase of the project activity. Following much discussion, the tentative RD for the next phase was suggested as being:

> A training initiative system to develop and share best practice in project management at the micro-level across sectors in education in Thailand. The system would be implemented initially by the British Council for a variety of clients in the Thai education sector increasing clarity, coordination, and accountability in projects funded by major donors.

This was discussed with and adjusted by Thai stakeholders and was subsequently accepted as a reasonable basis for further analysis and the development of a plan or agenda. The activity plan was to be the basis for a Phase 2 — arising from the TNA (Phase 1). It should be emphasised that the vision of the TNA at this stage was that Phase 2 would be expected to deliver a Project Management Workshop of some kind, but one focused on developing and sharing a picture of best practice — not on rolling out a prescribed training agenda.. In the next part of this article, this Phase 2 mission will be developed in terms of an action plan and a matrix of potential contents.

The conceptual model or action plan for Phase 2

By this stage of the TNA, the hardest work had been accomplished. The Kolb comparison had indicated areas of potential collaboration and the spray diagram feeding a primary task into the root definition had provided a mutually accepted 'vision' for transforming the situation. It now remained to understand what would be a useful selection of learning objectives to choose and then the range of tools, techniques, approaches, and methods which would best meet the objectives. This is an important point. The CCTA approach to TNA appears very focused on training methods and content. The approach of this TNA was focused on learning objectives: What do Thai education project managers want to learn and why? A top down-approach to TNA can easily be based on pre-judgements and therefore the TNA can take on an implicit pre-assessment where key questions become 'what is available to be known?' or 'what should be known?'. Throughout, the attempt here was made to keep the TNA learner-focused.

Since the initial drafting of the terms of reference for the TNA, my views had changed in terms of the expected delivery 'event' suggested for the next phase. Rather than a training course, a planning and brainstorming workshop might prove more appropriate.

There were two elements to the CM design. Element 1 refers to the development of the workshop or event which will comprise the next phase while Element 2 refers to the development of its content.

Design of the workshop or event

The design features or activities for the workshop, in line with the results of the analysis to date, are set out in Figure 5. A CM as interpreted and applied in this paper is expected to comprise a series of actions which come together to produce the transformation as originally set out in the RD. Such a CM can then be compared against the original rich picture (the spray diagram in this case) and discussed with stakeholders in order to arrive at a positive progression from the context as originally perceived. The contents of Figure 5 are unsurprising, but these were seen to conform to the transformation as agreed in with Thai professionals and set out in the RD earlier. Each element of the CM was further developed in collaboration into a set of sub-activities. Once again, the model arose from the discussions and conversations which I had during the week; as the model evolved I discussed the main items with local stakeholders. This CM provided the main series of actions which were required to develop the workshop. The next stage of the TNA was to set out the main form and content of the workshop itself.

Figure 5 Conceptual model of the 'event' plan

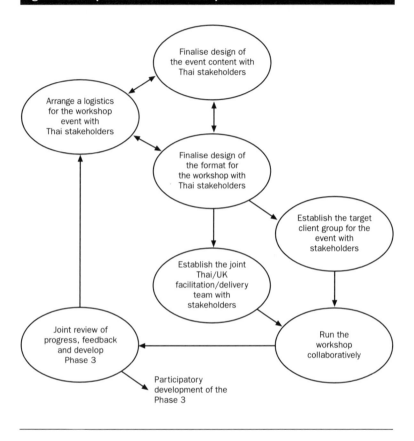

Content of the workshop or event

The TNA revealed a lot of enthusiasm for a brief initial workshop and so it was planned to be of five to seven days' duration focusing on the following five components — these five being the issues of main concern arising from the interviews undertaken during the TNA. (It was expected that the components would be worked on in the workshop in an iterative process with plenty of feedback between participants and facilitators.)

Component 1: assisted or joint brainstorming. The first component would focus on seeding ideas and sharing experiences about project methods and approaches that work and which are useful for various educational project contexts (probably with inputs from project directors and managers from Thailand and from outside). The result of the assisted brainstorm should be to focus the minds of all present upon the main policy and strategy issues which result in areas of project control, development, design, analysis, etc. which are of most concern; and to provide a basis for the more detailed work which was to follow. This first session might be thought of as *conceptual*. The brainstorming would prepare the way for the second component.

Component 2: methods and approaches. One of the observations relating to the TNA has been the near absence of methods for project work. During the second component, a variety of methods could be discussed and described — for instance the Team Up approach to projects, Soft Systems Approach, Total Quality Management and Learning Organisation — again with brief presentations relevant to Thailand followed by a process to select those which are seen to be useful in this context. During the TNA, this form of approach was selected as being of most value to those centrally involved with translating policy- and strategic-level decisions relating to projects into the purpose and outputs of the projects themselves.

Component 3: tools and techniques. This represented the major content of the event and a less Thai-focused TNA might have produced an event based around this element on its own. Two days would be set aside to review and consider the value of a range of project tools, all of which will have been identified by the participants in the previous two days and some of which are already applied in Thailand. The tools and techniques might be expected to include such items as proposal writing, procurement technique, log frame, financial planning, monitoring and evaluation, appraisal, participatory analysis, Gant chart, PERT chart, Management Information Systems, etc. Participants could be shown how these techniques could be applied (where possible with participants describing their own experiences) and would be given insights into their further development. Actual and potential project managers and their teams might work in small groups on their understanding of the various techniques.

Component 4: critical appraisal of the week, terms of reference, and action plans for the next component. The fourth component could provide the participants and facilitators with the opportunity to develop terms of reference and action plans indicating ways forward for their projects. Here, the team would review their progress over the event and set out the main lessons including:

- conceptual tools of value;
- methods and approaches of value;
- tools and techniques of value;
- major sites in need of further assistance;
- training needs.

Each small group in the training would be encouraged to settle on a single area to develop in the remainder of the event.

Component 5: in depth, small-group work on specific project elements: During this last component, the small groups would be expected to 'work out' some element of their project using some of the tools and techniques provided. During the afternoon it might be useful for each group to provide a brief presentation of their findings and it is hoped that senior policy-makers, Project Directors, and donor representatives would also attend the presentation stage. The small groups could then, if time allowed further develop their action plans and specify what further elements they might expect to receive from subsequent events. This would enable Thai decision-makers to determine their own areas of interest and specify the type of training which they considered most appropriate.

The items set out in the contents for the workshop were not expected to be in a definitive format. The ordering is in line with the interpretation of the outcome of the TNA in Thailand.

Reflections on the SSM/Kolb TNA

At the outset of the TNA, I set myself some rubrics for my approach (derived from Taylor 1995). In conclusion I will re-visit these rubrics and comment on my personal learning.

- Don't predetermine objectives. In honesty, practice almost always means that the researcher will come with preconceptions and understandings, which may prove to be erroneous. During the week of the TNA, I moved consciously from a pre-conception that training was needed and that the objective was thus 'provide training', to the conception that understanding is needed. Hence the objective became 'provide understanding of what international projects mean in effect'.

- Try to be open to assessing local capacities with which you are as yet unfamiliar. Other than a brief visit to Thailand in 1994, I was unfamiliar with the country and with the strengths, weaknesses, opportunities, and threats of the context in project terms. I found that my evolving understanding was further assisted by the use of SWOT (strength, weakness, opportunities, and threats) analysis and by daily review in consultation with my interviewees, I developed some useful insights into the context.

- Listen. This became my main job. Following a brief introduction, my task was to hear what Thai education sector professionals had to tell me about their experiences and problems. The main discipline here for me was to refrain from instantly assessing their experience in terms of my own prejudices and pre-conceptions.

- Continue to learn about the context. The TNA was planned as an evolving learning process. Both the Kolb cycle and SSM are learning devices — although I applied them in an adapted form here. Even at the end of the research period, I was still adjusting my thinking in line with the new insights with which the Thai professionals were providing me. A balancing act is required here in order consistently to match the continuing and developing complexity of the Thai context with the order and sequence of a complex but valuable training response.

- Develop trust. It is hard for me to comment objectively on this but my perception was that Thai officials were often disarmingly frank with me about their context.

- Don't develop training to address issues at a more structural level. As I set out in the introduction to this article, Thailand is at present undergoing a wide-ranging restructuring of its economy. This is disrupting all aspects of Thai life but the TNA could not hope to address or redress these issues. Throughout, the TNA was focused on developing an understanding of the main issues and tasks from the Thai perspective, and on providing an event that would to some extent allow decision-makers to react to the immediate training needs they were confronting. Only time will tell if this objective has been achieved.

Finally, as the TNA drew to a close, the root definition and conceptual model of the soft systems approach proved to be instant add-ins to the popular project planning approach called Logical Framework. The Logical Framework provides a hierarchy of projects from goal to purpose to outputs to activities. The root definition as I have adapted it here conforms to the purpose of the project whereas the adapted conceptual model provides a view of the activities needed in it. The integration of Kolb, soft systems, and logical framework planning will be the focus for a future paper.

Possibly the final word of any project should be about its resulting activity and value. The TNA as described here has been reported, the Phase 2 agreed (a participatory workshop event) has been undertaken and been favourably evaluated, and at the time of writing Phase 3 (further development of Thai-centred training in project approaches) is in development.

Acknowledgement

Special thanks to the British Council in Bangkok for support in the writing of this article.

References

Bell, S. (1996a) 'Approaches to participatory monitoring and evaluation in Dir District, North West Frontier Province, Pakistan', *Systems Practice* 9(2): 129–150.

Bell, S. (1996b) Learning with Information Systems: Learning Cycles in information Systems Development, London: Routledge.

Bennell, P. (1996) 'Privatisation , choice and competition: the World Bank's reform agenda for vocational education and training in sub-Saharan Africa', *Journal of International Development* 8(3): 467–487.

Boydell, T. (1983) The Identification of Training Needs, London: BACIE.

CCTA (1992) *Quality Training*, Quality Management Library 5, CCTA, London: HMSO.

Chambers, R. (1981) 'Rapid rural apraisal: rationale and repertoire', *Public Administration and Development* (1): 95–106.

Chambers, R. (1997) *Whose Reality Counts? Putting the First Last*, London: IT Publications.

Checkland, P. B. (1981) *Systems Thinking, Systems Practise*, Chichester: Wiley.

Checkland, P. and S. Holwell (1998) Information, Systems and Information Systems: Making Sense of the Field, Chichester: Wiley.

Craig, M. (1994) *Analysing Learning Needs*, Aldershot: Gower.

Denning, J. and C. Verschelden (1993) 'Using the focus group in assessing training needs: empowering child welfare workers', *Child Welfare* LXXII(6): 569–580.

Jacobs, C. and P. McLaughlin (1996) 'Making a difference: results of a pilot investigation into the impact of technical cooperation training on developing countries', *Public Administration and Development* 16(2): 123–129.

Kolb, D. (1984) Experiential Learning: Experience as the Source of Learning and Development, London: Prentice-Hall.

Open University (1987) 'T301 – Complexity Management and Change: a Systems Approach', Open University Systems Group, Milton Keynes: The Open University.

Taylor, H. (1995) 'From general training to projectisation : implications for learning processes and the roles of trainers', *Public Administration and Development* 15(5):481–494.

Matching services with local preferences: managing primary education services in a rural district of India

Ramya Subrahmanian

Introduction

As the World Bank notes, 'the state is in the spotlight' (World Bank 1997a: 1), with the focus on finding new ways to address problems of corruption, inefficiency, and social exclusion, particularly in the functioning of third world governments. The search for new ways of improving the record in the social sector in India is particularly urgent given the country's poor record in education. Disadvantages in access to education are particularly acute for the poorest households, and intensify by gender and caste. While resource allocation for primary education has been traditionally low, though steadily increasing, the evidence that funds that have been allocated for key education programmes have remained under-spent prompts us to focus on the content and management of education sector programmes and policies.[1] Urgent reforms are clearly needed to improve both the universal availability of quality basic services and universal access to these services.

Big questions remain to be answered. How can public services be structured to ensure maximum efficiency and equity outcomes in relation to basic services like primary education? Given the persistent exclusion of a significant percentage of the poorest, whose participation in education is constrained by a wide variety of factors operating both on the service provision side and household side, what structure of delivery can ensure the efficient provision of services that will secure the effective participation of the most disadvantaged? Advocates of decentralisation suggest that reorganising structures and relationships between levels of government, and/or between government and civil society or the market, offers a way to address chronic public sector management problems. It is suggested that decentralisation or the dispersal and distribution of power from the centre (Wolman 1990: 29) has several benefits that would help to address problems of inefficiency and misallocation of resources in public service delivery. In its 1997 annual report, the World Bank suggests that decentralisation 'offers the chance to match public services more closely with local demands and preferences' (1997a: 120), thus offering a more informed basis upon which to make decisions about the allocation of resources, a view that is supported elsewhere (Wolman 1990; Rondinelli et al. 1983; Bennett 1990).

The intention here is not to go deep into the debate about decentralisation, which is on-going, contested, and empirically rich and diverse. Rather, this paper attempts to think about users' 'preferences' in relation to primary education services, and to see how public service delivery may be improved if attention is paid to such preferences. This is done through empirical application to one particular aspect of education service delivery, school timings, among poor households in a village of Raichur district in Karnataka. The paper draws on interviews carried out with parents from poor households in one village, supported by interviews with local administrators, community members, and teachers. Some of the questions raised are: How are poor parents' 'preferences' revealed? What if their 'preferences' run counter to policy interests — whose preferences really count? How homogeneous can preferences be, even within a village? Can selected aspects of education delivery (i.e. school timings) be changed to match local preferences, or are local preferences symbolic of a more deeply embedded perspective on the role and importance of education, hence necessitating a re-think of the nature of the production of education services as a whole? The case used to explore these questions is 'micro', but serves to illustrate the complexity involved in making planning contextual and localised.

The equity and efficiency merits of decentralisation

Wolman (1990) identifies three core values identified with beneficial outcomes in decentralisation — efficiency values, governance values, and distributive values. *Efficiency* values arise when power is shifted to local levels of government covering smaller jurisdictions, thus enhancing the possibility of convergence of interests and preferences as the population is likely to be more homogeneous than in larger areas. *Governance* values include enhanced responsiveness of services and accountability to citizens, promotion of diversity and innovation in public policy, encouragement of public action and political participation, and establishment of countervailing loci of power to provide checks on corruption, and arbitrary behaviour in decision-making. *Distributive* values are associated with the redistribution of power and changes in 'the patterns of winners and losers from public policy' (ibid.). Reducing distances between government and citizens, whether through financial, administrative, or political decentralisation is considered to offer possibilities for greater efficiency and equity in service delivery.

Advocates of decentralisation are also united in cautioning against assuming that these benefits are unconditional outcomes (Wolman 1990; World Bank 1997a; Bennett 1990; Rondinelli et al. 1983). Wolman notes that many of the expected benefits of decentralisation are actually *a priori* judgements and require empirical scrutiny as they are based on assumptions about a wide range of important factors or variables. For instance, the organisational capacity of the units of administration to which power is devolved or management assigned will determine the extent of responsiveness, including the ability to plan resource allocation, and to monitor or regulate outcomes in service provision in keeping with local preferences (op.cit.). A second important factor is the extent to which local communities are in a position to access the information that is in theory more readily available — this will depend on existing social structures and settlements based on which groups within a community have relative power to take advantage of more localised government. Structural arrangements for decision-making and financial control also play a crucial role — the success of decentralisation strategies will depend on what is decentralised and how — the levels and the nature of control (e.g. are decisions over content of policy decentralised, or just management of pre-determined goals?), and whether control over budgets is also handed over to local levels of government. The case for decentralisation also will vary between sectors and on the type of service provision that is being decentralised.

The agenda for improvement in education service delivery in India

Assessments of the extent of failure in education provision in India produce mind-boggling statistics: half of the world's illiterate population is in India; 40–50 per cent of India's primary school-age children do not go to school according to some estimates,[2] while others claim that 32 million children of the 105 million children aged 6–10 years are out of school

(World Bank 1997b:3). The financial implications are proportionately huge — if all children of ages 6–10 are to be accommodated in school by 2007, the infrastructure requirement would possibly total 1.3 million classrooms, and 740,000 new teachers (World Bank, ibid.). Calculating the cost of making education for children in the age group 6–14 a fundamental right,[3] it was estimated that an additional 400 billion rupees would be required over and above existing levels of expenditure to educate all the children over the Ninth Five-year Plan period (Government of India 1997).[4]

The large and increasing scale of education requirement and provision in India (owing to population growth) has meant that the costs of providing education services for the goal of Universal Elementary Education (UEE) have been prohibitive and have increased with successive years of failure to invest sufficiently in infrastructure, particularly school buildings and teachers. World Bank assistance now constitutes 25 per cent of the total education outlay, with the help of which the District Primary Education Programme (DPEP) has been launched to inject much needed funds into districts with the lowest literacy rates and greatest gender disparities.[5] Two processes are evident in this programme: central control over education, which is considered necessary to ensure that resources are allocated and UEE policy is promoted as national policy; and a simultaneous emphasis on local participation to monitor and make government accountable, and to ensure that teachers attend, buildings are built, and that children do not drop out. DPEP emphasises 'contextuality' in education planning given local variations in education attainment and social diversity within the overall framework of UEE which emphasises access, retention, and achievement as three interrelated aspects (Government of India 1993:37).[6]

Addressing the huge scale of financial and management requirements in relation to providing UEE requires addressing the challenge of decentralisation: what aspects of education service production should be decentralised to what level, and how should controls over planning and budgets be structured to maximise equity and efficiency? In the Indian context, decentralisation of primary education refers primarily to inter-governmental restructuring, and not privatisation. High externalities result from education, with benefits accruing not just to the individual but to society at large. Returns to education are calculated at two levels: *private* returns or income benefits accruing to the individual, calculated as 'a measure of the expected yield of the investment, in terms of the future benefits, or income stream generated by the capital, compared with the cost of acquiring the capital asset' (in this case education) (Woodhall 1997:

220); and *social* returns, or returns that benefit not just the individual but also the society at large, such as 'better family health, lower fertility, and thus slower population growth' (World Bank 1997b: 1), and a more productive and better skilled workforce. Both private and social returns to primary education are considered to be higher than returns to secondary and tertiary education (Psacharapoulos, cited in Colclough 1991; Woodhall 1997), implying that both states and individuals have an incentive to invest in primary education.

However, because social returns do not accrue to individuals alone but to society at large, they are not internalised by individuals and hence the attractiveness of education investment in terms of perceived private returns may be lower than its full social benefits. Furthermore, private returns may be low for poor households, as these depend on a variety of factors, including structures of economic opportunity, ownership of capital, including land, and socio-political factors. For poor households, the incentive to invest in primary education is low on all three counts, whereas the incentive for the state to invest in education remains high.

A second case for state responsibility for education provision rests in the area of equality of opportunity. Social exclusion in India has deep structural roots and translates into systematic disadvantage in access to public resources, especially across axes of inequality such as caste and gender.[7] Enabling equal access of all to basic education remains an important part of the poverty alleviation and development agenda, and 'the dialectical relationship between educational progress and social change' (Drèze and Sen 1995: 109) provides governments with a central role in education. In India, central government's financial responsibility for primary education provision has increased recently, because states are not uniformly capable of coping with the huge financial costs of universal provision.[8] Thus, the decentralisation agenda for primary education in India has to be concerned with finding the most appropriate levels of government through which equity and efficiency goals in education are achieved.

Users' relationship to the education system in Raichur district

Policy concern with providing UEE rests on the assumption that households are in a position to use services if they are made available.[9] However, household-level capacity to invest in education is likely to vary depending on caste and socio-economic class, the social and cultural environment, and the economic opportunities available, which are all factors that impinge on household decision-making. In Raichur district, female literacy rates are the lowest for the state (22.2 per cent), compared with the state average of 44.3 per cent.[10] Economic opportunities in the district are curtailed by the poor irrigation infrastructure in some blocks which are drought-prone, resulting in a single agricultural season in a year, necessitating migration for small farmers to neighbouring areas in search of employment for half the year.

Elsewhere (Subrahmanian 1997), I outline some of the implications this has for education achievement, summarised here rather briefly. Even where primary schools are functioning regularly, a significant number of children attend school irregularly. A principal factor is that children from poor households miss school for long periods in the year when they accompany their parents during migration, or attend irregularly because of involvement in household activities. Some parents say that, despite their insistence, their children refuse to go to school, and for working parents it is impossible to monitor their children's activities. A few parents cite teachers' behaviour as a reason for not sending their children to school. Some of these are practical problems, solutions for which can only be found at the local level. Village Education Committees (VEC) have been formed in DPEP to facilitate and ensure better feedback from communities about the functioning of the education system, and to enable greater control over the behaviour of teachers.

The case of rural school timings

Rural schools in Raichur district run from 10.30 a.m. to 4.30 p.m. Despite high rates of school enrolment (nearly 100 per cent in the villages studied), in reality there is absenteeism as well as irregularity in attendance in primary school. Children's involvement in household activities such as animal husbandry, water, and fuel collection mean that they often interrupt school attendance to fulfil domestic duties.[11] Their participation in household activities also intensifies by season, including migration in the off-peak season. In the rural areas, children's involvement in household duties is not really 'labour force participation' — this is considered to be part of their contribution to household survival, fundamental to their sense of well-being, and not in conflict with children's participation in school, *provided the timings of school allow for both to co-exist*. While parents did not articulate this explicitly as a 'preference', their frequent references to the need for 'night schools' was an implicit plea for offering the option for children to be both educated and to continue carrying out chores for the household.

This was corroborated in interviews with two bureaucrats who had been carrying out micro-planning exercises with children to ascertain their motivation relating to schooling:

> We asked a lot of people about their preferences... We keep doing seasonal charts [with the children]. When they are very happy, it's actually season time, and they have a little money in their hands.[12]

> [Children] go to the fields, do the work, then they save their money and buy jugs and glasses for water [for the school]. ... 'I have earned and want to do something for my school' [they say]... If we gave them facilities to work and study at the same time, then it would be good. If you leave them to work for a little while then they will focus on their studies better, because they also have so many problems at home.[13]

These interviews, and informal discussions with children, indicate that they are closely involved in, and concerned about, household economic survival, and their sense of well-being is fulfilled by being able to help out and contribute to household work. Bureaucrats and parents interviewed also said that children were often scared to go late to school fearing teachers' reprimands, and hence often missed an entire day rather than just the time that they were away on errands. Forcing a choice between education and children's domestic contributions leads many parents to educate only some of their children, leaving the others free to help out at home. It is no surprise that the children who are more likely to get left out are female, given norms of early marriage for girls, low economic expectations and opportunities for girls, and concerns about adolescent girls' security.[14]

Accommodation of children's contributions to the household with their schooling would, therefore, be possible if school timetables were changed. However, this brings household preferences into some conflict with policy goals. UEE is promoted as the other side of the coin to child labour — it is considered essential to provide compulsory primary education services to ensure that children can be taken out of the labour force and participate fully in education instead. While policy preference for day-time school is not explicitly stated in policy documents, it is noteworthy that evening school is only ever suggested in the context of alternative, 'safety-net', non-formal schools for those children who are economically active.[15] Formal schools are very much the norm, and it is assumed that those who cannot attend formal schools with their fixed timings are 'outside the loop' and hence need a parallel schooling system. This view excludes the perspective that children's feeling of well-being and parents' strategy of risk-management may necessitate a different conception of 'formal' schooling.

Strategies for children's schooling pursued by poor households are fundamentally inter-linked with a range of other decisions about survival, security, and long-term household well-being (see Subrahmanian 1997). Parents whose children are involved in domestic chores send their children in and out of formal school in the hope that children may learn a few skills while continuing to help at home. The low expectations from education are not surprising — the encouragement of this ambivalent relationship to schooling is an outcome of parents' concerns for the future of their children. In the absence of any opportunities for economic betterment, it is often a risk to invest fully in a child's education, both in terms of short-term losses, and in terms of the oft-experienced phenomenon of educated youth who remain unemployed and yet refuse to return to work on family farms. The trade-off between long-term uncertainty and the vague possibility of gain is particularly evident with girls' education: with great social value being placed on girls' adolescent marriage, the barriers to girls' education are erected as early as puberty.

Underpinning parental decision-making on schooling are evaluations about the usefulness of education when applied to existing life circumstances. Decisions on investment in full-time schooling are based not just on immediate economic circumstances, but an evaluation of the medium to long-term prospects of household survival and economic security. Under such circumstances, participation in education on terms that satisfy national policy goals of UEE are not guaranteed, even if access is made universal. This immediately brings into question some of the centralised, standardised aspects of education policy which focus on building up a system of formal schooling in which all children, regardless of caste, class, and gender, can participate. Even if the investment in education is such that equitable access is ensured, getting households to participate in it is not such a simple matter, particularly where economic circumstances compel non-compliant household behaviour.

Some thoughts on 'preferences'

How are preferences revealed?

'Matching services with local preferences' assumes ease in the articulation or discussion of 'preferences', which belies the complex processes through which preferences are often, in reality, revealed. As evident in the case presented above, poor parents' 'preference' for flexible hours of schooling which allows for children to both work and learn something is not explicitly stated as preference, but reconstructed by an external researcher (the author) in the course of analysing wider education-related discussions and observations of behaviour. These 'preferences' are embedded in a wider context of perspectives and world-views, and are likely to emerge only through processes that fundamentally enable poor parents to have the confidence to express these views. Decentralisation may bring administrators closer to local realities, but this does not necessarily mean that preferences will be understood in the context of their complexity.

Whose preferences count in the context of conflict between local and policy perspectives?

Even where 'preferences' are picked up through participatory processes (as with the two administrators quoted above), they will not necessarily have an impact on the way services are managed. Upward feedback systems should be strong, and control over decision-making should be sufficiently devolved, to translate 'preferences' into systemic changes. A critical issue, however, is the recognition that policies, too, contain implicit 'preferences' in relation to the shape and design of services, which give rise to contradictions when couched in the language of participation and contextuality, and force the question — whose preferences count? Both household and state discourses are embedded in wider perspectives on poverty and its determinants; and, in the case of primary education, the critical question is that of understanding the role of children in managing poverty situations. While many authors have pointed out that over-emphasis on poverty as a causal factor in poor schooling can focus attention away from the crucial issue of the quality of schooling provision (see Drèze and Gazdar 1996), it is important to recognise the specific ways in which poverty structures both parents' and children's expectations and self-perceptions. Listening to 'preferences' and structuring services accordingly may go a longer way in encouraging participation and ownership among excluded groups than striving to push them into a schooling system without paying attention to their life-worlds.

Part of the conflict arises from the 'doublespeak' inherent in policy, where the push for UEE is tempered with the view that 'the Government would have to continue with its approach to motivate parents and children, involve communities and build up public opinion in favour of UEE' (Government of India 1997: ii). Winning excluded households over to the education system should involve making their preferences count, but there are barriers to this within the functioning of the policy process.

How homogeneous are preferences in a village?

Average school attendance is around 50 per cent a year in the village discussed, and the excluded are the poorest and often from the lower castes. Their preferences diverge from those of the better-off families who may see no need to alter the present system. The proposal that non-formal education (NFE) centres are established to serve as a safety-net for the poorest offers them a second-class schooling option with ill-equipped night schools and poorly-paid teachers, reinforcing a divide between those who go to formal school and those who do not.[16] Given that equality of opportunity is a policy goal, the solution lies not in continuing to divide village communities by class of education, but finding a system that suits the needs of all. Participatory processes of 'preference' articulation need to precede or accompany consensus-building in this area, with the state committing itself to solutions that work for the most excluded.

Can aspects of education services be selectively decentralised?

A practical consideration: if school hours are to be locally determined, then the work schedules and management of teachers would need to be reviewed. At present, teachers are managed by the bureaucracy, paid out of central or state funds, and recruited at state level through computerised district-based employment exchanges. Postings and transfers are managed by district education authorities, though teachers may move between districts if compelled by circumstances. Teachers' performance is monitored at the sub-district and district level.

Two implications emerge if services are matched with local preferences in this case. Firstly, as teachers' timings would need to be flexible in keeping with school hours it would be essential for teachers to live in the villages to ensure that they could perform their jobs. Given the situation where most rural teachers prefer to live in small towns or big villages and commute to their village posts,[17] this would be a challenge, and necessitate better investment in accommodation and facilities for teachers, as well as strictly enforcing rules regarding local residence. Secondly, this would necessitate placing teachers within more local control, to ensure accountability which may be best secured by also placing financial control at the local level. Within government, lines of authority are usually determined by control over salaries and financial resources, and hence it would be hard to see how teachers' accountability to local communities could be secured without changing the location of financial control.

Conclusion

This paper has attempted to think through broader issues relating to decentralised management of primary education services by applying questions about users' preferences to the case of rural primary schooling in a village of Raichur district. Some of the findings of the research on which this is based indicate that for UEE to be successful, there is a need to rethink the process of 'production' of education services from the viewpoint of the most excluded, incorporating livelihood concerns (in the widest sense) as well as the centrality of children to rural life-worlds, particularly in the context of poverty. Re-thinking the fundamentals would enable a more accurate perspective on users' preferences, and help set the agenda for the design of services and the structures of decentralisation that will bring services closer to these preferences.

Notes

1   A report in *The Times of India* indicates that Rs. 13.4 million of the budgets allocated for the Operation Blackboard scheme were not spent, leading to a reduction in the amount allocated for 1998–99 (8 June 1998).

2   A statistic revealed by the Union Minister for Human Resource Development in an interview with *The Times of India*, 10 June 1998.

3   Data from a UNICEF report 'In the Defence of the Child' cited in *The Indian Express*, 23 June 1998.

4   The proposal to make free and compulsory elementary education a Fundamental Right to be enforced through statutory measures through a Constitutional Amendment is in the process of being worked out by the Government of India. At present it is only a Directive Principle of State Policy (Art. 45 of the Constitution) and thus is a non-justiciable guideline.

5   Interview with Union Minister for Human Resource Development (ibid.)

6   Striking a balance between decentralisation and centralised control of education has been a long-standing quest in India and the subject of debates even in British India and newly-independent India in the 1950s (see Rai 1990 for some flavour of these debates). In fact, India's dismal progress in education in the early half of this century can be partly explained by constant shifts in control between the centre and the provinces.

7   The debate on the definition of social exclusion is rapidly growing and has largely emerged from developed countries (O'Brien et al. 1997), though it is seen to mirror closely work done in developing countries in the area of poverty, where processes of poverty are discussed not just in terms of income/consumption levels but also wider concepts such as 'relative deprivation, ill-being, vulnerability and capability' (ibid.: 4).

8   States bear most of the expenditure for education, but recently-launched schemes have considerably

increased the expenditure of the Central Government on elementary education (Government of India, 1993: 85).

9   Of course, the debate on what constitute acceptable minimum standards for education facilities is a major one, given financial constraints and management problems such as teacher absenteeism, high teacher-student ratios leading to multigrade teaching, non-availability of text-books in some cases, and so on.

10   Statistics are for 1991 (Gulati and Janssen 1997: 130).

11   Irregularly attending children tended to be from the poorer families where both parents were involved in livelihood management including migration; children from better-off families were often free to attend school all day.

12   Interview with local education administrator, 13 June 1997.

13   Interview with trainer, Block Resource Centre, Raichur District, 8 June 1997.

14   Not all villages have higher primary schools (for ages 10–14 years), and fears for girls' security (real or perceived) after puberty prevent parents from sending girls to school. This limits horizons for girls' education, and thus reduces incentives for parents to educate girls at the primary level.

15   A recent document of the Department of Education, Government of India, stated that 'Decentralisation of the education system holds out the possibility of introducing greater flexibility in the school system through measures such as shifting of school timings and adjusting the school/calendar timings to suit the local socio-economic conditions.' (1993: 48); however, the same policy document stresses at length the importance of non-formal education as a means of bringing working children into the education net. There are many contradictions within policy which point to a rather muddled perspective on how to resolve the education-poverty problem.

16   NFE is being promoted as a system which can provide equivalent quality of schooling to children outside the formal system, enabling working children to learn at their own pace. In effect, the government is committing itself on paper to funding two systems of schooling, which does not make much financial or other sense. The commitment is far from being realised, and NFE continues to be dogged by poor quality infrastructure, including a lack of teachers. Night schools (like most primary schools) often do not have electricity, or are plagued by frequent power cuts, and are far from providing an equivalent standard of schooling

17   Interviews with teachers indicate many reasons: family compulsion, problems such as lack of suitable accommodation, and critically, poor health and education infrastructure in villages which teachers consider essential for their own children, as well as broader, status considerations.

References

Bennett, R. (ed.) (1990) Decentralisation, Local Governments, and Markets: Towards a Post-Welfare Agenda, Oxford: Clarendon Press.

Colclough, C. (1991) 'Who should learn to pay? An assessment of neo-liberal approaches to education policy' in Colclough and Manor (eds.) States or Markets? Neo-liberalism and the Development Policy Debate, Oxford: Clarendon Press.

Drèze, J. and H. Gazdar (1996) 'Uttar Pradesh: The Burden of Inertia' in J. Dreze and A. Sen (eds.), *Indian Development: Selected Regional Perspectives*, New Delhi: OUP.

Drèze, J. and A. Sen (1995) India: Economic Development and Social Opportunity, New Delhi: OUP.

Government of India (1993) *Education for All: The Indian Scene*, New Delhi: Department of Education, Ministry of Human Resource Development.

Government of India (1997) *Report of the Committee of State Ministers on the Right to Free and Compulsory Elementary Education*, New Delhi: Department of Education, Ministry of Human Resource Development.

Gulati, L. and H. Jannsen (1997) *Gender Profile: Karnataka*, New Delhi: Royal Netherlands Embassy.

Lauglo, J. and M. McLean (eds.) (1985) The Control of Education: International Perspectives on the Centralisation-Decentralisation Debate, London: Heinemann Educational Books.

O'Brien, D., J. Wilkes, A. de Haan, and S. Maxwell (1997) *Poverty and Social Exclusion in North and South*, Working Paper 55, Brighton: IDS.

Rai, N. (1990) Centre-State Relations in the Field of Education in India, New Delhi: Atma Ram and Sons.

Rondinelli, D., J. Nellis, G. S. Cheema (1983) *Decentralisation in Developing Countries: A Review of Recent Experience*, World Bank Working Papers No. 581, Management and Development Series, No.8, Washington DC: World Bank.

Subrahmanian, R. (1997) '"If you build it, will they come?" Educational decision-making in the context of economic uncertainty and social risk', *IDS Bulletin* 28(3).

Wolman, H. (1990) 'Decentralisation: what it is and why we should care' in R. Bennett (ed.) 1990.

Woodhall, M. (1997) 'Human capital concepts' in A. H. Halsey et al. (eds.) *Education: Culture, Economy, and Society*, Oxford: OUP.

World Bank (1997a) World Development Report 1997: The State in a Changing World, Washington DC: World Bank.

World Bank (1997b) *Primary Education in India*, Development in Practice Series Washington: The World Bank and New Delhi: Allied Publishers Limited

The development management task and reform of 'public' social services

Dorcas Robinson

Introduction: public sector reform and the New Public Management

The 'New Public Management' (NPM), closely associated with public sector reform programmes currently in various stages of design and implementation around the world, emerged as a 'conventional wisdom' (Mackintosh 1997) in the early 1990s. Part of the appeal of the NPM for modern-day reformers lies in its apparent coherence as a model for re-organising public sectors. Drawing on the new institutional economics or rational choice theories, the NPM advocates:

> [the] disaggregation of public bureaucracies; competition in the public sector (for example contracting out, quasi markets); and discipline and parsimony in public spending. (Rhodes 1995)

This approach seems to offer solutions to the problem of developing social service systems that can respond to growing populations and changing demands without increasing the financial burden on the state.

Secondly, the NPM appears to provide a 'common-sense', 'no-nonsense' approach to public management, deemed appropriate to building probity and efficiency in large, poorly-funded government bureaucracies (Mackintosh 1997). It draws on 'managerialism', a body of thinking which extols certain supposed qualities of private-sector management, namely:

> ...hands-on, professional management based on private sector management experience which sets explicit standards and measures of performance and emphasises output controls. (ibid.)

But is the NPM up to the job? Does it, in fact, provide coherency and an adequately grounded appreciation of 'public' sectors and 'public' management to meet the challenges of shaping and managing viable and responsive public sectors in the coming years? This article proposes that three questions require more detailed consideration when talking about public sector reform:

- management of what?
- management by whom?
- how to manage?

These questions are discussed with reference to the philosophy and practice of Community Based Health Care (CBHC) in Tanzania. This discussion highlights aspects of 'public' sector management to which prevailing international and national Health Sector Reform debates and documents, from their inception, have paid only cursory attention. Firstly, the fact that 'public' sectors are geographically and historically context-specific, being constructed through processes of contestation and negotiation, including (and excluding) a range of actors. Secondly, that the fact of multi-actor involvement in public social services requires more than an output-oriented, efficiency approach to public management. It requires management of a wide array of relationships which cut across organisational and sectoral boundaries. Therefore, the questions raised here are relevant to all development managers — whether central government policy-makers, NGO activists, civic leaders, local government planners, for-profit entrepreneurs, or donor agency staff. For it is they collectively — at times inadvertently, at times with intent — who are constantly shaping and mis-shaping 'public' sectors and their management.

Management of what?

Community Based Health Care: what is it?

Originally developed by the African Medical and Research Foundation (AMREF) in Kenya, CBHC is the complement to the more familiar Institution Based Health Care (IBHC) approach to Primary Health Care (PHC). It is now widely used in Tanzania and Uganda. The focus of CBHC is on individuals and households within the community setting, and beyond the formal health service delivery unit. CBHC seeks to address the basic PHC problematic: that the majority of cases presented at rural village health posts and dispensaries are 'home-preventable'. They are health problems which tell the tale of poverty — in income, environment (sanitation, water sources, housing quality), education, power, and organisation. The CBHC approach recognises that these are issues that no health service facility can address alone, even where that facility is well-resourced and has the capacity to deliver quality health education and advice. Therefore CBHC seeks to develop people's health awareness and healthful practice within a framework of empowerment and collective action. The motivation behind this can be very simply expressed by the notion that a recurrently sick child is a burden on a mother's time, which is, in turn, an issue for the household. Recurrent and unresolved problems for a household are an issue for the community. And ultimately, what cannot be dealt with by the community is a concern for the nation. Thus, CBHC makes a direct link between individual health problems and public commitments, focusing on community members as key actors. Individuals are important not simply as individual consumers of health services, but as actors who take on their communal responsibilities and who are in turn supported by a national health and development system.

Through a process of facilitated dialogues and learner-centred training, CBHC trainers work within villages to build awareness and understanding of health as inextricably linked with all aspects of people's lives; to explore local needs, priorities and resources; and to develop confidence and capacities to take action. In the Tanzanian context, a common example of the use of such dialogue is with villages or wards which are organising for the rehabilitation of their local, usually government-run, dispensary. *De facto* responsibility for these physical facilities and ancilliary buildings such as staff houses, lies predominantly with the village government. Requests for additional support are usually processed through district government channels, and via these, to NGOs and other actors. This request provides an entry-point for questions and discussions with the villages involved about whether the dispensary is the real, only, or most immediate solution to the key health issues of the user community. Through these discussions, the motivating concern behind the proposed project is often revealed. For example, a high incidence of childhood morbidity or mortality linked to a particular illness such as diarrhoea, malaria, or other environmental health problems. Further dialogue about the cause and effect of the disease can lead communities to review their plans, deciding perhaps to tackle water supply and usage first, or to support the training of peer educators to carry health-related messages to their neighbours, or to reconstitute or revive the leadership of the village health committee so as to ensure they are more active or representative.

CBHC is about health education and awareness. It is also about building organisational and management capacities more generally. These capacities include consulting over the mobilisation and use of village resources. In the interest of better management of these resources, some CBHC interventions may also include start-up support for income generating activities, payment-in-kind for community health workers and services, and exploring schemes for managing community-based payment for, and distribution of, drugs and other material supplies.

CBHC is also about the larger system within which communities are located. For most proponents of CBHC that means the government health and development service system. In order to manage and promote improved health on an ongoing basis, villages have to be well linked to other development actors, in particular government. Most CBHC interventions seek to improve these linkages by working not simply with villages, but also with government departments. The idea is that better understanding on both sides will increase responsiveness and the relevance of support, whether this is the loan of the district truck for transporting building materials, allocation of new staff, or the inclusion of a village project in the next year's district development budget.

CBHC and public sector management

Much of the international health sector reform debate focuses on the formal health service delivery system, government programmes and units, and central policy mechanisms. In all the talk of public/private split, cost-recovery and 'basic essential health care' packages (World Bank 1993), it is easy to forget the history of health debate. Yet deep within this debate lies a fundamental question: what *is* the public sector in health? Is it government regulation of a market-mediated, professionally designed health *care* system, or a system which takes health *development* and the politics of access and equity to heart?

The CBHC emphasis on community involvement in health serves as a reminder of the PHC agenda articulated in the Alma Ata Declaration of 1978. That declaration, and ensuing programmes and publications, captured an international conviction that community participation, inter-sectoral collaboration and affordable technologies 'in the context of equity and social justice' (Monekosso 1992) are key to building better health services and better health in developing countries. With its emphasis on diversity of need between and within communities, CBHC also indicates that the 'public sector' encompasses an arena of action in which priorities, resources, and activities are various and contested. By advocating, for example, that health education needs to be based on local realities, institutions, and problem analysis — not simply on externally designed standard messages delivered from health facilities — CBHC identifies the need for an appreciation that policy design and implementation cannot just be the preserve of centralised technical experts. Policy design and implementation is about prioritisation, and the allocation of scarce resources. CBHC is one approach which seeks to give communities some space and voice in this arena.

At the same time, there are many limitations on the implementation of PHC. These provide a significant management challenge to those governments, which like the Tanzanian Ministry of Health, maintain their commitment to PHC as the basis for building a health system which will be 'cost-effective, efficient and sustainable' (Ministry of Health 1994a). The Ministry notes that PHC has tended to be misconceived at all levels. This means that in practice it has been reduced to specific programmes and interventions such as vaccination campaigns. In addition, the cooperation between sectors and agencies for which comprehensive PHC strives has been weak. These difficulties are neither uncommon nor surprising given the revolution in professional thinking and practice that comprehensive PHC requires, with its emphasis on 'the *promotion* of health through a partnership between health and other professionals and the community, as well as a system of treatments and curative care based on meeting the health needs of the majority' (MacDonald 1992). As MacDonald notes, however, there is a persistent tendency for health care provision to focus mainly on the curative care provided by medical professionals in formal service centres. This view of health care needs dominates health policy, restricting efforts to open up the debate.

There is also a continual need to reconcile community involvement in health with national frameworks and strategies. An overly macro-level focus on the part of policy makers can limit appreciation of diversity, but so too, a purely micro-level emphasis neglects the importance of potential national public concerns, such as ensuring national service coverage and equitable access. Currently, the proponents of the CBHC approach in Tanzania can be criticised for not grappling as effectively with macro-policy concerns as they could. But in its practice, CBHC is engaging with many of the problems that the Ministry of Health has identified in existing PHC policy and practice. This is because CBHC takes as its starting point a multi-actor, bottom-up, system of action which is based on local needs, existing resources, and improved lobbying for external support where necessary.

Management by whom?

Implementation of CBHC

The main actors involved in developing and implementing CBHC in Tanzania have been NGOs. The approach varies with context, history, and type of NGO. The local development office of a church may focus on training peer educators or CBHC facilitators identified through their parish system. Other NGOs work across groups of villages, describing these as cluster or area programmes. These groups of villages tend to fall within government administrative boundaries, and such programmes commonly involve the training of trainers within the ward and/or district government offices. These trainers may then be supported by the NGO in their interaction with village-level health workers, committees, and CBHC groups. Such an initiative may be part of an integrated development programme which also works on education, water, agriculture, and income issues. Alternatively, it may be health-specific, having emerged from Mother and Child Health (MCH) and other health promotion programmes. Some mission-run health service facilities have developed CBHC programmes from PHC outreach projects operating in the vicinity of their health centre or hospital. But if NGOs are the main implementors of CBHC, how do they fit into public sector management?

NGOs as 'private' service providers

International health policy debate has begun to recognise the significance of NGOs and other actors in the health sector,[1] but there has been inadequate attention paid to what their activities actually involve and how these are developing. While in many countries of Sub-Saharan Africa non-governmental health providers have consistently been responsible for a major percentage of health services (De Jong 1991) managed through fairly cooperative relationships with government (see Sivalon, 1995, on the Catholic Church as a service provider in Tanzania), Green and Matthias (1995) note a 'certain introspection' in health ministries which has produced a tendency to overlook this fact. When NGO activity in health is recognised, ministries tend to focus on particular sub-sections, such as mission-run hospitals. This neglect of NGOs arises in part from confusions about what NGOs actually are. Green (1987) notes a tendency to lump NGOs with the 'private' sector, and this is certainly the picture painted by the World Bank in its 1993 World Development Report, *Investing in Health* (World Bank 1993).

Yet the example of CBHC shows that while mission hospitals are active in community-based approaches to PHC, they are far from being the main actors in this area. Many other non-governmental agencies are not direct health service providers, but are working to build CBHC into existing government systems, with the intention of moving out of this activity in the medium-term. So if NGOs working in CBHC are not adequately described as private service providers, what are they?

NGOs as 'community activists'

Alternative views are provided by Gilson et al. (1994) who identify at least four categories of NGO action in health, more than one of which may be supported by a single organisation. These are: service provision; social welfare; support to the health system through training, supplies and so on; and, research and advocacy. The latter aspect can range from being 'community activists' — developing the PHC concept and training Village Health Workers (VHWs) — to advocacy and lobbying at the national and international level. Given its community-based activities, CBHC implementation puts NGOs in the 'community activist' category. Most CBHC facilitators would see themselves as change agents, not just supporting shifts in people's awareness and understanding of health, but ultimately working with communities to enable them to become more effective managers of their local and collective actions.

NGOs as 'public' actors

However, CBHC activities also highlight another area of NGO work which is rarely discussed. In the same way that NGOs should not be narrowly defined as private service providers, they should also not be lumped simplistically into 'civil society and all that'. A focus on community development is central to the work of most NGOs, but a not uncommon strategy in pursuing this goal is, for many agencies, to provide support to governments. Although this support may be primarily related to the NGOs' operational needs, they are not simply acting as implementors ('gap-fillers', contractors and so on) in government-defined systems, but as change-agents setting out to influence government policies and practices.

In terms of *government practice*, while NGOs may be the main initiators and implementors of CBHC initially, they seek to build the approach into existing systems, and this usually means local government. For example, in 1988 AMREF began a CBHC programme in

Rukwa Region, at the request of, and in collaboration with, the Ministry of Health and district governments. The agency trained and supported government CBHC teams, withdrawing its direct input during the mid-1990s. A similar example is provided by the Community Based Health Care Council (CBHCC). This council emerged from an earlier multi-agency (NGO and government) PHC Coordinating Committee, registering as an NGO in 1992. Initially supported by Oxfam GB, the Council's first work-plan covered nine regions and involved the training of key government staff within the hospital and regional or district structure. This initiative has left CBHC-trained personnel within the government structure, some of whom have successfully lobbied for support for extending CBHC from other NGOs. In some cases this may involve government staff informally liaising with an NGO, or being formally seconded to the agency for a period.

Direct training and support of government staff in CBHC is only one aspect of this NGO-government relationship. Many NGOs also link their CBHC activities with other health support services they provide. For example, NGOs which are involved in the delivery of government vertical health programmes, such as family planning, HIV/AIDS, and malaria control may integrate these with their CBHC programmes, supporting community-based care for AIDS patients, and providing communities with information and education prior to vaccination programmes in addition to providing logistical support (drugs, transport, and funds) for these campaigns.

A history of interaction between NGOs and local governments in these areas has led to localised attempts to build cross-agency collaboration, which range from informal networks that aim to share information, training, and community development approaches, to formal committees with some planning function.

In terms of *government policy* some NGOs have gone further with the promotion of CBHC. The incorporation of CBHC into the Proposals for Health Sector Reform (1994) is in no small way due to the relationship between AMREF's CBHC unit and groups in the Ministry of Health. Having worked with AMREF in Rukwa Region, the Ministry invited AMREF to conduct a study of CBHC in 1993, and the agency subsequently worked with the Ministry on the design of the National CBHC Guidelines (1994b). This example highlights how NGOs can also act as innovators beyond the local level, in some cases as active (though rarely acknowledged) contributors to public policy.

Reforming the system: the public action approach

The piloting, development and implementation of CBHC by NGOs provides just one example of how public policy and public sector management involves complex relationships between a variety of agencies, many of which are not governmental. Yet, whilst most development managers would acknowledge this reality, few are armed with the tools for thinking about its implications for their work. For example, while the Tanzanian Proposals for Health Sector Reform (1994) note that CBHC offers an approach which will 'empower communities to organise their health and health services within well defined Government administrative structures' (Ministry of Health 1994a), the health reform policy process itself has provided few opportunities for effective inputs from groups and organisations outside central government.

The example of CBHC highlights a need for a broader understanding of 'public' if reforms are to reflect what is happening in practice, and if they are to allow for more effective involvement by a range of key actors and stakeholders. The notion of *public policy as a process of public action* offers a way of thinking about the public arena which goes beyond a narrow focus on government systems or on policy as a matter of technical expertise.

> Public action is ... not just a question of public service delivery
> and state initiative. It is also ... a matter of participation by the
> public in a process of social change (Drèze and Sen 1989, quoted
> in Mackintosh 1992).

Taking this definition one step further, Mackintosh suggests that public action also incorporates action on behalf of sectional interests, which would include for-profit actors. So what you have in the idea of public action is a recognition that the public arena is open to collective and purposeful manipulation by a whole range of actors. Therefore, public policy, and what is deemed at a point in time to constitute the public interest and the public sector, are social constructions which emerge from a dynamic political process. Having recognised this, what are the implications for the actual task of public management?

How to manage?

What does CBHC suggest about the task of public management?

'I am not a manager... I am a facilitator, an animator' (personal communication 1998).[1]

This government PHC/CBHC coordinator clearly does not see himself as the 'hands-on professional' manager of the NPM (Rhodes 1995). His perception of himself as a facilitator is resonant of the 'soft' aspects of management, which have long taken commercial sector managers far beyond a simplistic focus on goals, performance, and output, to the process and people aspects of management.

In the implementation of CBHC there are at least three groups engaged in the task of managing — communities, NGOs, and government. Not everyone in these groups would call themselves a manager. Few of those outside government employment will think of themselves as 'public' managers. Yet in their practices they are engaged in managing an ongoing process of defining public interests and taking public action. Their activities include lobbying for resources for projects, awareness-raising and discussion, formal meetings to allocate resources, training sessions to build skills, and joint planning activities. The CBHC approach recognises that this is not a set of activities which can be pre-defined and controlled so much as a process of building understanding and cooperation between parties which have diverse perceptions, needs, priorities, relationships, resources, and capacities.

CBHC does not offer a panacea for more effective public management. A study of its implementation simply highlights aspects of current practice, some of which CBHC facilitators set out to change. Many of these have a long history — lack of information-sharing, weak or non-existent consultation mechanisms, poorly defined agendas, externally defined priorities, limited resource control — which reflect limitations in structures and capacities on all sides. Proponents of community involvement in health stress the need for professionals in the health system to adapt their approaches, emphasising their role in 'negotiation, compromise, advocacy, teaching' (Hildebrandt 1994). These skills apply equally to government, NGO, and civic managers.

Unfortunately, in much of the debate surrounding health sector reform, limited attention has been paid to the implications of pluralism in organisation, agendas and action, or to the shifts in philosophy and practice which are required to manage this. The efforts of the 1980s to operationalise PHC by taking district health management as the logical focal point can be criticised for their over-emphasis on the government system to the exclusion of appreciating the role of, and relationships with, other health actors. A limitation in the current health reform agenda is its excessive faith in the power of policies to create an 'enabling' environment (Save the Children Fund 1993). The 1993 World Development Report talks of decentralisation without reference to the sophisticated debate about the notorious political and practical difficulties of actually implementing this. And despite a lot of current rhetoric about partnerships for health, there are few who have considered and explicated the management implications of privatisation, de-regulation, dis-aggregation and the like, either for government managers or their counterparts in other organisations.

Developing the capacities: public management as management of interdependence

There are significant problems in moving from a state-centred, hierarchically managed view of public policy based on notions of control, to a more decentralised and pluralistic system. In the current health management system in Tanzania, the district government role has not been conceived of as a policy role. There is little emphasis in practice on information analysis, team work, or strategic thinking. The district has been treated as the implementing arm of central government. Similarly, at no level of government are other actors such as NGOs or community groups explicitly thought of in any capacity other than implementation, despite their impact, however localised, on health infrastructure, management, and systems. Finally, non-governmental actors of all kinds often fail to think through their own roles *vis-à-vis* government systems and policy. What is commonly missing is an appreciation and analysis of *interdependence*.

Recognising that public managers are operating in a pluralistic world, caught in an 'increasingly complex net of interdependence', Geoffrey Vickers suggested that goal-setting approaches to public management were insufficient to the task (Vickers 1983, cited in Rhodes 1995). He advocated that public management should be understood as regulation, or the task of:

... maintaining through time a complex pattern of relationships in accordance with standards or within limits which have come somehow to be set as governing relations. Its regulative function consists partly in maintaining the actual course of affairs in line with these governing relations as they happen to be at the time and partly in modifying these governing relations....

... the goals we seek are changes in out relations or in our opportunities for relating: *but the bulk of our activity consists in the 'relating' itself.*

(Vickers 1968, quoted in Rhodes 1995, emphasis added)

For Vickers, public managers are engaged in a task of 'appreciation' and of making 'multi-valued choices' through this process of regulating interdependence. All too often, proponents of the NPM gloss over these more qualitative aspects of public management by adopting the language of pragmatism, but as Rhodes (1995) points out:

...management in the public domain has distinctive tasks, purposes and conditions. For example, it determines collective values out of the mosaic of conflicting interests. NPM is confined to the values enshrined in the '3 Es' of economy, efficiency and effectiveness, and it does not encompass broader notions, such as the public interest and public accountability.

Conclusion

The NPM would not be the first in a long line of management 'theories' which say more about the way the world *should be* or is *assumed to be*, than about what *is*. The promotion and implementation of CBHC reveal some important aspects of what *is* happening. Firstly that the 'what' of the public sector is not just a set of definable government functions which can simply be privatised and dis-aggregated. It is constantly being redefined in an arena of public action which is home to a range of non-governmental agencies. These are continually initiating action in the name of improved public health, defining new areas for government support, and of public concern. This is the second point: the 'whom' of public sector management includes non-governmental actors, from direct health service providers working within the formal health system to broader development agencies concerned with grassroots empowerment and community development. These agencies are actively involved in relationships with various parts of governments, in the interest not just of implementing CBHC, but of shaping the nature and focus of public management. This fact has implications for the 'how' of public management. These relationships are complex, political, and often fragile. They require management, and of the kind which goes beyond target setting and quantifiable outputs.

The notions of public action and interdependence offer a way of thinking which can be applied by all development managers to the context within which they work. One of the key challenges for the architects of public sector reform is to use these perspectives on public management as a starting point for building the structures, incentives, and capacities on all sides to manage the process of continual re-negotiation of what is being managed, by whom, and in what ways.

Note

1 For example, the World Bank notes that NGO spending on health in developing countries was estimated to be US$1 100 million in 1990 (US$830 million from NGOs' own sources, US$242 million from bilateral donors, US$21 million from the UN system, and US$7 million from foundations), at a time when total external financial assistance to the health sector from donor countries was US$4,794 million (World Bank 1993).

References

De Jong, J. (1991) 'Non-governmental Organisations and Health Delivery in Sub-Saharan Africa', World Bank Population and Human Resources Department, WPS 708, Washington DC: The World Bank.

Drèze, J. and A. Sen (1989) *Hunger and Public Action*, Oxford: Clarendon Press.

Gilson, L., P. D. Sen, S. Mohammed and P. Mujinja (1994) 'The potential of non-governmental organisations: policy options', *Health Policy and Planning* (9)1: 14–24.

Green, A. (1987) 'The role of non-governmental organisations and the private sector in the provision of health care in developing countries', *International Journal of Health Planning and Management* 2: 37–58.

Green, A. and A. Matthias (1995) 'Where do NGOs fit in? Developing a policy framework for the health sector', *Development in Practice* (5)4: 313–323.

Hindebrandt, E. (1994) 'A model for community involvement in health (CIH) programme development', *Social Science and Medicine* 39(2): 247–254.

MacDonald, J. (1992) Primary Health Care: Medicine in its Place, London: Earthscan.

Mackintosh, M. (1992) 'Introduction', in M. Wuyts, M. Mackintosh, and T. Hewitt (eds.) *Development Policy and Public Action*, Oxford: OUP/The Open University.

Mackintosh, M. (1997) 'Managing Public Sector Reform: The Case of Health Care', *Development Policy and Practice Working Paper 37*, Milton Keynes: The Open University.

Ministry of Health (1994a) *Proposals for Health Sector Reform*, Dar es Salaam: Government of Tanzania.

Ministry of Health (1994b) *Guidelines on Community Based Health Care activities in Tanzania*, Dar es Salaam: Government of Tanzania.

Ministry of Health (1995) *National District Health Planning Guidelines*, Dar es Salaam: Government of Tanzania, Version 1.0.

Monekosso, G. L. (1992) 'An organisational framework for achieving health for all in developing countries', *International Journal of Health Planning and Management* 7: 3–22.

Rhodes, R. (1995) 'Foreword: governance in the hollow state', in M. Blunden and M. Dando (eds.) *Rethinking Public Policy-making: Questioning Assumptions, Challenging Beliefs*, London: Sage Publications.

Save the Children Fund (1993) 'A response to the World Development Report', unpublished report, London: SCF.

Sivalon, J. (1995) 'The Catholic Church and the Tanzanian State in the provision of social services', in J. Semboja and O. Therkildsen (eds.) *Service Provision under Stress in East Africa*, London: James Currey.

World Bank (1993) *Investing in Health*, World Development Report, Oxford: OUP.

An endogenous empowerment strategy: a case study of Nigerian women

P. Kassey Garba

Introduction

Several studies have shown that women in private and public sector organisations generally participate very minimally in decision-making compared to their male counterparts (see, for example, Foner 1982; Muna 1991; and Odubogun 1995). Even when women do participate, their level of participation is shown to be insufficient to exert significant influence on the major decisions made by the bodies to which they belong. In a highly patriarchal context such as Nigeria, where men have always dominated the core decision-making organs of society, there is an obvious and pressing need for the empowerment of women so that they can meaningfully participate in processes whose outcomes will affect their lives. This need is made more acute, since the interests of men and of women are very likely to diverge. When conflict does occur, their empowerment may be women's only protection against attempts to subordinate their interests.

This article argues that the enhancement of women's capacity to influence and participate in making decisions that directly or indirectly affect their lives is a key issue in raising their standard of living and protecting their rights to full participation in the processes of development. In other words, empowering women is a means to an end; the end being to improve their lives and protect their rights to participate in decisions that affect them. Strategies for empowering women need to be evaluated for at least three reasons. The most obvious is that strategies are necessary to facilitate women's empowerment in order to improve their economic, social, and political status. Secondly, the observation that most women do not participate as much as men in decision-making processes, despite attempts to empower them to do so, implies that these strategies need to be reviewed. And thirdly, the apparent failures of previous empowerment strategies mean that we need to seek more effective ones.

This article is in four parts. In the following section, we provide a conceptual clarification of the term 'empowerment', both to show that the way in which empowerment is conceptualised predetermines strategies to achieve it, and to develop the argument for an endogenous empowerment. Section three presents a critical review of empowerment strategies that have been implemented in Nigeria, with the aim of identifying the requirements for more effective ones. The structure of an endogenous empowerment strategy is then developed, and this is followed by a concluding section.

Basic issues in the empowerment process

Conceptual clarification

There are two dimensions of the empowerment concept with respect to women: the static, and the dynamic. The former defines the empowerment of women in terms of their capacities to participate in making decisions that directly or indirectly affect their lives, and to influence those decisions. This refers to the notion of women having an effective voice. Consequently, women are assumed to be disempowered when they cannot influence decisions that alter their lives (Odubogun 1995). This view may suggest that an effective voice could be given to women who do not have one, or that disempowered women could be exogenously empowered.

The dynamic concept regards empowerment as a process of developing the capacity of individuals (in this case women) to participate effectively in making and implementing decisions that directly or indirectly affect them. Viewed as a process, empowerment is something an individual or a group of individuals acquires over time. It is not something you can give to people, although the conditions could be created to increase their chances of acquiring it by themselves. Of course, this also means that it is possible to create conditions that block people's capacity to empower themselves.

The distinction between the static and dynamic concepts of empowerment is significant because it is likely to lead to different empowerment strategies. Specifically, the former may lead to exogenous empowerment strategies while the latter may lead to endogenous ones. Exogenous strategies are those built on the premise that disempowered groups can be empowered by external individuals or groups. By contrast, endogenous strategies are those whose underlying premise is that external groups can only facilitate empowerment by creating enabling conditions for disempowered groups to empower themselves. The exogenous empowerment strategy implies a top-down approach while the endogenous strategy implies a bottom-up one.

Disempowerment is the consequence of some combination of social, cultural, economic, political, and historical processes. For instance, where individuals lack the capacity or competence to participate in decision-making, their disempowerment may be explained by humanly devised rules that foster inequalities and ordinate-subordinate relationships among groups of people within a society. A woman would be unable to contribute to the planning and design of development projects in her community if the prevailing rules of human interactions prevent her from being educated. Even an educated and highly skilled woman cannot contribute to the planning and design of development projects in her community if its culture and religion forbid women to sit and talk with men. A woman in purdah and/or seclusion [1] is usually not allowed to mix freely with the opposite sex even on a professional basis.[2] In other societies, social standards of wealth, preconditions for participation in professions, politics and government, and so on, are both cause and effect of societal structures that make some people superior to others in the same society, (Odubogun, ibid.). In Nigeria, as in many parts of the world, women do not enjoy the same privileges, opportunities, power, influence, and recognition, as men.

Empowerment is unlikely to be granted to the disempowered because some individuals or groups benefit from the disempowerment of others and are unlikely freely to give up the resulting 'privileges'. Consequently, a quick-fix solution, which the static concept seems to suggest, is unlikely to be feasible or effective. The dynamic concept is more likely to lead to effective empowerment strategies because its perception of empowerment and disempowerment as the consequences of social processes, is more realistic. The endogenous notion of empowerment implies both that much of the effort to achieve empowerment depends on the disempowered and that exogenous forces can enable or accelerate the endogenous process, particularly if these do not treat empowerment as a gift. Thus, the exogenous enabling conditions for endogenous empowerment become the key point of reference in evaluating empowerment strategies for Nigerian women.

Exogenous enabling conditions for endogenous empowerment

Karl (1995) offers a useful framework for identifying the exogenous enabling conditions for endogenous empowerment, describing four stages in the empowerment process with respect to women: awareness; capacity-building and skills development; participation and greater control in decision-making; and action for change. The basic proposition is that the capacity for awareness and skills can be developed and will tend to increase the capacity to participate in, and exert greater control over, decision-making, while empowerment is realised by the use of the awareness and skills acquired.

We extend Karl's four-stage process in two directions. Firstly, we add two more stages in order to facilitate a more systematic analysis of the empowerment process, one that is more applicable to the empowerment of Nigerian women. Secondly, we explicitly recognise the significance of institutions in disempowering women. This implies that a more effective strategy would first target the capacity and motivation of women to break institutional barriers to empowerment and then provide a framework for changing those humanly devised rules that support women's disempowerment. The differences in the humanly devised rules of disempowerment can be significant and changing these would make endogenous empowerment easier.

Figure 1 shows a six-stage empowerment process namely: awareness; skills and capacity assessment; capacity-building and skills development; participation and greater control in decision-making; action for change; and evaluation. The capacity and skills assessment stage increases the chance that the requisite capacity and skills will be developed. It also has an important methodological implication, which is that a needs assessment must be based on the objective conditions of a specific problem of disempowerment. In other words, a general doctrine of empowerment would not work in all cases; nor would exogenously deduced approaches work. The sixth stage (evaluation) is a feedback mechanism.

Being aware of the current situation of disempowerment and of options for empowerment is a necessary condition for achieving it. It is easy to accept a situation if one is either not aware of it or of better options. Consequently, building awareness about discriminatory practices against women, about laws that undermine their interests, and cultural and traditional norms that perpetuate women's subjugation and subordination, are the necessary building-blocks of an endogenous empowerment strategy. Awareness of the rules of disempowerment is potentially conflictual.

Figure 1 A six-stage hierarchical empowerment process

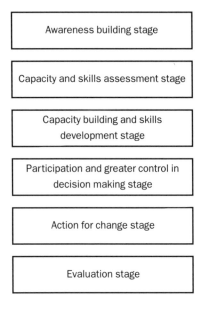

Awareness building stage

Capacity and skills assessment stage

Capacity building and skills development stage

Participation and greater control in decision making stage

Action for change stage

Evaluation stage

Source: A modification of Karl (1995)

It is important to recognise this, and its implications for the empowerment process. The history of feminism shows that winning the vote in Europe and the USA after World War I was the result of a long struggle and sacrifice by women during the war. So being informed of the costs of empowerment is a key part of the process of awareness.

The second stage involves identifying the capacity and skills which are needed for effective participation but which the individual or group lacks. This assessment will realistically show what changes should take place before the targeted person(s) can be expected to participate effectively. A major disadvantage of not carrying out a needs assessment is that inappropriate skills and capacities may be given to a person who actually needs something else. For example, if a large number of women are represented in the lower echelons of an organisation and are, as a result, unable to influence major policies, a needs assessment may show that education is a key to their empowerment. If, on the other hand, the needs assessment shows that women are given low status jobs even when they do have the relevant education to occupy management positions, educating women who are already educated is obviously a waste of resources. An efficient assessment of needs may show that artificial barriers, such as those created by the tradition and culture, are responsible for the problems identified; and this would require a different kind of capacity and skills development than giving formal education. In general, a needs assessment will reveal the enabling conditions for empowerment in any given case of disempowerment.

The third stage of the empowerment process involves taking deliberate steps to build capacity and develop relevant skills as suggested by a needs assessment. Programmes of enlightenment may require building capacity for planning, organising, coordination, and resource and personnel management. These and other relevant skills and capacities are frequently needed in order to participate more meaningfully in decision-making.

The fourth stage calls for the use of the skills and capacities that have been acquired to participate in actual decision-making and to exert a greater control over what happens in the home, the workplace, and in the larger society. Acquiring skills and developing capacities is meaningless if these remain unused. On the contrary, such skills and capacities should lead to more adroit decision-making as well as improving women's bargaining power and deterring the potential agents of disempowerment.

The fifth stage consists of deliberate action on the part of the empowered person(s) or group(s) to bring about change to redress the problems highlighted earlier. The entire process is successful only if the acquired skills and capacity built are used to bring about desired changes in the lives of the individuals or groups concerned, and in the lives of others in their communities.

The last stage, evaluation, is important to assessing the success or failure of the entire process, the results of which can be used as feedback into the next cycle of the empowerment process. In other words, empowerment is not seen as a 'once and for all' activity but one that is gained over time and frequently updated. New information fed back into the awareness stage often means building new and fresh capacities and skills in order to gain more decision-making power for positive action. A woman is never fully empowered but must continue to update the skills and capacities necessary to be an effective participant in ongoing decisions that surround her. It should also be emphasised that evaluation is a continuous process in a dynamic scheme of enabling endogenous empowerment.

The scheme shows that empowerment assumes concrete forms in stages four and five,[3] and that stages one, two, three, and six are points of exogenously enabling or accelerating empowerment.[4]

Assessing the strategies used in empowering Nigerian women

This section presents an historical review of the general problem of empowerment in Nigerian society, and evaluates some empowerment strategies that have been used.

Historical origins of disempowerment

Nigerian women had a long history of empowerment before colonial rule. In fact, women were far more empowered (politically, socially, and economically) before colonialism — the alien culture and beliefs brought in by colonialism negated most of the rights and privileges hitherto enjoyed by them. Alongside men's political association, in most parts of Nigeria, women also had their own well-organised political groups which were solely managed by women leaders in the various communities. For instance in Yoruba land (one of the major ethnic groups in Nigeria), an *Iyalode,* or woman leader, is appointed to the *Ala'afin* or *Ooni's* (the king's) council of chiefs to represent women in the community. In most southern Nigerian palaces, women, just as men, had their own governing and chieftain councils headed by the Iyalode, which administered the needs of women and made representation to the various king's institutions. The Iyalode works to protect the interests of women and to ensure that their dignity is maintained. Although this arrangement still exists in Nigeria, the powers of the Iyalode have been substantially reduced because of, and since, the colonial period. Although they still function in their areas of the palaces, more of the women's problems for which they were once responsible are now dealt with by the modern law courts. It is debatable whether these have been as effective as the Iyalode system in dealing with women's issues. Men did not consider the arrangement a threat. Moreover, it minimised social conflicts and offered protection to women and children.

The unique (centralised and totalitarian) administrative structures of the colonial period destabilised the otherwise well-established culture and structures. Not only did the colonial administrative structure result in the politics of class and the identity of individuals taking on new meaning, it also stripped women of most of their basic rights to administer their own affairs and protect their own future. In other words, the Nigerian people, and especially women, lost their autonomy and most of their rights.[5]

Alongside the traditional structures of governance and administration, there is a long history of very active and effective and autonomous women's organisations, particularly in the south. Ibo women, a dynamic trading group in the south, have always had (before and after the colonial period) appreciable political and economic influences through established associations that are well managed and solely run by them. Their power and influence goes beyond issues that affect their trade to issues of governance at the state level. Despite the problems brought about by the colonial administrators, Ibo women's movements and some others in southern Nigeria, have struggled to maintain some respectable level of power and influence in their communities.

Many of the pre-independence struggles of Mrs Fumilayo Ranson-Kuti in Western Nigeria, of Margaret Ekpo and the Aba women riot of 1949 in Eastern Nigeria, and Hajiya Gambo Sawaba, targeted the colonial assault on women's rights. Historical documents reveal that women were political leaders and led war campaigns of their people.[6] Thus, there is little doubt that colonialism did not improve the rights of Nigerian women. This is hardly surprising, since colonialism could only thrive under a regime of extreme and general violations of human rights and divide and rule tactics; and considering that women in Britain were themselves marginalised by their society at the time.[7]

Evaluation of dominant strategies for the empowerment of women

The strategies fall into two groups. The first attempts to empower women by improving their entrepreneurial capacity to become more self-reliant. This is approach is common among development agencies and government. The approach assumes the form of:

- economic interventions, i.e. improving women's economic status by providing them with employment, improving their capacity to be involved in income-generating activities, and improving their access to credit facilities;

- integrated rural development which, in addition to improving the entrepreneurial self-reliance of women, focuses on the satisfaction of basic needs, education, literacy programmes, and reproductive health issues (such as family planning programmes).

The latter approach targets individuals and their capacity to become self-reliant. The Better Life for Rural Women programme (BLRW) of

Mrs Maryam Babangida (Nigeria's first lady from 1985 to 93) which was under the supervision of the National Commission for Women (NCW), and the family support programme (FSP) of her successor, exemplifies this approach.

Women's and non-governmental organisations mostly use the second dominant approach. Empowering women is conceived as awareness-building, particularly about gender inequities in their societies, building capacities and developing skills necessary to ensure that women effectively participate in present and future decision-making, and then organising women into groups which take action to bring about desirable changes, focusing on greater equality between men and women in all decision-making. So, rather than targeting the capacity of an individual to become more economically self-reliant, this approach actually attempts to empower women to participate not only in policy implementation but also in policy formulation, design, implementation, control, and evaluation. Rather than being recipients of development policies, this strategy enables the process of empowering women to participate in shaping development policies.

The NCW was established to oversee the activities of all women's groups in Nigeria, and was funded by the government during the Ibrahim Babangida military administration. The NCW was, however, never adequately funded, which raised doubts as to how genuine was the desire to protect the interests of women. Even the real benefits of the BLRW, a strategic area of the NCW, were never known. What were known were its most advertised attributes: glamorous meetings that celebrated the elites that made up the national, state, and local leadership. The real benefits in terms of the empowerment of rural women, whom it was expected to target, were never recorded in relation to the level of public funds used to finance it.[8] [9] This may explain why the programme did not survive after the Babangidas 'stepped aside'.

The Country Women's Association of Nigeria (COWAN) stands in sharp contrast with the BLRW and the FSP, both of which were set up, funded, and managed by the federal government. Though initiated by an individual (Mrs Ogunleye) in 1982, COWAN approached the empowerment of rural women using a 'bottom-up' approach. 'It is the only organisation in the country where the Board of Directors are rural women with Mrs Ogunleye as the secretary' (The Guardian, 28 September 1996). Its main goal, according to Mrs Ogunleye, is to 'empower rural women towards achieving self-sufficiency'. The success of COWAN in empowering rural women tends to confirm the basic proposition that 'using a "bottom-up" approach, where the rural people are allowed to say what they want and do the planning themselves, is a more feasible and effective strategy of empowering women than top-down programs which assume that rural women and men are too ignorant that you have to teach them everything'.[10]

Several other women's organisations of different origins have been engaged in engineering some kind of empowerment of women. These include the Nigerian chapters of international women's organisations and those originating in Nigeria. The latter could be classified into four categories: (a) professional groups (e.g. NAWIB, NAWOJ, SWAN); (b) activist women's groups (e.g. WIN); (c) research-driven groups (e.g. WORDOC); and (d) women's religious groups. The Nigerian chapters of international organisations concentrate mainly on philanthropic activities and the basic philosophy underlying most of their activities is that of 'trickle-down'. The Nigerian office of Soroptimist International is possibly one of the few attempting to extend its activities to the problem of women's voice, but it is, unfortunately, as elitist as other 'Nigerian chapters' of international women's groups. As a result, they are not representative of a large percentage of the female population of Nigeria, especially since their ways of working are fashioned around the conventions of their parent organisations. As a result, though these bodies do improve opportunities for some less privileged individuals (children, women, and men), they are unlikely to be the tools for empowering Nigerian women.

The focus of the various professional women's organisations is limited to the struggle to empower women in their respective professions. Most professional women use these groups to have a voice and to boost women's capacity to influence decisions that affect their careers and their professions. Any success is thus limited to the women in the respective associations. This notwithstanding, the chances of success are higher given that it is consistent with endogenous empowerment.

Formed in the early 1980s, Women in Nigeria (WIN) is an organisation that has struggled for the total emancipation of Nigerian women and has remained committed to the eradication of any form of class inequality and oppression (Imam 1994). Through participation in public debates, organising seminars, workshops, and conferences, and using all available legal, political, and social processes, WIN appears to have a uni-directional goal of struggling for the economic, social, and political conditions for women's autonomy without placing limits on such autonomy. However, its successes are limited to: prosecution of incidences of abuse of 'child-wives'; raising awareness about discrimination against women, and about early marriages and its negative consequences; and, rendering financial assistance to indigent females wanting to be educated.

Other attempts at empowering Nigerian women have come from such organisations as the Women's Research and Documentation Centre (WORDOC) which is the coordinating body for most research and documentation efforts of many women research groups in the country; and from women's religious groups such as the Young Women's Christian Association (YWCA) and the Federation of Muslim Women Association of Nigeria (FOMWAN), both active in empowering women to understand more about themselves, their roles as women, and how they can use their position to influence decisions, especially in their families.

Overall, the empowerment of women is a complex and difficult process. But while a single group or programme is unlikely to bring it into being, the adoption of a bottom-up strategy is more likely to facilitate the process. A programme that purports to empower women must begin by listening to them and allowing them to determine what they want and how they think it they would be empowered, because the 'empowerment buck' stops on the crown of each disempowered woman. Of course, widening the information content of a woman's choice (through awareness programmes) and enhancing her capacity to make her own choices (through skills and capacity assessment, capacity-building and skills development programmes, and evaluation) would enable to her to make better choices and to act on them.

Endogenous empowerment strategy for women's effective participation within organisations

The basic tenets of this article are firstly that the effective participation of women is necessary if they are to protect their interests within their organisations, and, secondly, that empowerment buck stops at the desk or on the head of each woman.

The first proposition justifies more effective participation of women in organisational decision making while the second, which was deduced from a dynamic conception of empowerment, suggests that the enabling conditions for endogenous empowerment offers a reference point for any external intervention. Consequently, the strategy outlined below focuses on the enabling conditions previously discussed, where we stated that a potentially effective intervention is one that seeks to enable endogenous empowerment by raising awareness, developing the skills and building the capacity which a needs assessment reveal as constraints to empowerment, and conducts regular evaluations. We also noted that that organisational environments differ. Hence, the barriers to female participation may also differ. Some of the barriers that may constrain the full participation of women in organisations include: hostility of men, family or domestic constraints; lack of access to information; cultural constraints; lack of education and skills; established societal stereotypes; and, lack of self confidence (Garba 1997). These barriers could be relaxed by awareness building; skills acquisition and capacity-building; and, socio-cultural changes.

Awareness building

Three types of problems call for an awareness programme, namely inadequate information about the objectives of unions or other organisations, male hostility, and domestic constraints.

Awareness programmes could be undertaken by the various women's organisations, some of which have been discussed above, to enlighten women through workshops and seminars designed to encourage discussion, question and answer sessions, and case study analyses. Issues arising could be thrashed out at the relevant fora. In general, the focus of the awareness campaign would be determined by the problems facing women in any given organisation.

Issues of men's hostility and domestic constraints are particularly problematic in Nigeria because they have their roots in the rules of disempowerment. Therefore, the basic awareness issue with respect to male hostility is to make women appreciate that this is intended to undermine their own interests and that it generates from insecurity among the men who perpetrate it. In an awareness programme, the benefits of asserting women's rights need to be explicitly balanced against the costs of accepting male domination.

Skills acquisition and capacity-building

In general, a successful programme of skills development and capacity-building must begin with a proper assessment of what skills and capacities women already have, what they lack, and the relative importance of the skills to be imparted. Needs assessments would ensure that only identified gaps are filled. Failure to undertake these may result in duplication of existing skills and capacities, or offering those not directly relevant to the case at hand. Usually, there is a dire need for training programmes that will help increase the political and management skills of women in organisations. Being politically skilful means, among other things, being able to understand and assimilate diverse political opinions, participate intelligently in political debates, express one's own views coherently and effectively, and being able to use different viewpoints to analyse issues and to make useful decisions. Obviously, a woman who lacks good communication skills, the capacity to listen effectively, and to work well in groups, cannot to be an effective participant in any political organisation. It is not enough for women to attend meetings. If they are thought to be deficient in some way, they should be trained to have the self-confidence to participate effectively through active speaking and listening. They should, like every other participant, rise above their shyness and timidity so that they can, without trepidation, contribute to debates and decision-making processes.

Changing discriminatory traditional and cultural norms

Most of the problems confronting women would not exist in the first place but for the very conservative, traditional and cultural norms of most societies, such as those of Nigeria. For instance, most societies are hostile to women's involvement in political activities. Women are seen as weak, fragile, and should not be involved in 'men's work'. Women who do attempt to get involved are considered over-aggressive, which is not tolerated in many societies. The hostility of men to the participation of women in 'gender-neutral' organisations, and the imposition of a trade-off between participation in such activities and domestic duties, are rooted in the rules of disempowerment of the society. For instance, a male participant at a workshop where an earlier draft of this paper was presented, justified his resentment of women workers or managers and their participation in economic activities, with the following words:

> They have no business competing with men. In fact, I have allowed my wife to work only reluctantly, and very soon she would want to be an active member of a union in her company. I think women should stay in the roles that God meant for them instead of competing with their husbands and leaving their own domestic duties unattended to.

Most of other men at the workshop shared his perceptions, essentially the use of sex abuse as a means of domination. However, what was most disturbing was the fact that women participants in the seminar seemed to have lost the will to fight against this form of mental abuse and the demeaning analyses of what their presence in the world really is about.

This example of how some men view women justifies the need to focus not only on women but also on men in raising awareness about undesirable behaviour towards women, and the harm such behaviour has on the proper development of both men and women in society. Gender sensitivity training can assist people to differentiate between appropriate and inappropriate social behaviours, and to show how appropriate behaviour can lead to the development of individuals and groups. It can also help to give suitable management skills for eradicating various forms of undesirable behaviours, and promoting gender equality.

Most forms of domination against women in Nigeria will only be eradicated through enforceable laws. All rules of disempowerment ought to be changed. But changing these rules requires political action which only a broad-based women's rights movement could bring about. Though this is difficult under the general state of disempowerment that prevails in Nigeria now, women must be active participants in the struggle for constitutional rule, and then use their leverage to outlaw discriminatory practices and to provide for its effective enforcement. Active participation in the struggle for constitutional rule could be facilitated by political education.

Unfortunately, even women frown at other women who attempt to change the status quo, reflecting many years of 'brain washing' and submission to the rules of disempowerment. A long-term solution to the problem of women's poor participation in political activities rests in awareness that the culture of disempowerment is unjust and unfair. Further, that submission to this culture is to believe, erroneously, that one human being is inferior to another because of gender, ethnic origin, religion, and so on. Levelling the playing field and respecting the humanity of women becomes the primary focus of struggles for emancipation. This implies that changing the discriminatory culture of treating women as inferiors, is necessary to their empowerment.

Conclusion

This article has sought to show the ineffectiveness of the exogenous methods that are currently being used to empower women. Using Nigeria as a case study, it argues instead for an endogenous strategy that sees empowerment as a dynamic concept, and as a process of developing the capacity of women to participate effectively in making and implementing decisions that directly or indirectly affect them. This, we have shown, is more likely to generate an effective empowerment strategy. The dynamic concept leads to a proposition that the empowerment buck stops at the head of the disempowered woman herself. In other words, an external agent cannot grant empowerment as a gift. However, the conditions within which disempowered women could endogenously empower themselves can be fostered. Even then, however, the content of any enabling conditions must be determined by the objective realities of the disempowerment in question. Thus, a bottom-up, rather than a top-down, strategy is to be preferred.

To illustrate this, we modified Karl's four stages of empowerment to a six stage process in order to pinpoint ways in which the empowerment process could be enabled or accelerated, and explicitly recognising the constraints posed by the rules of disempowerment that are entrenched in societal norms and laws. One of our modifications of Karl's empowerment model locks in programmes that are designed to develop capacity and skills to needs revealed by a prior assessment. The strategy we suggest is influenced by the actual problems that are revealed by earlier studies. Thus, the strategy requires enabling conditions that would enhance the capacity of women to overcome the barriers, as well as to participate more effectively in removing them. Consequently, we recommend a three-pronged strategy consisting of: interactive and family-oriented awareness programmes; skills and capacity development programmes, especially in the areas of communication and organisational and political management; and, political action to change the rules of disempowerment that are the underlying cause of most of the disempowerment of women in society.

Notes

1 Women in purdah are usually Muslim married women whose bodies, except for the parts required to see (and sometimes smell), are totally covered. This is usually done to prevent men apart from their husbands from looking at and desiring them. Women in seclusion are those who are usually confined to parts of their husbands' homes where other persons, particularly men, apart form their husbands, are neither allowed to see nor communicate with them. This is so even when such women are educated and highly skilled.

2 For instance, the Taliban-led government of Afghanistan has decreed against females being educated or working. In the short term, the decree disempowers women, notwithstanding their competence and potential contributions to their families and to their societies. In the long term, even when the decree is abrogated, women will lack the competence to participate effectively in making decisions that affect them and their societies.

3 At both stages, the disempowered group is the active agent. Unless the group participates and induces desired change, empowerment is not achieved.

4 External agents can facilitate endogenous empowerment at these stages by improving awareness and facilitating the development and acquisition of requisite capacity and skills.

5 Prior to the colonial period, there was a structure of collective decision-making among representatives of all groups (men, women, and children being represented by their parents). People's views were seen as crucial to all decision-making processes in order to maintain peace. No one individual or group dominated others as there was no benefit attached to — nor the incentive for — dominating other people. However, the colonial administration changed this. With the appointment of Nigerian colonial officers, who received incentives and power to dominate other members of their society, some individuals felt for the first time superior to others. Power, once experienced by a few, corrupted the laid-down norms and rules of behaviour which before had promoted reasonable levels of equality, and assumed that every person's views were important to decisions affecting all. With the new power structure, everyone who was too weak to be appointed a colonial officer was seen as inferior. Since the colonial 'masters' never felt that women were important enough to be appointed officers, women were automatically seen as inferiors who had to be dominated by the superior officers — men. Every man had a chance of being made an officer, so all men were, by extension, perceived as superior to all women. Along the way,

not only did many traditional male organisations lose their powers, but women were almost totally disempowered. Class and power struggles began then, and have remained since.

6 For instance, Efunsetan, Madam Tinubu and Moremi (Western Nigeria); Queens Amina and Kambasa (Northern Nigeria); Om. Owe (Eastern Nigeria) and so on.

7 For instance, British feminists convened for the first time in 1855; female property rights were legalised in 1870; and women won the right to vote after World War I. The marginalisation of women's rights in the colonies was thus consistent with the practice in the centre.

8 The funding of the programme was not reported in government budgets or other such documents, nor was any account rendered. This prompted Chief Gani Fawehinmi to sue the government and the First Lady for abuse of office and misuse of public funds.

9 While a few rural people actually had access to and enjoyed the benefits accruing from BLRW resources, many only got promises, which were never fulfilled. In many cases, production machines were purchased for small-scale rural producers without training given on how to use and maintain them efficiently. Many faulty machines were not repaired which, in most cases, created additional burdens for the rural dwellers (women and their husbands) whom the programme was meant to relieve. In fact, the various problems faced by many rural dwellers as a result of the programme led people to the conclusion that the benefits accrued more to the urban wealthy women who were closer to the resources intended for the programme activities.

10 That the food we eat is produced by these so-called, ignorant farmers suggests that much of the ignorance lies, ironically, with those who assumed them to be ignorant. Consequently, factual and logical fallacy underlies many of the observed failures of 'top down' programmes.

References

Foner, P. S. (1982) Women and the American Labour Movement: From the First Trade to the Present, New York: Macmillan.

Garba, P. K. (1997) 'A strategy for empowering women: application to trade union activities' in Garba, Akanji and Isiugo-Abanihe (eds.) 1997.

Karl, M. (1995) Women and Empowerment: Participation and Decision Making, London: Zed Books.

Muna, O. T. (1991) 'Women Participation in Trade Unions: A Research Study of the Nigerian Bottling Company PLC, Ibadan Plant', unpublished Master's Thesis, University of Ibadan.

Odubogun, P. K. (1995) 'Extent of the economic empowerment of Nigerian women' in Osotimehin, Erinosho and Olawoye, (eds.) (1995) Women's Empowerment and Reproductive Health, Ibadan: Social Sciences and Reproductive Health Research Network.

Fundraising in Brazil: the major implications for civil society organisations and international NGOs

Michael Bailey

Introduction

This paper looks at the opportunities for civil society organisations (CSOs) in Brazil to increase and diversify income and considers some of the attendant risks and challenges. The Brazilian experience is relevant to middle-income countries in Latin America, where similar, though more incipient, trends in local fundraising are evident, and it may also be relevant to the more industrialised Asian and African countries where the state manages significant resources and there is a substantial middle class, as in India.

There are tens of thousands of CSOs in Brazil that assist the disadvantaged. This paper focuses on those that, in addition to providing services, represent or support the interests of the disadvantaged in the wider society. In Brazil as elsewhere in Latin America, these organisations include rural and urban unions, Amerindian groups, women's associations, the social action institutions of the Catholic church, community-based organisations (CBOs), and NGOs working in specific fields such as human rights and the environment. Many were born out of the opposition to the military dictatorship, which lasted from 1964 to 1985, and were influenced by progressive social thinking and liberation theology. Because of the size and sophistication of the state in Latin America and its key role in poverty reduction, the work of most of them has a public policy dimension, be it municipal or national. They are the typical counterparts of international NGOs (INGOs) in Europe and North America.

In Brazil, these CSOs, though numerous, dynamic and boasting a solid record of social achievements, manage extremely small amounts of money in relation both to the scale of poverty and hardship in the country and to the size of the economy and population. A key question for them is simply how to increase income. A second, related, question is how to reduce high levels of dependence on INGO funding, which may become scarcer in future. The need for diversification was highlighted in 1994 when currency revaluation reduced the purchasing power of grants from abroad and threw many social movements and NGOs into financial crisis. However, tapping new sources has far-reaching implications for the nature and ways of working of these CSOs.

The paper draws on recent experiences in Brazil to demonstrate the range of potential new sources of funds, including the Brazilian public, commercial activities, and government institutions. The role of volunteers is also addressed. The pivotal institutional and cultural changes CSOs need to undertake in order to mobilise these resources are highlighted, along with associated risks, such as diversion away from their representational and advocacy roles, loss of political independence, and bureaucratisation. The paper then suggests specifically how aid agencies might fulfil their responsibilities to help counterparts bolster income and raises the possibility of more inter-institutional collaboration in what is increasingly a global rather than national activity. Finally, some comments are offered regarding the funding priorities of the INGOs, given the new income opportunities facing CSOs; the main recommendation is to concentrate on supporting advocacy work rather than service provision.

Though the focus of this paper is on financial sustainability, it is important to register at the outset the crucial link for CSOs between raising money and building public support for their concerns — these are two sides of the same coin. Since many Brazilian CSOs working for the disadvantaged aspire to influence government policies, they need both credibility and political weight. The credibility may come from the quality of their ideas but the weight comes from having a social base capable of being mobilised around specific proposals. Fundraising from the public enables an organisation to broaden its constituency, bring attention to its causes, and stimulate political action. Raising money can also be linked to the aim of changing society's attitudes. Brazilian NGOs working on HIV and AIDS, for example, have poster campaigns that bring in money and communicate positive images of people with HIV/AIDS.

Discussion of financial sustainability raises broader issues, such as the desirable relationship between civil society and the state, between the voluntary sector and the private sector, the appropriate role of the voluntary sector in social service delivery, etc. There are complex and controversial debates around these topics, which, sadly, cannot be explored here.

Increasing and diversifying income

In 1995, a survey jointly made by Oxfam and ISER (Instituto de Estudos da Religião) of the major North American and European aid agencies and foundations registered an annual flow of US$74 million for development programmes and related public policy work. The dollar volume may have dipped since then, and its value in local currency has fallen by about 25 per cent. Unless Brazil becomes highly unstable economically or politically, flows will probably decline gradually and might reach considerably lower levels within a decade — a worrying scenario for Brazilian CSOs, especially development NGOs.

There are negligible data on CSO income, so quantification and analysis of trends is difficult. However, over the last few years, it has been possible to observe myriad incipient developments in funding which, over time, will change the face of the whole sector. The principal innovations are:

- fundraising from supporters and the general public using a variety of sophisticated techniques;
- growing corporate philanthropy;
- commercial activities;
- greater access to government resources;
- direct funding by official aid organisations.

Predictably, most of the new resources are being generated for welfare, the environment or 'safe' development activities. Environment NGOs, for example, now generate an impressive 80 per cent of their income domestically. Organisations with a rights focus, or seeking to tackle the roots of poverty and suffering find less favour with the economic and political establishment. Nevertheless, the boundaries of what is 'safe' are undoubtedly wider than a decade ago, and some controversial causes like the movement of landless farmers (*Movimento dos Sem Terra* — MST) succeed in appealing to a broad public.

It is also evident that there is an easier fundraising environment in the more developed parts of the country, because of higher personal incomes and favourable cultural propensities. However, this public could be approached to support emergency and development programmes in poor regions such the Northeast and Amazonia.

The potential for mobilising the community around poverty issues was demonstrated in the early 1990's when the anti-hunger campaign known as *Ação da Cidadania contra a Fome, a Miséira e pela Vida* (Citizens' Action against Hunger, Misery and for Life) became a national institution. It attracted massive media coverage and motivated hundreds of thousands of individuals, unions, businesses, churches and civic associations to donate food and clothing to the poor through a network of local groups. The late Betinho de Souza, the charismatic founder of IBASE, a Rio-based NGO, led the campaign. Stressing the responsibility of both the individual and the state to respond to suffering, he called for charity with political action. This landmark movement shifted the outlook of many Brazilians: the left revised its critical view of charity and welfare work, which it had considered a diversion from the issues of structural change, and the business and cultural elites were encouraged to take up social causes.

One factor affecting the willingness of individuals and companies to give money for good causes is lack of confidence in the state as a provider of health, education, and other services. The public believes the state is inefficient and, especially in the case of the social security system, corrupt. In addition, people are now more aware that government spending is highly regressive. Evasion of personal and corporate taxation is widespread. Better-off people who feel a responsibility towards the underprivileged do not, therefore, see paying tax as a way of 'doing their bit', and may increasingly look to non-governmental alternatives. This is rather a mixed blessing, since rebuilding the public sector and redistributive taxation are key elements of any anti-poverty policy.

So what is the potential for fundraising? The answer is less generic if the four main sources — individuals, companies, commercial activities, and governmental institutions — are examined separately.

Individual supporters

In Brazil, as elsewhere in Latin America, many of the CSOs working for the benefit of the disadvantaged are CBOs such as rural unions, urban neighbourhood organisations, women's groups, etc. Partly because it has been easier to negotiate grants from abroad, these have generally not prioritised raising money from their constituencies. Arguably, there is potential to do so, despite the fact that many members live in poverty and, in some cases, in even greater poverty than 20 years ago. There would be significant side benefits from tapping this potential, such as a heightened feeling of ownership among the rank and file and greater downward accountability of leaders.

Members' contributions, frequently in the form of food, lending a room or paying a bus fare, need to be stimulated by the organisation. Cash can be mobilised through events, raffles, and the simple 'whip round'; and in some organisations there could even be a regular subscription, especially now that hyper-inflation has ended. The hardest problem, almost insuperable except in the case of labour unions, is to get resources passed on to second and third tiers of organisation, e.g. from a local farmers' association to the regional association and on up to the national association. This is where funding agencies have traditionally come in. Probably the best example of 'internal' fundraising is the MST, whose settlements contribute a percentage of their production so that other groups can gain access to land, reflecting their faith in the cause and trust in the leadership.

Because of the grossly unjust distribution of income in Brazil, fundraising from the general public principally means targeting the better-off. The middle classes are about the size of Britain's and, in the case of the upper-middle and middle-middle ranges, have a higher disposable income. And the rich are astoundingly rich. A significant proportion of the middle classes, particularly the university-educated, is progressive and concerned about social issues, making it a potential source of finance for CSOs concerned with rights and poverty. At the same time, though the lower income groups do not have much money to spare, the culture of solidarity is stronger and they can be valuable supporters of local causes. Given that the British public supports innumerable civic and non-profit organisations with US$22 billion a year, it is reasonable to think that within ten years several hundred million dollars a year more could be raised in Brazil, even without the benefit of the North European charitable tradition.

Understandably, well-off Brazilians are attracted most easily to concerns which have some bearing on their own lives, though local disasters also generate a response, as demonstrated in 1996 by the support given to the victims of flooding in Rio de Janeiro. The causes with the most appeal are probably the environment, AIDS, women's rights, children's welfare, and law and order. According to a World Wildlife Fund (WWF) survey, over the half the income of environmental groups comes from their membership. Greenpeace's Brazilian chapter raised US$150,000 in 1997, which is set to increase sharply following huge investments in television and direct mail promotion during in 1998. Stimulated in part by the ubiquitous presence of street kids and the violence they suffer, there are thousands of local projects for children that raise money from the community. It is very common to see collectors with banners and tins at traffic lights. The largest fundraising operation for children is UNICEF's television campaign, which finances about half its US$25 million in-country spending, much of which benefits local NGOs. NGOs working on social violence and law and order issues like penal reform, drug abuse, reform of the police force, etc., have been less adventurous in looking for money, but have great potential to mobilise resources from a middle class which lives in daily fear of crime.

Catholic social action organisations such as the Pastoral Land Commission and Indigenous Mission Council have a natural constituency they can approach for resources, though currently this potential is little exploited. The Catholic Bishops' Conference is developing fundraising via its annual Lenten Fraternity Campaign, which seeks to raise public awareness and promote solidarity around a social theme. There are more advances in fundraising in the Spiritualist centres and evangelical Protestant community, though this is largely for welfare provision. World Vision now raises substantial amounts, much of it from the wealthy state of São Paulo where it targets a small number of rich people for big donations.

Box 2 Volunteers

CSOs depend heavily on people who, with or without qualifications, give their time. In organisations representing disadvantaged people, such as rural unions or *favela* associations, this voluntary effort, whether focused around local self-help or national political issues, has been the heart of the vitality demonstrated by CSOs in Brazil over the last decades. Levels of participation are the product of a complex set of social, economic, and political factors and are therefore hard to predict. One negative factor has been the sharp increase in the hours of paid employment people need in order to meet household needs, thereby reducing the time available for social militancy. However, organisations can improve the ways they attract and sustain voluntary effort — e.g. childcare provision, training, recognition, etc. 'Northern' experience in this may be instructive.

These organisations and other non-profit bodies can take advantage of people who are not 'interested parties', but have a sense of social responsibility. The pool includes university students, often as volunteers or through job experience schemes, and the retired. The latter constitute a quite exceptional resource in Brazil as many public employees, including teachers, university professors, doctors, social workers and administrators, retire on full pay in their forties and fifties. Companies and public sector institutions could increasingly lend qualified staff. For example, the consultancy firm McKinsey releases people for advice work with NGOs, while the Luis Freire Centre, an NGO in Recife working on education and public security policies, has had up to six professionals on long-term paid secondments from state and local government.

Corporate philanthropy

The private sector is emerging as a significant donor for social and environmental programmes, despite the lack of philanthropic tradition in Brazil's business culture. Members of the *Grupo de Instituiçõcs e Fundações Empresariais*, an association of some 40 philanthropic organisations which includes multinationals like Xerox and Alcoa, disburse US$300 million each year. The Bradesco Foundation alone, linked to the bank of the same name, spends US$70 million a year, largely on schools.

Growth in private sector giving has several motives: public relations advantages; a genuine, albeit embryonic, recognition of the moral responsibilities of corporate citizens; and, in common with the middle classes, a fear of social explosion and distrust in the state's capacity to administer defusing programmes. Nevertheless, much of what is called corporate philanthropy is, in fact, investment that will generate direct benefits for the donor. A company can offer literacy courses for its employees and the neighbouring community and present this as philanthropy, but essentially it is training its workforce. Another may spend money on environmental improvements but be largely cleaning up its own mess. At worst, philanthropy is thinly disguised tax evasion. Foundations also receive government resources for their initiatives, a factor which swells the figures.

Box 3: Toymakers come top of the class

The best example of creative philanthropy-cum-fundraising is the Abrinq Foundation, established by the toy manufacturers' association, which supports children's rights. In 1994 the Foundation received US$160,000 for its first major investment in fundraising. Current annual income US$8 million, 94 per cent raised inside Brazil and three quarters from companies. The Foundation campaigns against the use of child labour and is developing 'child friendly' product labelling. It not only seeks resources for its own work but also acts as an intermediary between donors and third-party projects, like many INGOs.

Corporate *pro bono* support is beginning to appear for CSOs. TV Globo's free air time for *Ação da Cidadania* and the UNICEF appeals is the most obvious case, but there are other initiatives such as American Express helping IBASE raise US$90,000 by mailing its cardholders. Affinity credit cards, through which a percentage of the consumer's spending is passed to a non-profit organisation, are now offered by a number of commercial banks. The Women and Life Collective in Recife, which works on gender violence and teenage prostitution, has obtained free help from media companies to mount a campaign involving TV, tele-marketing, poster sites, and direct mail; the telephone company has also agreed for donations to be collected by addition to customers' bills.

Commercial activities

Commercial activity by CSOs is in its infancy, but considering the purchasing power of the middle and upper classes there is reason to believe it has significant potential. The principal obstacles are the lack of business skills in CSOs and the astronomical cost of borrowing, as well as the rather volatile economy. Business activity can be loosely divided into two types: conventional and 'solidarity'. An example of the former is TV Viva in Recife, which successfully sells video services to corporate clients, whose interest is getting a quality clip at a competitive price, and not the social objectives of the supplier. Some Brazilian development NGOs are also entering the consultancy market or tendering to run the social components of government development projects. IBASE, for example, has a major contract to evaluate the impact of the federal government's special credit programme for family farmers.

Most businesses, however, will have a solidarity dimension, since the client or consumer is motivated partly by the social objectives of the supplier, as in the case of Abrinq's US$1.5 million income from cards and wrapping-paper sales through the door-to-door saleswomen of a cosmetics company. There are a growing number of smaller-scale initiatives such as the Women and Life Collective in Recife setting up a hotel for women and GAPA-Bahia selling T-shirts in boutiques. A network of Amazonian grassroots groups and NGOs has held a trade fair in São Paulo to promote regional products in the domestic market. There is also potential for expanding Fair Trade exports, especially foodstuffs and niche products like Amazonian *babassu* soap, and for social tourism — though growth prospects depend on currency devaluation.

Brazilian state resources

Brazilian CSOs enjoy increasing access to governmental resources, be they municipal, state, or federal, in line with the global trend. However, the amounts involved are still insignificant from the state's perspective, and no special budgets have been created. President Cardoso and the technocratic élite seem keen on CSO participation in social service delivery but many politicians disagree, either because they wish to conserve Brazil's sophisticated system of *clientilismo,* or because they have a state-centred view of economic and social development. Many civil servants in the powerful bureaucracy also believe the state should provide all services. Another factor limiting the transfer of resources to CSOs is the modest operational capacity of the CSOs themselves. Despite these constraints, the outlook is for a gradual increase in funding that will have a major impact on the voluntary sector as a whole.

However, not all government monies finding their way to CSOs are purely for service provision. Firstly, organisations can sometimes make a legitimate margin on these services, which becomes 'unearmarked income'. Farmers' unions, for example, can generate income by supplying technical advice to groups receiving government credit. Secondly, there are progressive municipal and state governments, and the occasional federal institution, which are prepared to help CSOs with their more political roles of representation, lobby and campaign, rather as some local councils did in Britain in the early 1980s. The Josué de Castro Centre, an NGO in Recife, received money from the City Hall to give courses to community leaders on the new participatory budgeting process, thus equipping the disadvantaged population to negotiate better with it. Though funding for 'strengthening civil society' is not common, it is coming under discussion and could well increase, especially at municipal level.

Box 4 Legal and fiscal environment for CSOs

The creation of non-profit civil associations is easy, but subsequent control by the authorities is negligible. A new legislative framework for CSOs is under negotiation; this would include requirements regarding governance, audits and public disclosure of information that would help increase the confidence of the donating public. However, if the state went beyond the minimal level of regulation that facilitates public scrutiny, there could be problems of political interference, bias, and inconsistency. Self-regulation and voluntary codes of conduct could help foster credibility in NGOs, but there is a long way to go before any standards become widely accepted. The fiscal framework for CSOs, which includes some tax benefits as well as incentives for donors, is under review. The worst abuses of this system have been curbed, but the weakness of control mechanisms still impedes progress towards more generous and transparent arrangements.

Bilateral and multilateral development aid

Official aid monies have long been reaching CSOs via international NGOs. However, there are growing opportunities for CSOs to deal directly with official institutions, both bilateral and multilateral. Increasing CSO sophistication combined with the decentralisation of official aid management facilitates this trend.

The European Union has global budget lines open to CSOs, including resources for disasters, which larger Brazilian NGOs are well placed to tap. There are also special programmes for Brazil, such as the fund created for projects with children at risk. Some of the UN bodies also finance CSOs directly, though on a small scale. Many embassies, including the British and Japanese, administer expanded funds for small CSO projects.

World Bank monies are increasingly finding their way to CSOs, either directly through grants or loans, or indirectly through the government projects it funds. The latter has become quite significant: as of April 1997 there were eight projects channelling some US$150 million to CSOs. The bulk of this is for credit programmes, but there are significant amounts for health and other social projects, as well as for contracting consultancy, research, and training services from NGOs. There are also resources reaching NGOs from the Global Environment Facility and the G-7 Programme for Tropical Rainforests. Direct support to CSOs is, however, still on a tiny scale, with the notable exception of US$19 million for AIDS programmes.

Much of the money reaching CSOs from the Inter-American Development Bank (IDB) is also for credit programmes though, unlike the World Bank, this can be accessed direct. There are also grant budgets to which Latin American CSOs can apply, such as the Indigenous People's Fund and the new Women's Leadership Fund. Most interestingly, the Brazilian Association of NGOs has negotiated a US$150,000 grant to study the feasibility of creating a foundation to raise money from within Brazil and draw in matching funds from multilateral banks and official aid. The foundation would provide grants of US$50–70,000 and capacity building services to local NGOs.

Box 5 IDB loans

NGOs can apply for capital for loan programmes to the Small Enterprise Development Facility of the IDB's Multilateral Investment Fund and to the Small Projects Programme. Cearah-Periferia, an NGO in the Northeastern city of Fortaleza, is negotiating a US$500,000 loan for housing credits and a US$250,000 grant for advice and training to the beneficiary communities.

The multilaterals also encourage Brazilian state institutions to see CSOs as 'partners in poverty alleviation' and to incorporate them as delivery agents in social programmes. This influence is exercised in the design stage of specific projects, such as the World Bank-funded Planafloro Natural Resource Management programme in the Western Amazon, through technical assistance in drawing up sectoral policies, and through seminars and publications on state/civil society partnerships. The banks are also fostering private sector involvement in poverty alleviation.

Organisational development

To understand the organisational challenges facing CSOs today, it is necessary to understand their cultural, political, and institutional roots. In the 1960s and 1970s, most social movements and NGOs concerned with rights and poverty radically questioned the economic, social, and political order, many from a Christian socialist perspective. Even though some organisations expressed the concerns of moderate, pro-democracy sections of the middle-class, they all operated outside the establishment and their attitude to the state and to business was highly critical. In order to survive, many depended on a low profile and discretion about their funding and activities. The wave of new NGOs and movements that emerged in the 1980s, including women's organisations, were often led by people who had been political activists, exiles, or prisoners. Organisations evolved in 1980s and 1990s in the context of gradual democratic consolidation at home and the collapse of communism abroad, and became more numerous, diverse, pluralist, and institutionalised.

Though political violence and authoritarianism persist, especially in rural areas, CSOs now operate in a more open society, with greater access to the media. They are having to change internal cultures, ways of working, skills and, crucially, their relationships with other actors — notably the state, business, the general public and, not least, their own membership. INGO donors have been one source of pressure for organisational changes, having themselves discovered 'management' in the 1980s, but most Brazilian CSOs perceive the need to evolve, thus reducing both the friction with funders and, more importantly, the danger of adopting inappropriate institutional paradigms.

Today, to survive and grow, a CSO needs to demonstrate that it is effective and efficient with the time and money given by its members, the general public, or institutions. Achieving overall quality depends greatly on improving the skills of staff and the management systems. Since the results of CSO work are often by their nature difficult to evaluate, the quality of internal organisation often serves as a proxy impact indicator for donors and supporters. Institutional fundraising, particularly, demands further development of the organisational disciplines of planning, financial management, and reporting.

Transparency and accountability are other keys to successful fundraising. At the moment, few CSOs publish annual accounts or reports or have boards which properly steward funds donated for the organisation's declared aims. However, many have external audits, and accountability is now squarely on the CSO agenda, not least because those that wish to call the state or corporate sector to account know they have to put their own house in order. Building commitment and trust among stakeholders also requires an effective communications policy, as lights under bushels are invariably short-lived.

A trend already evident amongst Brazilian NGOs is specialisation, partly to develop institutional competence, and partly to build public support. An institution needs to have a clear identity and role — if the profile is woolly, nobody will identify with it. Specialisation also facilitates gaining the know-how to manage more complex projects that will attract resources from government and official aid sources.

Organisations need to bring in more professional fundraising and marketing skills, and some now seek to do this. Brazil has the advantage of having a well-established advertising industry, including specialist companies in telemarketing, direct mail and database management, though costs are high and availability is limited in the less developed parts of the country. Most CSOs cannot afford in-house fundraising departments, but they do need people to oversee the function, which should be closely tied to the rest of the organisation's work, especially campaigning.

Applying the management manuals is of limited benefit, however, if staff and members lose faith in the cause. The hardest task in organisational development is building enthusiasm and consensus around the many choices and changes being made, and managing the permanent tensions in attempting to respond to both 'institutional and development imperatives'. Moreover, it is hard to convince the public or an institution to give money to an organisation if the people in it do not firmly believe in what they are doing.

Managing the trade-offs

So what are the risks for a CSO arising from the active pursuit of income? In the worst scenario, the consequences are political neutering, diversion away from its more strategic roles, loss of its institutional qualities, and even its soul. These outcomes are certainly not ordained, but some trade-offs are inevitable — their size and nature being a function of institutional choices and the quality of management.

Governmental funding of CSOs brings the well-known danger of loss of political independence and critical spirit, especially in Brazil where the political culture does not (yet) consider 'biting the hand that feeds you' to be acceptable behaviour. Even nibbling at the fingers can lead to funding cuts. For example, IBASE lost a substantial contract from the Ministry of Education when Betinho, its director and leader of *Ação da Cidadania*, criticised government social policies. It is important, therefore, that INGOs do not press counterparts too hard to take government money on the mistaken presumption that the political compromises and risks involved will be as modest as those in the USA or UK. The same considerations apply to funding from business.

Some Latin American CSOs have felt that by taking money to deliver basic social services, especially from 'social compensation funds', they legitimise government and multilateral banks' macro-economic policies, which they consider prejudice the disadvantaged. This has been less of an issue in Brazil, where CSO fears are more about sanctioning the transfer of services to the private sector. Brazilian CSOs, though, increasingly argue for services to be managed by the community on a non-profit basis, with the state acting as funder and regulator. Espousing this 'non-state public sector', as Brazilians call it, allows greater scope for involvement in service provision without endorsing privatisation.

In the long run, the greatest risk posed by governmental funding is the gradual diversion of organisations away from their representational or advocacy role. This is because, even though entering into partnership with government might theoretically increase access and influence, so much extra effort, especially by key staff, has to be invested in simply managing the service. Clearly, if the funded activity fits well with other strategic change objectives and the opportunity costs are minimised, the net benefit is more likely to be positive.

Similarly, if CSOs prioritise doing what individual and corporate donors want, they may find themselves in the politically more comfortable corners of poverty alleviation, at a distance from sensitive issues and the broader agenda of social and economic reform. But, with skill and conviction, public opinion can be lead to some degree. Moreover, organisations can develop more sophisticated ways of appealing to different constituencies simultaneously.

Box 6: Give them bread, or give them land? Or both?

The potential tension between fundraising and advocacy objectives was illustrated by *Ação da Cidadania* in the third year of campaigning when it focused on the issue of agrarian reform. While this certainly made some supporters more aware and helped prepare the ground for the MST's later burst of popularity, it distanced and demobilised others, who essentially wanted to help their neighbours. *Ação da Cidadania* could perhaps have reduced the trade-offs by more actively safeguarding its appeal to the good neighbours while not compromising its campaign.

Finally, the organisational and cultural changes required to be a successful fundraising institution may lead to loss of the desirable NGO characteristics of innovation, flexibility, and risk-taking. Even core values are at risk if the welfare and future of the institution, or indeed of the staff, becomes the paramount concern, or if the business side of the venture and related culture of growth and competition take over.

Reviewing risks highlights the fact that the pursuit of money has to be managed extremely carefully and that, even then, there will usually be downsides for an organisation. Careful management includes:

- making informed and calculated choices about the costs and benefits of a fundraising strategy, not just in financial terms but in development and institutional terms;
- administering the inevitable tensions between different institutional objectives;
- having a clear definition of the organisation's mission so that the appropriateness of any action is more easily judged;
- having checks, including an effective external board, to keep the organisation on the straight and narrow.

The role of INGO donors

The opportunity for Brazilian CSOs to diversify and increase income has three principal implications for INGOs. Firstly, although US foundations and a few European agencies such as Oxfam GB have been making grants for fundraising and developing fundraising capacity, there is great need for further investment. Secondly, support could increasingly be offered through formal partnerships, reflecting the now globalised nature of the fundraising business. The relationship between 'Northern' organisations and larger Brazilian CSOs will change as the latter participate as more equal partners in worldwide networks. Thirdly, INGOs should concentrate investments in activities and regions less easily funded from Brazilian sources, including some of the more politically sensitive areas of social development such as campaigning and lobby for the rights of the disadvantaged. These implications are now looked at in more detail.

Box 7 Do INGOs ever abandon counterparts?

Although INGOs have a moral responsibility to assist local counterparts on the road to greater independence, it is not uncommon in Latin America to see them withdrawing from projects or entire countries on the grounds of 'new priorities' and 'thematic and geographic concentration', without seriously trying to secure the future of the work supported. Funders should have a franker dialogue with counterparts about their long-term plans and, in cases of withdrawal, there should be long notice periods and active support for income diversification.

Support for income growth and diversification

INGOs can provide grants or loans for the following activities by counterparts:

- fundraising from the general public (events, concerts, media campaigns, direct mail, membership drives, etc.);
- commercial initiatives, such as setting up businesses and marketing professional services, including preparation of tenders;
- preparation of projects to be financed by government sources or official aid;
- creation of endowment funds;
- acquisition of assets, such as premises, which reduce overheads;
- staff development, recruitment of qualified personnel, creation of small specialised departments, and development of the use of volunteers;
- research and publications on fundraising, training courses, and exchanges 'North–South' and 'South–South';
- research and lobby on legal and fiscal frameworks for CSOs.

These are necessarily long-term investments and some, especially fundraising from the public and business ventures, can be risky — at a minimum, failures will be more obvious than in the case of much social development work. But this is no reason not to finance them; it simply underlines the need to monitor experiences so that lessons are learnt.

Many INGOs possess vast experience of fundraising and related issues such as tax regimes benefiting charities, codes of conduct, fundraising ethics, fair trading etc. that could be shared with Latin American organisations. There are also specialist advisory organisations that can be contracted, such as Catalyst in London; and the British Charities Aid Foundation, which has recently opened an office in India. It is necessary to be careful when transferring 'Northern' institutional and fundraising practices to places where the culture and challenges are different, but there are many relevant principles, techniques, and lessons.

More modestly, INGOs can stimulate local fundraising throughout their normal grants programmes. When talking to counterparts, they can assess more carefully the 'local contribution' that appears in income plans and discuss in detail proposals for longer-term financial viability. Grant funding can be linked to advances in fundraising from local sources — a policy common in the UK and USA. However, it is essential to avoid situations where a counterpart loses a dollar of external subsidy for every dollar raised locally — the immense effort needed to raise funds needs to be rewarded, not penalised.

In much of Latin America, a more strategic policy option for INGOs is to use their money and know-how to help develop the capacity of local institutions to advise and train others. Services already established in Brazil include a course in non-profit marketing at the Getulio Vargas Foundation, a nationally-known Quango, and advice on social programmes for companies, offered by Dialog, a Rio-based NGO. A complementary policy is to promote the socialisation of successful local experiences within the region. The Ford Foundation and Ashoka have an annual competition for pioneering fundraising initiatives in Rio de Janeiro and São Paulo that serves to disseminate new approaches. Oxfam GB has contributed a grant in order to extend the competition to the poorer, north-eastern states.

New forms of partnership

Fundraising is already a globalised activity, with the concomitant emergence of new types of competition and collaboration. For some INGOs, the long-term strategy will be to fundraise with Brazilian counterparts for specified programmes. This could mean applying in consortium to official aid budgets or, more ambitiously, fundraising together from the Brazilian public. In both cases, the 'Northern' partner can contribute risk capital, fundraising know-how, and its 'name'. It can also provide managerial or technical support to the programme itself and help place a check on the influence of official donors. Fair Trade partnerships are yet another opportunity for collaboration.

Joint efforts may well develop within broader frameworks of international inter-institutional cooperation that cover emergency and development programmes, related lobby and campaign work, learning, and publications, etc. This cooperation will take different forms. Some front-runners in fundraising in Brazil, such as Greenpeace and World Vision, are local chapters of internationally-federated organisations with 'Northern' origins, several of which have developed a membership in Brazil. Alternatively, established Brazilian NGOs may decide to apply to join networks like Oxfam International or the International Save the Children Alliance. Over time, these international associations may lose their overwhelmingly 'Northern' character. There is also scope for greater cooperation between Catholic social action organisations in Brazil, which play an important role in development and strengthening civil society, and the Catholic aid agencies.

Funding priorities

As Brazilian CSOs diversify and increase income, INGO funding will become more complementary, seeking the parts other monies do not reach. Firstly, as local fundraising will develop principally in regions with propitious cultural and economic conditions, INGOs may further concentrate spending in the poorer parts of the country, such as the north-east. Secondly, they may reduce grants to the larger CSOs that fundraise successfully and concentrate instead on seed-funding new, innovative social entrepreneurs. Thirdly, since fundraising will be easier for some issues than others, donors may focus on 'Cinderella' themes. NGOs working on the environment or children's rights, for example, are clearly more attractive to the general public than labour rights or leadership training programmes run by rural unions. Fourthly, as more government and official aid monies reach service-orientated programmes run by CSOs, INGOs may cut back spending in these areas, though they may continue to fund 'practical' development work where this underpins a group's advocacy capacity and empowerment.

In the western Amazon state of Rondônia, the World Bank-financed Natural Resource Management Programme (Planafloro) has allocated US$22 million for social and economic programmes, to be channelled via grassroots organisations and NGOs. Projects include innovative experiences which could later influence public policies — the type of work many aid agencies fund in Brazil. The challenge for CSOs in Rondônia is not to search for funds but how not to drown in them, even though there are generous budgets for technical assistance. At the same time, they face another great challenge — how to maintain their capacity to politically represent or advocate on behalf of small farmers, the landless, rubber tappers, Amerindians, and rural women vis à vis local government, the World Bank, and society at large.

Government and official aid monies will not generally be used to strengthen the advocacy and representational capacity of disadvantaged groups and their allies — indeed, it would probably not be conducive to healthy civil society if they were. And building such capacity will not appeal to most corporate and well-off donors, who may feel their interests are threatened if the disadvantaged become protagonists in their own causes. In the longer term, CSOs may be able to count on a significant number of lower- and middle-income Brazilians to understand and financially support this function, particularly if efforts are made now to recruit that support. Until this happens, resources from NGOs abroad will have a vital and distinctive back-up role to play. This is, arguably, the most effective contribution they can make to poverty reduction in Brazil.

Acknowledgement

Thanks to many friends and colleagues for contributions, notably Cecília Iório, Guillermo Rogel, and Simon Collings.

Routes of funding, roots of trust? Northern NGOs, Southern NGOs, donors, and the rise of direct funding

David Lewis and Babar Sobhan

Introduction

Debates about the roles and importance of NGOs in promoting social change and development have grown more complex in recent years as the diversity of organisational types and contexts has become apparent. Contexts are changing rapidly. In many countries, Southern NGOs (SNGOs) now receive funds and other forms of support from many different sources including Northern NGO (NNGO) 'partners', international foundations, and official bilateral and multilateral donors. Donors may support SNGOs directly or indirectly through NNGOs. As SNGO competence and capacity has increased through their own efforts at professionalisation, through wider recognition and support from government, and by the provision of 'capacity building' partnerships with NNGOs, these Southern organisations have taken up positions within the burgeoning 'third sectors' of aid-recipient countries alongside the governmental and business sectors.

These changes, while proceeding at a very different pace in different parts of the world, have profound implications for the relationships between NNGOs, SNGOs, and donors. This paper sets out to address two main themes in the context of Swedish aid to NGOs in Bangladesh. Firstly, as bilateral donors provide an increasing proportion of their resources to NGOs, how can sound and responsible funding relationships be built between bilateral donors and NGOs? Secondly, how can NNGOs work usefully in contexts where the number and capacity of local SNGOs has expanded significantly?

The growth of direct funding

The recent growth in direct funding of SNGOs by official donors (as distinct from funding them through NNGO intermediaries or as participants in wider bilateral multi-agency projects) has been noted (Bebbington and Riddell 1995; Edwards 1996). For official donors such as the Swedish International Development Authority (SIDA) there are two main routes through which funds are transferred to SNGOs: the *indirect* route in which resources are provided to Swedish NGOs which then work with SNGO 'partners' in the country concerned; and the *direct* route in which funds are given directly to SNGOs via the donor's country office.

However, there are risks associated with the rush by donors to fund NGOs directly. For example, Bebbington and Riddell (1995) conclude their discussion of the changing relationships between NNGOs, SNGOs, and donors with three main issues for further consideration: (i) that donor support to NNGOs has tended to rest on a view of NNGOs as effective aid delivery mechanisms rather than as organisations capable of assisting SNGOs in the wider strengthening of 'civil society'; (ii) that there may be a danger in direct funding that SNGO agendas may be distorted to fit donor objectives; and (iii) that while the trend towards increased direct funding is sometimes perceived as a 'threat' to NNGOs, it may also be viewed as an opportunity for creative thinking about enhancing the effectiveness of donor, NNGO, and SNGO roles and relationships.

Following from the third point, Edwards (1996) has drawn attention to a potential crisis of identity and legitimacy among NNGOs, as increasingly effective SNGOs take over most of the activities previously carried out by organisations from the North. In the case of Bangladesh in the late 1990s, there may be very little a NNGO can bring to a third sector which is increasingly dominated by a range of highly professional local organisations and ideas. The changing environment in which NNGOs now operate therefore raises a set of important questions about their possible future roles.

This paper discusses issues arising during a recent SIDA study in Bangladesh, which attempted to compare direct and indirect funding routes. The study was commissioned by SIDA in order to assess whether its two forms of NGO support were complementary, and whether they were effective in contributing to SIDA's development assistance goals. Although the study was commissioned by a specific donor in relation to a particular country, we suggest that the issues raised are of wider relevance to NNGOs engaged in thinking strategically about their future roles, and to donors seeking to develop sound and equitable funding relationships with NGOs.

What criteria were used to assess the effectiveness of Swedish NGO assistance in Bangladesh? The main themes considered were: (i) the relevance of NGO activities to ongoing development efforts in Bangladesh; (ii) the sustainability of NGO activities and the extent of the 'sense of ownership' being fostered among clients and 'beneficiaries'; (iii) the feedback provided by NNGOs and the level of accountability to Northern publics; and (iv) the implications of the Swedish experience in Bangladesh for the future of NNGO development roles.

After some introductory comments on the respective histories of Swedish and national NGOs in Bangladesh, these issues are discussed in turn and illustrated with selected examples. In conclusion, the paper briefly explores the importance of building trust in the changing relationships between NNGOs, SNGOs, and donors.

NGOs in Bangladesh

Bangladeshi NGOs

Bangladesh is unusual in the scale and importance of its NGOs. The origins of many of its NGOs can be found in the aftermath of the Liberation War of 1971, particularly in the processes of national reconstruction alongside the international relief effort mobilised after the 1972 cyclone which immediately followed independence. Gradually, these organisations grew in size and in scope, and many began shifting from a relief to a development focus. In particular, Bangladeshi NGOs worked with the growing numbers of landless rural people, a target group whose needs were generally ignored by government agencies (Lewis 1993).

The largest and best-known of the Bangladeshi NGOs, such as the Bangladesh Rural Advancement Committee (BRAC), Proshika, and Gono Shahajjo Sangstha (GSS) — and to some extent Grameen Bank, a private non-profit bank which is often associated with NGO initiatives — have pioneered development approaches which seek to work with rural and, more recently urban, landless households through a combination of consciousness-raising (for example, providing information about legal rights), service provision (such as credit for income generation, education, and health care) and group formation (for building solidarity among disadvantaged households). Some NGOs have combined these with wider lobbying and advocacy for legal and policy reforms.

The two military governments which came to power in post-independence Bangladesh saw the growth of a local NGO sector as a threat to both their access to foreign funds and to their legitimacy, especially as many NGOs began the shift from relief activities towards longer-term development work which focused on the structural causes of poverty. Much of this work was a direct response to the failure of government agencies to deliver basic services and respond to essential needs. Some of the NGO leaders were former student activists, who found comparatively sheltered arenas to work for social change within the precarious climate of authoritarian rule.

However, opposition political parties, including those on the left, looked on with alarm as NGOs began to form links with their erstwhile constituencies (the rural poor), and with suspicion as they received increasing quantities of foreign funds from official donors and from NNGOs. The availability of these foreign funds drew many NGO field workers away the cadre ranks of political parties towards the NGOs. This process was seen by some as undermining the potential for a genuine mobilisation of the poor by focusing on the symptoms rather than the causes of poverty.

While many Bangladeshi NGOs were initially funded by international NGOs such as Svalorna (Swedish Swallows), Canadian University Service Overseas (CUSO), and Oxfam GB, there were few questions asked about their relationship with government at this time and the NGOs were largely seen by the government as general welfare agencies. However, as they grew in size, NGOs began to access funds directly from foreign donors, many of whom viewed NGOs as dynamic alternatives or complementary support to government-based assistance. By the late 1980s, a polarisation of views existed in Bangladesh about the role and the status of the NGOs, supported with very little informed public debate. Relations between NGOs and government, at least at the formal level, became generally poor.

A reaction to these problems was the establishment of an NGO Affairs Bureau by the government in 1989. The aim was to speed up processing the growing flow of NGO project proposals which required approval by government, while creating a new mechanism for the government to monitor resource flows to the NGOs and to oversee NGO activities around the country. The government felt that NGOs needed to be regulated as part of civil society rather than simply standing apart from it. Despite NGOs' misgivings about dealing with this new layer of bureaucracy, the new policy contributed to the opening up by many NGOs to the possibilities of working constructively with government. The World Bank (1996) report on NGO-government relationships is the most explicit example of the donor view that NGOs and government can usefully complement each others' efforts. However, relations between NGOs and government may still remain highly dependent upon personalities.

Swedish NGOs

The history of Swedish NGOs in Bangladesh has firm roots in the post-1971 relief efforts. In the case of church-based organisations, a connection with Bangladesh can be traced back to missionary work dating from the nineteenth century. Swedish NGOs were found in the study to be driven by a range of domestic religious, political, and social agendas and answered to different domestic constituencies, where their roots were to be found in Swedish popular movements. For example, the Swallows developed out of the humanitarian concerns of the Emmaeus movement, which originally focused on homelessness in Europe during the 1940s. Diakonia and the Swedish Free Mission (SFM) grew from different sections of the Swedish Church. Other sections of Swedish society reflected in Swedish NGOs working overseas were the trade unions and the cooperative sector, as well as the international humanitarian federations such as The Save the Children Fund, which affiliated with Swedish counterpart agencies. Like many of the Bangladeshi NGOs, Swedish NGOs which started with a relief and welfare focus have, to varying degrees, begun moving towards a more developmental approach.

There are 12 Swedish NGOs presently working, or funding projects, in Bangladesh, a surprisingly high number given Sweden's size and the fact that there are no special historical links between the two countries. Seven Swedish NGOs came to Bangladesh immediately after independence and began implementing their own projects. A continuing preoccupation with implementation delayed links with the growing local NGO movement. However, partnership with Bangladeshi NGOs gradually developed, changing the role of some Swedish NGOs from direct implementation towards partnership and funding roles. In some cases Bangladeshi partner organisations quickly outgrew their donor NGOs and went to SIDA for direct funding. This was true for Swallows in the case of Proshika and for Diakonia with regard to BRAC and GSS.

The work of many Swedish NGOs remains influenced by this history. For example, Lutherhjälpen is still committed to work only with the Rangpur Dinajpur Rural Service (RDRS) in northern Bangladesh and the Swedish Free Mission (SFM), mainly on Bhola island, working on initiatives established as far back as 1970. Rädda Barnen still has its Mirpur clinics and the Swallows work with Thanapara village — though interestingly, both organisations have tried to end direct implementation of these projects.

The Swedish NGOs and their partners too have a diverse set of roles in Bangladesh. These broadly mirror the national and local NGOs' efforts, though some have found themselves unable to move away from more traditional service roles, such as running local clinics. The particular opportunities for international NGOs to provide specialised support to local NGOs (aside from mere funding), and their advantageous position for internal networking and lobbying, are only beginning to be explored by most Swedish NGOs.

SIDA support to NGOs in Bangladesh

In order to receive funds, NGOs must comply with SIDA's five development assistance goals: these are (i) economic growth; (ii) economic and social equality; (iii) economic and political independence; (iv) democratic development; and (v) environmental quality. Aside from these goals, SIDA support to NGOs is guided by several other factors, although there is no formally-stated NGO policy. Swedish NGOs are required to contribute a minimum of 20 per cent towards total project costs and in order to qualify for SIDA funds NGOs must be non-profit organisations, have a democratic structure, and be able to implement planned projects. In addition, NGOs applying for Swedish funds must ensure that their activities are sustainable, and must support the strengthening of democratic processes (SIDA 1993: 34). Support to Swedish NGOs is also designed to raise awareness in Sweden in that it:

> ... provides a way of stimulating people's interest in development issues in Sweden. This should increase public awareness of international development trends, of the role of development cooperation, and of how worldwide changes may influence Swedish society.

How do the two modes of funding work? The direct mode of support provided by SIDA to Bangladeshi NGOs is illustrated by Figure 1 while indirect support to Swedish NGOs is shown in Figure 2. There are several types of direct funding, such as that provided through bilateral projects, including the General Education Project (GEP), to which SIDA contributes, and which has considerable NGO involvement. There is also a separate, though far smaller, democracy and human rights funding channel, through which the electoral monitoring NGO, Bangladesh Mukto Nirbachan Andolon (BAMNA), is supported, for example. In the case of indirect funding, the Swedish NGOs may implement their own projects or be working with local partners. Some Swedish NGOs such as Swallows are also engaged in networking on an international level.

SIDA regards these two principal modes of funding as being essentially complementary forms of NGO support, with indirect funding coordinated from the SIDA NGO Division in Stockholm, while the direct funding is managed by the SIDA Development Cooperation Office (DCO) in Dhaka. However, the two modes are each intended to serve different purposes in Bangladesh within SIDA's overall aid programme. Through indirect funding, Swedish popular organisations (as Swedish NGOs, which are taken to include trade unions and cooperative societies) can be supported in their work in Bangladesh, forming links between the non-governmental sectors of both countries. Through direct funding, innovative SNGOs can be supported by SIDA in their efforts to generate experimental or pilot approaches, such as credit provision to the landless or a progressive model of primary education, which may subsequently be used within the public sector; and in activities, such as electoral monitoring or social mobilisation, which can contribute to strengthening the democratic process in Bangladesh (SIDA 1992).

In Stockholm, SIDA makes block grants to the larger Swedish NGOs or to groups of smaller NGOs. In what has become known as the 80:20 funding ratio, SIDA supplies up to 80 per cent of the funds provided the NGO contributes a minimum of 20 per cent of the project costs. In 1992–93 Swedish NGOs received a total of 21.4 million Swedish Krona (approximately US$2.75 million) for work in Bangladesh. As we have seen, these NGOs include Rädda Barnen (Swedish Save the Children), a range of church-based NGOs, the Swedish Red Cross, the Swedish Organisation of the Handicapped (SHIA), the Swedish Swallows volunteer organisation, and the LO/TCO Swedish trade union umbrella organisation. Some of these operate their own projects but most work with local partners. The Swedish NGOs are active in various sectors including health, education, and rural development. SIDA's support to these organisations is rooted in their origins within the Swedish non-governmental sector, whose votes help to determine the Swedish parliament's allocation of aid expenditure.

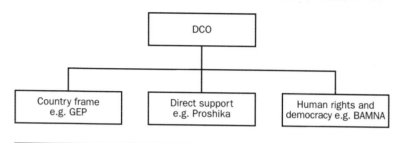

Figure 1 Types of NGO assistance given by SIDA through the Development Cooperation Office [DCO] (SIDA direct support)

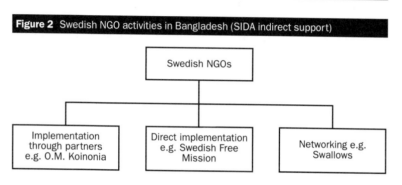

Figure 2 Swedish NGO activities in Bangladesh (SIDA indirect support)

Direct support to SNGOs is a more recent trend within the Swedish aid programme as a whole, and this only takes place in three countries in which SIDA is active — Bangladesh, India, and Sri Lanka, of which Bangladesh is by far the largest recipient. The main reason for this has been the development of an influential and innovative indigenous NGO sector in the country which, among others, includes BRAC and Proshika, two of the world's largest private development agencies, both of which have received SIDA support. In 1992–93 this brought SIDA funds worth 28.8 million Swedish Krona to Bangladesh (US$3.7 million), or 21.4 per cent of total disbursements.

How relevant is NGO assistance?

SIDA is concerned to ensure that its NGO assistance is relevant to its own wider objectives and to local priorities. According to Lewin (1994), SIDA uses the term 'relevance' in the sense of whether or not the proposed inputs have solved or contributed to the solution of a particular set of problems. However, the expectations of SIDA and other donors has contributed to two sets of problems for NGOs.

The first is that of conflicting pressures and expectations generated by different donors and their consultants who may fund the same organisation or programme. These pressures are illustrated by the case of SIDA support to the Comprehensive Nutrition and Blindness Prevention Programme of the Worldview International Foundation where different donors have moved the organisation away from the initial intention of carrying out a general mass campaign, towards a more specifically poverty-focused campaign (a Norwegian agency), and group formation and income generation activities (a Dutch agency). The task of managing these different donor expectations, while widening an NGO's choices, may add to the its administrative burden and potentially limit its autonomy.

The second is the possibility that while support may be relevant in the narrower sense of meeting donor expectations, it may be less relevant in the wider context of Bangladesh. For example, pressure from Swedish women's organisations to earmark funds specifically for women's groups does not always fit with current SIDA policies for 'mainstreaming' gender concerns within broader SIDA activities. To give another example, SIDA's support for trade union education and training in Bangladesh has tended to assume that the Bangladesh trade unions are similar kinds of organisations with comparable roles to those found in Sweden, which in many cases they are not. One visit which we made to a major Bangladeshi trade union which was being supported in this way showed quite clearly that it was primarily an organisation of the government party and not a democratic trade union in the Swedish social democratic sense. It is also difficult for Swedish NGOs to achieve relevance given the increasing scale and effectiveness of Bangladesh's own non-governmental sector in the form of organisations such as BRAC and the Grameen Bank (Lovell 1992; Holcombe 1995).

The study found that greater relevance was more likely to be achieved by direct than by indirect funding because, true to the spirit of the Swedish NGO tradition, Swedish NGOs receive no overall coordination from SIDA in Bangladesh. They are left to situate themselves within the local context as long as they keep within the broad terms of SIDA's objectives. The SIDA office in Bangladesh on the other hand has been able to identify more relevant local NGOs for direct support, which can be coordinated within the overall country programme. In the case of gender issues it was found that the Bangladeshi NGO supported by SIDA worked primarily with landless women and had developed local analyses of gender-based development problems. By contrast at least one of the Swedish church-based NGOs took a paternalistic view of Bangladeshi women's needs, which rested more strongly on outsider preconceptions than on local social and cultural realities.

Sometimes an ideal complementarity has been achieved between direct and indirect support. SIDA support to the education sector includes four complementary approaches: general support to NGOs participating in the GEP through the SIDA country frame with a broad impact in the education sector as a whole; direct funding of specialised education NGOs such as GSS; support to the Campaign for Mass Popular Education (CAMPE) network which seeks to bring government and NGOs together; and support to BRAC, whose education programme aims ultimately to strengthen the government system through training and innovation. However there is no Swedish NGO involvement.

Which funding route is the more efficient method of disbursing development assistance for SIDA? Within the direct route, the SIDA office in Dhaka has opted for a small number of quality relationships with NGOs, characterised by a trusting, 'hands off' approach supported by frequent contact and communication. Efficiency is perceived by NGOs and by SIDA to have been increased by donor coordination among the so-called Like-Minded Group of donors (an informal donor liaison group which includes the Nordic donors, the Dutch, and the Canadians) and by the formation of a donor consortium to coordinate the funding of larger Bangladeshi NGOs such as BRAC.

Although it was not possible to quantify this during the present study, it is likely that there are increased costs associated with the indirect funding route through Swedish NGOs, which play the role of intermediaries between SIDA and the SNGOs, thus adding an extra layer of administrative costs. Some Swedish NGOs also take a directive approach to their partners which was criticised by local NGO partners. One example was the Swedish Free Church-based NGO Diakonia, which insisted that all of its ten partner organisations seek to conform to a single strategy and approach.

On the other hand, there may be value added to the relationship by the link created by indirect funding between Bangladesh NGO partners and the Swedish public, which supports the work of Swedish NGOs internationally. The administrative burden on the SIDA office staff in Bangladesh in the direct funding links can be heavy, and considerable local knowledge may be concentrated in personal relationships which are easily lost when expatriate staff are transferred to other countries. This has potentially negative implications for sustainability.

There are also examples of the 'hands off' policy causing confusion, such as when the Bangladeshi NGO Prodipon managed to access SIDA funds through three different funding routes without the full knowledge of the DCO staff — as a partner of Diakonia, through a legal aid partnership with the volunteer organisation Swedish Swallows, and through Rädda Barnen for work in the slums. With three separate Swedish NGOs funding the same NGO for different project components, largely without coordination either among themselves or with the SIDA office, programme cohesion and learning opportunities may be being lost.

Is the support building sustainability?

The concept of sustainability has long preoccupied SIDA and other donors, but there is a lack of clarity about its meaning. It has financial, environmental, and institutional dimensions. The definition of sustainability used by SIDA is drawn from its own evaluation manual (Lewin 1994) which states that:

> ... a development programme is sustainable when it is able to deliver an appropriate number of benefits for an extended period of time after major financial, managerial and technical assistance from an external donor is terminated.

However, this type of definition has led to sustainability being viewed by many NGOs primarily in financial terms but less in other forms of capacity. For example, the Swedish NGO Adventist Development and Relief Agency (ADRA) has emphasised the micro-level financial sustainability of its credit programme which manages to break even. The Young Men's Christian Association (YMCA) is building a large rentable office block in order to cover their operational costs. However, what seemed to be missing from these strategies as the realisation that unless the impact of the work of these NGOs is sustainable, then the fact that the books may balance, while obviously desirable, may be of limited relevance in development terms.

The Bangladesh Unemployed Rehabilitation Organisation (BURO Tangail) is an NGO which has begun thinking in terms of two levels of sustainability. The first level is the more familiar financial one, and involves charging an appropriate fee to users for credit delivery in order to cover the NGO's costs. The second is that of local capacity-building at the grassroots, through training and organisation building and strengthening, in order to sustain new ideas and structures emerging from current experience.

Another key to sustainability in Bangladesh lies in the ability of NGOs to link their efforts with wider government policy in order to secure lasting improvements in services. This has been taken up more successfully by directly-funded NGOs such as BRAC and Proshika, which are active in attempting to influence policy in the education and the forestry sectors respectively, than by Swedish NGOs and their partners who may hand over a project such as a clinic to the government even when there are few public resources with which to keep it running.

The question of ownership refers to the relative strength of voice between the NGO and the beneficiaries or target group. Here there were no straightforward generalisations possible between the two funding routes. Rädda Barnen was engaged in moving out of its traditional operational role, in which it implemented projects, towards a new niche involving low-profile support to local NGO partners in combination with an advocacy agenda in the area of child rights. While this work has sometimes brought the NGO into politically sensitive and difficult areas of activity, it was felt that the chances of playing a role in securing wider, longer-term change was greatly increased. However, there is no straightforward solution for the problem of handing over the Mirpur clinic which the NGO has been operating for many years to a local organisation or to the government, and there is presently much discussion on this topic. Many other Swedish NGOs have remained primarily operational and traditional (e.g. running clinics or schools) in their approaches. These findings were also born out more widely in SIDA's NGO assistance in a later evaluation across four countries in which it was noted that overall Swedish NGOs have found it difficult to built processes of resource-generation among the poor, or maintain sustainable local service delivery which continues after the initial SIDA-funded intervention (Riddell et al. 1994).

Questions of sustainability also remain difficult ones for Bangladeshi NGOs funded through the direct route. There are as yet few real examples from which to learn of NGOs withdrawing support from their beneficiary groups and leaving behind sustainable structures to carry on development activities. The case of RDRS is interesting in this regard because it is currently engaged in the process of transforming itself from an international body into a national NGO, as well as from an implementing agency into a sponsoring organisation. By creating an advisory board consisting of appointed Bangladeshis drawn from a broad representation from civil society, the first stage has been taken towards the eventual aim of establishing an executive board with additional representation from staff and beneficiaries.

Feedback and accountability to a Northern public

This section briefly considers how well SIDA and the NGOs are learning from the experiences of funding NGO activities in Bangladesh. Perhaps ironically, the SIDA office in Bangladesh appears to know far more about the directly funded NGOs than it does about the indirectly funded ones. In keeping with the spirit of Swedish aid and the autonomous Swedish NGO sector, the Swedish NGOs are free to play autonomous roles and need have no formal relationship with the SIDA office in Dhaka. In contrast with the constant feedback of information which emerges from directly-funded NGOs to the SIDA office, there is no systematic linkage with the Swedish NGOs working in Bangladesh. This is largely an outcome of SIDA's strategy of seeking to preserve the independence of the Swedish NGOs.

All project information relating to SIDA block grant allocations (i.e. those made by SIDA for indirect funding) is a matter between the NGO Division of SIDA in Stockholm and the headquarters of the Swedish NGOs. While the indirectly funded NGOs are required to keep the Dhaka office informed of their activities, not all of them actually do in practice. Few of the Swedish NGOs have felt the need to make external evaluations of their work in Bangladesh, nor has SIDA requested that such evaluations should take place. By contrast, detailed project applications and reports are received under the direct NGO support arrangements. The Bangladeshi NGOs which receive direct SIDA support are monitored by SIDA locally. The formal or informal funding consortia in which SIDA participates have initiated a number of external evaluations and a considerable amount of knowledge has been brought back to SIDA. There are very few links constructed between the experiences drawn from SIDA direct support in Bangladesh and the indirect support by the Swedish NGOs. The information potential of the Swedish organisations may therefore be under-utilised when it comes to their own project involvement in Bangladesh, but it is totally untapped as regards SIDA's direct NGO support.

As a government agency, SIDA cannot reach out with information about development to Swedish civil society with the same effectiveness as the Swedish NGOs, because these are popular organisations with their roots in Swedish public life. One of the important motivations for SIDA's funding of Swedish organisations is the role they can play in promoting understanding of Swedish development aid and improving SIDA's accountability to the Swedish public. Swedish NGOs have, over the years, built up valuable experience, which can be used for campaigning, development education, advocacy, networking, and the promotion of North-South dialogue.

Swedish NGOs pool their information within Sweden for development education and awareness-raising purposes through the umbrella NGO BIFO based in Sweden. Bistandsinformation (BIFO), which has 60 Swedish NGO members, works with NGOs to strengthen Swedish public awareness of development issues. Information is also sent back to SIDA about the directly-funded NGO work, and while there is evidence of institutional learning, it would appear that the system facilitates more specialisation than integration, where information is sometimes lost between the NGO division, sectoral departments, and the human rights and democracy office.

Does the transfer of knowledge between the Swedish NGOs and the public actually take place? There have been a number of activities undertaken successfully in the past, such as a Diakonia Bangladesh exhibition which has been used in churches since the 1980s. Swedish Swallows have made information work a major priority in recent years, and they have campaigned in Bangladesh and Sweden over environmental issues, such as the controversial Flood Action Plan. However, the indications from discussions with Swedish NGOs and with SIDA are that, in practice, very little new or challenging information about Bangladesh presently reaches the Swedish public. This is partly because Bangladesh is not usually considered newsworthy in Sweden unless there happens to be a disaster, and also because many Swedish NGOs have larger operations underway in other parts of the world which take precedence in their publicity.

An added constraint is the poor 'fit' which often exists between the views of NGO supporters in Sweden and other Northern countries, particularly those with a more traditional welfarist outlook, and more radical NGO initiatives in Bangladesh. Diakonia, in its recent efforts to develop a more activist approach in Bangladesh, has run the risk of becoming isolated from its traditional church-based support in Sweden. Whenever there is a mismatch between the aims and assumptions of the constituency and the actual work carried out, the organisations's ability to communicate experience with its constituency at home will be undermined.

In the need to secure funds from the public, it is tempting for some Swedish NGOs to opt for over-simplified messages based on their work (such as their success of building and maintaining an orphanage) rather than genuine development education which shares complex, difficult, and ambiguous realities (such as the problem of strengthening child rights).

This may be the most severe limitation of relying on primarily operational organisations (such as the Swedish NGOs) to transmit educational messages on development issues. Advocacy roles for the Swedish NGOs working in Bangladesh might include the support of human rights, among them women's rights, and the democratic process in Bangladesh, and the need to change public perceptions of Bangladesh as a passive victim of disasters. With the notable exceptions of Rädda Barnen (child rights) and Swallows (environment), most Swedish NGOs working in Bangladesh did not see themselves taking advocacy role either in relation to Sweden or Bangladesh. SIDA and BIFO cooperate in Sweden on educational projects and public seminars, but this is not clearly linked with Swedish NGO experiences drawn from the indirect funding route.

Conclusion: direct funding and changing NNGO roles

Direct support has been a useful strategy for SIDA in Bangladesh. Although Bebbington and Riddell (1995) draw attention to the dangers of the distortion of SNGO agendas by direct donor funding, the present study found little evidence for this in the SIDA case. For many of the Swedish NGOs working in Bangladesh, the problem was more a lack of imagination and adjustment to changing local conditions than a problem of being 'instrumentalised' by the objectives of a donor.

By contrast, SIDA's direct support to a relatively small number of generally important Bangladeshi NGOs has made good sense in terms of SIDA's overall development assistance objectives and the objectives of the SNGOs with which it is working. However, direct funding has tended to benefit the large, well-established NGOs such as BRAC and Proshika, where economies of scale, and English-language abilities among more educated NGO leaders, make management of the funding links relatively straightforward. Smaller, less formalised local NGOs may be less equipped to access a donor directly. The direct funding approach clearly does not supersede indirect funding in any simple sense.

What are the wider implications of this study? The first is that it throws light on what constitutes effective and responsible funding relationships between bilateral donors and SNGOs. In a recent study of grant and contract funding Mowjee (1997) lists the various key factors influencing funding relationships as trust, communication, understanding, shared assumptions and values, experience, and knowledge of desk officers and the donor's institutional framework. This is a useful model for analysing funding relationships, and from the case of SIDA in Bangladesh it is clear that both local knowledge and personal trust are important ingredients in the success of direct funding.

There is now considerable interest in the social sciences about the importance of the level of trust in a society to its management of economic affairs (Fukayama 1995). One of the reasons for SIDA's apparent success with its policy of direct funding of NGOs in Bangladesh has been the culture of trust which has been built into its relationships with NGOs. This has been achieved through partnerships built by individual SIDA staff in the Dhaka office with local NGO leaders. Underpinning this relationship has been the fact that two SIDA country office staff had worked previously in the Bangladesh NGO sector as volunteers or staff members with progressive Swedish organisations.

This fact neatly underlines the potential future value of building interdependent ties of trust between donors, NNGOs, and SNGOs. Although relations of trust no doubt also exist between SIDA in Stockholm and the headquarters of the Swedish NGOs, this is a more generalised relationship which has not apparently improved the relevance of Swedish NGO activities in Bangladesh. A level of trust based on good personal relations and an understanding of each type of agency's objectives has, therefore, in this case allowed high quality relationships to develop within a coherent, locally rooted programme. Within this relationship, SIDA has not considered its growing support to Bangladeshi NGOs as an all-purpose solution to Bangladesh's development problems, but as a continuing dialogue around the issues of sustainability, relevance, NGO relationships with government, and the dangers of a possible duplication of efforts. This trust-based model of partnership may have wider implications for other donors reviewing their relationships with NGOs.

The second set of implications relates the changing role of NNGOs working in aid-recipient countries. In particular, this comparison of SIDA's two funding routes in Bangladesh raises a number of important wider questions about the future roles of NNGOs in countries in which indigenous NGO capacity is relatively strong:

1 NNGOs need to strengthen their capacity to adjust to changing local realities in many Southern countries. There may be little value in continuing operational roles in countries with strong NGO sectors, but NNGOs can support SNGOs with training, information, and international coalition-building where appropriate.

2 Partnerships between Northern and Southern NGOs can be analysed critically by both partners so that they diversify beyond funding into more reflective, dynamic relationships in which the capacity of both sides is strengthened.

3 NNGOs may have a comparative advantage, as well as a moral obligation, to build stronger links between their own publics at home and development issues, through development education, networking, and lobbying their own governments.

4 NNGOs can raise the level of accountability of official development assistance by making connections between issues which are important in both Northern and Southern contexts (such as environmental pollution, women's rights, deforestation, corruption, and the effects of privatisation).

The growth of direct funding of SNGOs by donors therefore provides a useful opportunity to rethink the form and style of funding relationships along with NNGO approaches. There is a growing responsibility for NGOs and donors to build a more genuine form of partnership, which may or may not in future include financial resource transfers, around a greater level of trust.

References

Bebbington, A. and R. Riddell (1995) 'The direct funding of Southern NGOs by donors: new agendas and old problems' *Journal of International Development*, 7(6): 879–894.

Edwards, M. (1996) *International Development NGOs: Legitimacy, Accountability, Regulation and Roles*, Discussion paper for the Commission of the Future of the Voluntary Sector (CFVS) and the British Overseas Aid Group (BOAG).

Fukayama, F. (1995) *Trust: The Social Virtues and the Creation of Prosperity*, London: Hamish Hamilton.

Holcombe, S. (1995) *Managing to Empower: The Grameen Bank's Experience of Poverty Alleviation*, London: Zed Books.

Lewin, E. (1994) *Evaluation Manual for SIDA*, Stockholm: SIDA.

Lewis, D. J. (1993) 'Bangladesh country overview', in J. Farrington and D. J. Lewis (eds.) *NGOs and the State in Asia: Rethinking Roles in Sustainable Agricultural Development*, London: Routledge.

Lovell, C. (1992) *Breaking the Cycle of Poverty: The BRAC Strategy*, Dhaka: Dhaka University Press.

Mowjee, T. (1997) *Donors and NGOs: Case Studies of Grant and Contracting Models*, paper presented at Centre for Voluntary Organisation Open Day, London School of Economics, April.

Riddell, R., A. Bebbington, and L. Peck (1994) *Promoting Development by Proxy: The Development Impact of Government Support to Swedish NGOs*, London: Overseas Development Institute.

Sahley, C. (1995) *Strengthening the Capacity of NGOs*, Oxford: INTRAC.

SIDA (1992) *SIDA Country Review on Bangladesh 1993/94–1995/96*, Stockholm: SIDA (memo dated 18 December 1992).

SIDA (1993) *SIDA's strategies*, SIDA Internal Document, Stockholm: SIDA.

World Bank (1996) *Pursuing Common Goals: Strengthening Relations between Government and Development NGOs*, Dhaka: Dhaka University Press.

Relevance in the twenty-first century: the case for devolution and global association of international NGOs

Alan Fowler

Introduction[1]

In 1992, *Development in Practice* published an article setting out the decentralisation choices and trade-offs faced by Northern and Southern non-governmental development organisations (NGDOs) (Fowler 1992).[2] This paper reviews what can be learned since then and what might lie ahead for Northern NGDOs (NNGDOs).

What does organisational decentralisation mean? What types of decentralisation can NGDOs choose from, and what appears to be occurring? Answers to these questions are set out in the next section, which is followed by an analysis of the pressures and forces involved in choosing between different forms of decentralisation. These point towards devolution as a preferred option. The final section argues that globalisation calls for a truly international response from NGDOs, namely the formation of global associations. Together, 'downward' devolution and 'upward' association are the strategic response that international NGDOs must follow if they are to be relevant players in shaping the type of 'globalisation' they want in the twenty-first century.

The discussion is complicated because decentralisation takes on different features for different types of NNGDO. Specifically, important differences emerge between those which are themselves operational, such as CARE, ActionAid and World Vision, and those which fund but do not themselves implement programmes in the South, such as NOVIB and many US foundations. To distinguish the two, operational NNGDOs will be referred to as transnational NGDOs (TNGDOs), and non-operational funders as international NGDOs (INGDOs). Together they form the Northern NGDOs referred to in this paper.

A word of warning is needed. There is little publicly available documentation about what lives within NNGDOs as they strategise and make their choices and moves towards decentralisation. Consequently, this paper must be read with caution as, of necessity, much herein is based on observation and conversation, not on freely available documentary evidence.

Decentralisation for Northern NGDOs: concepts and practices

What does decentralisation mean and why is it significant for NGDOs? This section begins by answering these two questions. It continues with observations on what is happening in terms of the options available and the choices that NNGDOs have been making.

What is decentralisation in the context of NGDOs?

At its core, organisational decentralisation has to do with the distribution of authority, i.e., power, over goals and decisions about how resources are gathered and applied. Put another way, decentralisation is about the degree to which power is held in a central place — usually the top — or distributed downwards within, or outwards from, an organisation. This is not the same as, but is often confused with, the allocation of responsibilities for the tasks over which authority is exercised. For example, a programme manager's task may be to create and oversee a budget but not then to approve expenditures within it. In this set-up, he or she has responsibility without authority.

There are basically three types of decentralisation:

- *deconcentration:* responsibilities and tasks are allocated downwards in the organisation, but authority remains at the top or the centre;

- *delegation*: both responsibility and authority are assigned to lower levels of the organisation, e.g. to regional or country representatives or directors and, perhaps, to area or local managers and/or to field workers;

- *devolution*: is far-reaching in that authority for achieving an organisation's goals, mandate, and functions are allocated outwards to — and hence shared with — (legally) autonomous organisations.

There is always an element of NNGDO devolution in effective micro-development. Why? Because best practice in working with communities of poor and/or marginalised people (whether organised in community-based organisations (CBOs) or in grassroots organisations (GROs)) requires the creation of empowering relationships with them. This calls for authentic participation, which means negotiating key development decisions with the people. To some degree, the sharing of authority with CBOs or GROs always places decisions outside a manager's or staff member's sole span of control. While a significant factor in the effectiveness of an NGDO's development work, this paper does not look at the critical aspect of 'devolution' to CBOs. Instead, our focus is on delegation within, and devolution between, NGDOs.

What have been the trends and why?

It is ever more difficult to find examples of long-term deconcentration in NNGDOs. Why? Because, for example, decentralising tasks to regional offices, without giving these any substantive authority, adds a layer of bureaucracy without significant gains. It can also introduce conflicting advice and, for Southern partner organisations, confusion in communication with the real decision-makers, especially in the North. These were some of the reasons why, in 1992–3, NOVIB phased out its regional offices, replacing them with local consultants.

Experience also suggests that to equate decentralisation with simply replacing expatriates with indigenous staff — often as a cost saving measure — creates a veneer of change that, for reasons of culture and allegiance, is not readily matched by a continuity in trust with the new incumbent. In reality, while power may appear to remain the same for indigenous staff, often there is a subtle re-concentration of authority. There have been enough problems and negative feedback from indigenous staff within NNGDOs to show that this approach to decentralisation is seldom viable in the long term.

Where deconcentration remains, it tends to be in the form of specialist technical support functions (either staff or local consultants). These human resources typically assist in writing proposals, capacity building, and designing evaluations; and act as the eyes, ears (and uncertain voice) of those far away. A cost-reducing variant is to locate regional technical staff within country offices as a way of reducing overheads and, on occasion, because of registration and work permit problems. Trends suggest that, overall, deconcentration seldom generates significant organisational returns when set against the costs. This paper, therefore, focuses on the other two types of decentralisation.

For reasons detailed below, internal delegation is becoming almost a common approach to decentralisation among NNGDOs. Normally, this involves allocating authority to regional and/or country staff, typically bounded by a centrally approved strategic plan and annual reports. However, we argue here that internal delegation will, in fact, need to be seen as an interim step to eventual devolution and new forms of NGDO organisation that are truly international.

Why (not) decentralise?

Under most conditions, decentralisation through internal delegation or external devolution makes NNGDOs more effective because it helps them better respond to the diverse, often unstable, settings in which they work. In principle, allocating decision-making authority closer to the point of action enables participation that is more meaningful and greater potential for empowerment of local NGDOs and CBOs. Both are essential factors for gaining local ownership, commitment, and sustainability of impact (Craig and Mayo 1995). Common drawbacks to decentralisation, however, are: a possible erosion of NNGDO identity; more complex and hence weaker accountability; empire-building; unhealthy dominance or interference of funders due to their physical proximity; loss of quality control; and, enhanced potential for fragmentation of effort, typified by incoherence in development approaches and conflicting interpretation of policies. These factors reflect both strategic and operational drawbacks that decentralisation can produce.

The issue for NNGDOs is how to reinforce the benefits of decentralisation while limiting the costs. This challenge is made more complicated by the context of aid thinking and practice within which all NGDOs must function in the next century. Specifically, Northern NGDOs must approach decentralisation in a context where the service-delivery and policy-influencing capacity of *local* institutions are seen to be fundamental to success in sustained poverty reduction, as well as being a prerequisite for the strong civic expression associated with good governance.

Forces pushing towards Northern devolution

Since the late 1980s, several factors have been pushing NNGDOs in the direction of decentralisation in general and devolution in particular. At least six forces are significant:

- pressure from Southern NGDOs;
- donor policies and preferences;
- direct, in-country donor funding;
- concerns about NGO performance;
- enhanced communication technologies;
- within globalisation, economic and political regionalisation.

Southern pressures

Although uneven across the world, Southern and Eastern NGDOs are increasingly uncomfortable with their Northern counterparts doing development for them. The arguments against an in-country operational role for TNGDOs stem from many things. These include: nationalist sentiments; disappointment with supposed partnership arrangements; inconsistencies due to staff turnover; and, perhaps most importantly, increasing support for the notion that the problem of development is less to do with lack of resources to be made good by aid transfers and expatriate expertise than with the local leadership, institutional arrangements and capabilities, and the policies required to mobilise and use existing resources well (Riddell 1996). This perspective diminishes the justification for the presence of foreign agencies.[3]

It is beyond the scope of this paper to assess the evidence and merits of this position. Nevertheless, they would appear to be firm enough to adopt, as a working proposition, that the nature and measure of development cooperation are shifting from issues of quantity to quality, and to a diminishing contribution of aid in how countries eradicate poverty and injustice. Consequently, the strength of *indigenous* NGDOs in terms of their number, size, diversity of activities, economic rootedness, and mutual and social relations, becomes a critical factor in national development capacity. This points to devolution as a long-term NNGDO strategy.

Many governments of the South and East are also becoming less happy with NNGDO operations and presence. For example, Eritrea recently asked a number of NNGDOs to leave the country. Why? One reason is that NNGDOs are seen as an embarrassing signal of the failure of local institutions to do development themselves. Foreign-funded services and agents may also provoke public questioning about the soundness or legitimacy of the regime and government. In general, NGDOs are also perceived to fragment service-delivery, while diverting resources from public provision. In addition, foreign NGDOs are viewed with suspicion, in part because of a coupling of the aid and foreign policies of Northern governments on whose funds many NNGDO increasingly depend (Bowden 1997). Further, NNGDOs adopt positions on national issues and exert influence in the international arena and media, especially on donor policies, without meaningful political accountability (Jordan and van Tuijl 1997). In doing so, they further erode an already aid-threatened sovereignty. This state of affairs is creating a G-24 backlash (Mohammed 1997), typified by more stringent registration and operational requirements, restrictions on tax privileges, work permits and so on. Pressures to leave or become local are on the increase. Again, devolution is one solution.

Donor policy pressures

Often, using the arguments of capacity building and sustainability, Northern donors are encouraging or requiring NNGDOs to work with and through, or even to become, local NGDOs. For example, as a condition of further financing, USAID required Family Health International at the local level to incorporate the country structures it had established as part of its AIDSCAP project. Generally speaking, and tied to the policy of direct funding described below, donors are increasingly interested in financing local organisations or tying their domestic NGDOs to this strategy. The premise is that donors' capacity-building goals are served by having more local NGDOs to work with; and transforming a foreign project into a local NGDO is one way of achieving this. One usefully documented example of a transition from a donor project to local NGDO is PACT/PRIP in Bangladesh (Holloway 1997).

The connection that donors make between devolution and capacity building seems clear cut. However, the link between devolution and sustainability is fuzzy. What seems to be at play is the idea that a local NGDO will be in a better position to raise alternative, local, or complementary finance than a donor-funded project. Hence, there is assumed to be a greater chance of continuity once the donor withdraws. In other words, pushing for NNGDO devolution is, in fact, part of a donor exit strategy.

Direct funding

Recent years have seen a significant shift in the availability of resources within countries of the South and East. Occasionally, this shift arises from budget allocations made by national governments, as in India. More often, however, the origin is bi- and multi-lateral aid that is increasingly disbursed directly from agencies' local offices, or via governments from development loans (Patel and Jorgensen 1998). Examples of the first are to be found with British government funding in Bangladesh and Kenya. An example of the second are the social development and adjustment compensation loans made available by the World Bank, and which have a strong NGDO implementation component (Heiser 1994).

Given this trend, it makes economic sense for NNGDOs to delegate authority for in-country fund-raising, which are what many are doing. For example, the country offices of CARE-US now raise some 60 per cent of development (not relief) finance within the South and East. As Smillie (1995) points out, in taking this step TNGDOs have advantages over their local counterparts. Why? First, a transnational with a presence in donor countries can lobby at both ends. Second, they can transfer (people with) knowledge about donor quirks and practices across countries. Sharing this capacity makes proposal writing, negotiation, and so on much easier. Third, donors are still predisposed to 'tie' their aid to their domestic NGDOs. They do this in part to maintain an aid lobby back home, in part because communication in national languages is easier, and in part because of a higher degree of trust and ability to sanction, using domestic pressures, studies, procedures, and laws.

All of these factors place Southern and Eastern NGDOs at a significant disadvantage. However, it appears that size and strength of the local NGDO community can determine the extent to which NNGDOs can get away with the lion's share of direct, in-country financing. This does not happen in Brazil, India, Bangladesh, or the Philippines, though it does in Cambodia and Ethiopia. Making good the weakness of a local NGDO community by locally incorporating and then devolving foreign NGDOs is one route. This strategy can respond to criticism of unfair advantage and also bring with it a useful transfer of donor-oriented 'technology'.

NGDO performance

It would appear that NGDOs do not perform very consistently or well overall when it comes to achieving their strategic goals and missions. A series of (disconnected) donor-funded studies suggest that NGDOs are generally effective at producing outputs from development projects. However, they are seldom as effective in achieving impact, if this is understood as the sustained alleviation of poverty for really poor people or the communities with which they work (ODI 1996; Kruse et al 1997; Fowler 1998). A number of reasons are attributed to this.[4] One is the lack of authentic participation due to the dis-empowerment of NGDO front-line staff who do not have sufficient authority really to negotiate with communities. Hence, people's 'voice' does not become translated into shared power over decisions. This failing has negative consequences for the local ownership that sustainability requires. Consequently, to improve performance, pressure builds up to empower from within by spreading authority downwards. The issue — especially for TNGDOs in the short term — is not if, but how, to decentralise in an integrated way, and to do so in a way that capacity limitations are not shifted from one place to another, thus giving rise to additional problems.

Communication

Improved communication can also act as a force for or against decentralisation. On the one hand, satellite telephones and e-mail make it possible to keep managers in the North frequently informed about problems and possibilities on the ground and ask for their decisions. In other words, centralisation could work better. On the other hand, better communication can act as a confidence-building measure for the centre when authority is delegated or devolved. In other words, modern communication can facilitate decentralisation. It does so by helping to mitigate the fragmentation that can easily occur when reasonably autonomous parts of an organisation do not know and share information about what they are doing with each other, as well as with the centre. On balance, it looks as if the availability of modern, mobile communication is being used as a factor supporting the other pressures for decentralisation described here, so adding to their weight.

Regionalisms

Globalisation has become the buzzword in today's NGDO strategic thinking. Less talked about, but of equal significance, is the economic and political regionalisation going on within global integration (e.g. the European Union, the Southern Africa Development Community [SADEC], the Economic Community of West African States [ECOWAS], the Association of South East Asian Nations [ASEAN], the Mercado Común del Cono Sur [Mercosur], and the North American Free Trade Area [NAFTA]).[5] Having a regional approach has long been part of NNGDO organisation, but their regions are cobbled together without a firm developmental logic. The advent of regional groupings, which are meaningful in economic, political and institutional terms, calls for a similar approach from NGDOs. For example, the influence of preferential trade areas (PTAs) on local producers needs to be seen from a regional rather than a global perspective. Analysis of, and effective impact on, regional institutions requires being there. This, in turn, acts as another force for decentralisation.

NGDOs can also define regions in terms of their own insights. For example, in East Africa, regionalisation chosen by Norwegian Church Aid (NCA) derived from its analysis of, among others, human (seasonal) migration, patterns of insecurity, flows of refugees and internally displaced persons, informal cross-border trade, and ecological factors.[6]

Overall, devolution is emerging as the preferred response to both internal and external pressures facing NNGDOs today. But devolution to more national and local NGDOs must not lose the necessary perspectives, linkages, and advantages of international relations, and the capacity to act globally. This is where investment in global associations comes in.

Building upwards: forming global membership associations

Crudely speaking, devolution is a case of letting go downwards from a Northern centre to autonomous NGDOs with shared ideals. But this investment in local capacity must also respond to the interdependent poverty-inducing, marginalising forces being propagated by globalisation and its instruments: the World Trade Organisation (WTO), the Multilateral Agreement on Investment (MAI), the Bretton Woods Institutions, and transnational corporations, to name but a few (Korten 1995; Malhotra 1997). Consequently, to increase their impact, NGDOs within a given country need to link and ally upwards. In order to do so, there are major associational variants from which NNGDOs could choose.

From the perspective of a global association between devolved, autonomous entities, membership-based options seem most appropriate. It is beyond the intention of this paper to detail the major alternatives and differences between them. Relevant publications are included in the references and more are sure to come because of the intense attention the issue is receiving (Young et al. 1988; Edwards 1998). However, NNGDOs such as the World Wildlife Fund and World Vision are already well along the way to a fully international status, no longer rooted in, and governed by, one national history. Both comprise locally incorporated organisations world-wide, with global governance made up of all national bodies. This does not, yet, mean that all are on a democratic par with each other, because the members providing funds can inevitably end up as the first amongst equals. But the necessary foundations for a democratic, truly international, NGDO have been laid.

Other NNGDOs have already started to invest in a variety of types of global association. The Save the Children Alliance and Oxfam International are emerging examples. Already, Southern NGDOs operating under the Save the Children name are included in the Alliance, though this is not yet the case with the Oxfam 'family'. Others, such as CARE International and Plan, are governed solely by the funding countries and do not have locally incorporated and governed entities in countries of the South or East.

Experience shows that there is no one path to form global associations of whatever type. It depends very much on who you are and where you are starting from. But there are some important pre-conditions:

- A sufficiently strong, clear and shared vision of what the association is to be.

- The vision must be allied to a strong enough set of shared ideals for independent entities to be willing to forego part of their sovereignty for the common good, and agree on sanctions and modes of compliance when doing so.

- There must not be too severe an imbalance in terms of resources, size, experience, and domestic constituency. If there is, the stronger members must see it as an obligation, and in their interest, to invest in the weaker members for the common good. Without this principled acceptance, the first-among-equals syndrome will stand in the way of developing a shared global identity and truly international — as opposed to a 'many-nations' — reputation. The result will be a supranational shell that does not become more than the sum of its parts. Is this outcome worth the investment?

- In associating globally, NNGDOs must face up to, and be prepared to overcome, the psychological barriers of their relative disempowerment, for this is a necessary condition for the empowerment of the South and East — seated around the same table with the same voice, votes, and rights. Few global associations emerging from NNGDOs are yet close to this condition.

In conclusion, the rule of thumb is not to embark on forming global NGDO associations if the pre-conditions are not in place and cannot be created.

Conclusions: towards true democratic internationalism — balancing devolution with federation

Together, the forces described above are seriously challenging NNGDOs, especially the TNGDOs, to transform themselves. The demand is to move from being transnational in name to truly international in organisational perspective, nature, and practice (Taylor 1997). To do so requires balancing devolution with the evolution of truly international forms of NGDO organisation and global systems of governance.

Upward federation brings with it international democracy, for democracy is not solely an issue of the politics of governments and states; it is a weakness for many, if not most, NGDOs. Organisational democracy is a necessary condition if truly international NGDOs are to be able to improve both internal and external accountability. It is also a necessary condition if, as a part of civil society, international NGDOs are to push for democratic reforms, global governance and corporations. In other words, devolution and federation are a strategic contribution to a global citizens' agenda of gaining 'civic compliance' both from those who regulate and enforce, and from those who control production and distribution of the goods and services that society values (Bendall 1998).

This paper argues for a long-term future, where devolution to local entities will be a central feature in the decentralisation of NNGDOs. This is likely to be a contested view, in part because of the radical implications that this move implies. But, in fact, the argument for devolution is simply a logical consequence of realising the goals in local capacity development and policy advocacy that most NNGDOs already espouse (James 1994; World Vision 1997). Achieving this future will, therefore, be a sign of success, not failure. The challenge is to factor this desired outcome into the long-term thinking, vision, and journey of self-development of Northern NGDOs.

Notes

1 A revised and shortened version of a paper presented at a seminar organised by the International NGO Training and Research Centre (INTRAC) in December 1997.

2 As a shorthand, North is used for the OECD countries and the corresponding domestic NGDOs that are involved in international aid and development. The South corresponds to the traditional recipients of aid, and East for countries of Eastern Europe and the former Soviet Union that are now also receiving foreign assistance.

3 It also raises the question of whether or not solutions to internal limitations of leadership and capabilities —rather than lack of external inputs — are amenable to time-bound (project) aid (Fowler 1997).

4 An important omission in these studies is that they do not take into account the pre-conditions for NGDO effectiveness set up by donors in the first place. By concentrating on the impact of NGDO projects, donors have shielded themselves from critical investigation. This is not only unfair, it doesn't help in improving the system, which is what is needed. Donor behaviour is part of the problem as well as part of the solution to enhancing NGDO effectiveness.

5 According to *The Economist*, tariffs within PTAs are being reduced more quickly than they are between trading blocs, which may lead these to use tariff borders as a way of keeping other blocs out.

6 NCA Regional Strategic Plan 1996.

References

Bendall, J. (1998) 'Citizens' cane? Relations between business and civil society', paper presented at the Third Biennial Conference of the International Society for International Development.

Bowden, M. (1997) 'The New Africanism', Discussion Paper, London: SCF.

Craig, G. and M. Mayo (eds.) (1995) *Community Empowerment: A Reader in Participation and Development*, London: Zed Books.

Edwards, M. (1998) 'Structure, Governance and Accountability in CARE-International: Options for the Future', report to the Lead Member Model Review Group, Brussels: CARE-International.

Fowler, A. (1992) 'Decentralisation for international NGOs', *Development in Practice* 2(2): 121–124.

Fowler, A. (1997) *Striking a Balance: A Guide to Enhancing the Effectiveness of Non-Governmental Organisations in International Development*, London: Earthscan.

Fowler, A. (1998) 'An assessment of the performance of NGOs in social development: the case for quality not quantity in international aid', paper presented at the 3rd Biennial Conference of the International Society for Third Sector Research.

Heiser, T. (1994) 'Socio-Economic Development Funds: An Operational Guideline', Social Dimensions of Adjustment Project Unit, Africa Region, Washington DC: The World Bank.

Holloway, R. (1997) *Exit Strategies: Transitioning from International to Local NGO Leadership*, New York: PACT.

James, R. (1994) 'Strengthening the capacity of Southern NGO Partners: A Survey of Current NGO Approaches', Occasional Paper No. 5, Oxford: INTRAC.

Jordan, L. and P. van Tuijl (1997) 'Political Responsibility in NGO Advocacy: Exploring shapes of global democracy', Washington DC: World Bank Information Center/NOVIB.

Korten, D. (1995) *When Corporations Rule the World*, London: Earthscan.

Kruse, S-M. et al (1997) *Searching for Impact and Methods: NGO Evaluation Synthesis Study*, Vol. I Main Report:8, Helsinki: Finnish Ministry of Foreign Affairs.

Malhotra, K. (1997) *Globalisation and its Implications*, Bangkok: Focus on the Global South.

Mohammed, A. (1997) 'Notes on MDB conditionality on governance', *International Monetary and Financial Issues for the 1990s* III: 139–145.

ODI (1996) *The Impact of NGO Development Projects*, Briefing Paper No. 2, London: Overseas Development Institute.

Patel, R. and L. Jorgensen (1998) *Direct Funding from a Southern Perspective: Strengthening Civil Society?*, Oxford: INTRAC.

Riddell, R. (1996) 'Trends in international cooperation', paper presented at the Aga Khan Foundation Round Table on Systematic Learning: Promoting Support for Canadian Development Cooperation, Ottawa, Aga Khan Foundation.

Smillie, I. (1995) *The Alms Bazaar: Altruism Under Fire — Non-Profit Organisations and International Development*, London: IT Publications.

Taylor, M. (1997) 'Past their sell-by-date?: The role of NGOs in the future of development', Bradford Annual Development Lecture, London: Christian Aid.

World Vision (1997) *Transnational NGOs and Advocacy*, Discussion Paper No. 5, Milton Keynes: World Vision UK.

Young, D. et al. 'Strategy and Structure in Managing Global Associations', unpublished paper.

Northern words, Southern readings

Carmen Marcuello and Chaime Marcuello

Introduction[1]

This paper presents two sides of the same coin: certain words used in the North, and a reading of their effects in the South. Firstly, we summarise the recent evolution of Spanish non-governmental development organisations (NGDOs), which have gained in social visibility and prestige as a response to socio-political changes that have taken place in Spain. We then present a reading of the work of these NGDOs from the perspective of various Southern actors. We show instances of a kind of perverse inertia that undermines precisely what it is they are seeking to do. Thus, in Central America, recipients of foreign aid identify two extremes which we call *living by the wound* and *the project culture* (also known as 'projectitis'). If NGDOs want to meet their goals, they must guard against these unintended effects.

Northern words...

Spanish NGDOs

Like other social movements in Spain, the history of NGDOs is tied up with the country's socio-political evolution. To understand the backgrounds of these social movements, we must take into account the almost 40 years of the Franco dictatorship (1939–1975) and subsequent developments. The dictatorship conditioned the forms, models, and history of social movements, within a highly authoritarian context. Political and social action was thus defined as either conservative, national-catholic, or anti-communist. Following Franco's death, the transition to democracy was marked by great ebullience. Trade unions and clandestine organisations came out into the open, and new ones were born. These became the protagonists and very core of citizen action. As democracy was consolidated, social movements took on new missions and explored previously prohibited possibilities. The predecessors of today's NGDOs first had to survive the dictatorship, then pushed for democratisation, and finally came to occupy second place in terms of citizen action during the first decade of democracy.

We can discern two stages in their evolution. The first is characterised by their *social invisibility*. Neither before nor during the 1980s were NGDOs relevant to Spanish public opinion. Their activities were largely associated with missionary fundraising campaigns. This image began to change only very slowly. In 1982, the Socialist Party came to power. This brought about qualitative changes in the government's development aid policies. The term NGO came into being for the first time, though little attention was paid to NGOs. The second stage is thus marked by the achievement of *social visibility*. This was a gradual process. The '0.7% platform' mobilised many citizens (Marcuello 1996a). At the same time, there was more information about the desperate situations in the South. Social invisibility was thus converted into *social prestige*.

NGDOs acquired this social recognition because of three factors:

First, free advertising in the mass media. Second, the coopting of their language and successes by the politicians. Third, their growing presence as sponsors of the campaigns of private and public companies. These are three spaces conquered not by magic, nor by altruism on the part of the newspapers, the politicians and the companies: if they did not have 'social prestige' nobody would be supporting a concert for Rwanda, for example. (Marcuello 1996b)

NGDOs want this fragile achievement to continue, because they know that it has only just begun and that there is still much to be done within Spain. They know that they have come to represent something within the collective consciousness, and that there has been a qualititative change in how NGDOs are perceived. But more remains to be done.

Thus, Spanish NGDOs now face a kind of adolescent crisis, a time time of search, internal discussion, and social consolidation. The challenge is more complex than ever, but Spanish NGDOs now have some experience. Most of them, and certainly those which belong to the federation, want to affirm their identity because they know that their greater social visibility imposes greater precision on their work and activities.

The collective discourse

The NGDO Committee was founded in 1986 and brings together about 90 organisations in Spain. It has become a major reference point for NGDOs, public institutions, and society. Admittedly, the Committee represents an unstable balance given the diversity of its members. Nonetheless, it is acknowledged as the leader of 'joint action in cooperation with the peoples of the Third World'. In the Committee's own words: 'our general objective is to increase and to improve international development cooperation and to accomplish common actions in response to the interests of the peoples of the Third World'. Its objective is, 'to change the unbalanced and unjust relationships of dependency of the South on the North and to raise public awareness of the need for change'. [2]

Its members fight for a model of development that is sustainable, endogenous, balanced, and global: *Sustainable*, that guarantees the welfare of the present and future generations, based on the protection of natural resources and of Human Rights. *Endogenous,* based on the direct participation of the beneficiaries, and where foreign aid constitutes a stimulus to the development, but never a new kind of dependency. *Balanced*, based on questioning the social, economic, and political conditions that produce inequality among the countries of the North and the South and among the different sectors of the population. *Global,* based on the need profoundly to transform Northern development models, being the principal cause of the imbalances and the relationships of dependency between North and South.

On paper, the general perspectives are very clear. It is a Northern discourse, well formulated, well written. It represents years of NGDO experience and summarises the conventional wisdom on overseas development assistance. But how is this discourse seen by the Southern counterparts? How do they translate into practice? What reading do the beneficiaries have of what is done in the name of these high-sounding words?

Southern effects...

In general, the answers to these questions are positive. But now we focus on the 'perverse inertia' of this Northern discourse. For there are darker sides to all NGDO actions — Spanish NGDOs included. Despite their short experience in the international arena, they have adopted the rhythms and procedures of other Northern NGDOs, repeating once again the same development paradigms and rhetoric about North-South relations.

Perverse inertias

Effects and tendencies that are the opposite of what was intended are what we call 'perverse inertias'. In this case, these are the effects of Northern-funded development cooperation projects, whether non-governmental or official. We look at this in the light of our own work in El Salvador, Nicaragua, and Guatemala, and on the basis of visits by aid recipients from these countries. Their differences notwithstanding, these three countries serve as a basic reference or model of how international cooperation works.

Our research focused on both quantitative and qualitative issues and was conducted during 1995–1997. Here, we present our partial conclusions on some of the qualitative elements. Our methodology included interviews, discussion groups, and participatory action-research. These techniques allowed us to capture people's actual words. We then analysed what they had said in order to get a sense of the central elements within their worldviews. Here, we offer a selection of the most significant readings of the Northern aid discourse, by some of its recipients in the South.

Translating words into reality is difficult. Often, development projects do not respond to the recipients' felt needs — endogenous development — but to Northern NGDOs' own project repertoire. As the beneficiaries said:

> We need support, and as we want to ask these people for money, know that we must request it for certain things. Since we're going to ask so-and-so for money, we have to focus on women and ecology ... that's the fashion today. Perhaps we don't really need a cattle-raising project, but we know that they will fund this or nothing. So we get hold of the 25 cows even though they are going to ruin much of our land.

This happens frequently. The North sets the agenda. The recipients know that neither the rhythms of cooperation nor the cash intended for them are in their hands:

> For example, the European Community gives money for rural development, but only for agro-forestry or forestry. So, either you request a project for rubber-tapping or to collect plants for tea-infusions — to give a silly example — in other words, a project which does what they want of you, or you won't get anything.

But it is not only the macro-policies of government institutions that define the scope and funding of international cooperation. Northern

NGDOs are also responsible. These have the resources to work with their Southern counterparts, but almost always do so according to their own logic — the plans, standards, and models for action of the Northern NGDOs themselves.

> Look what happened to us. We were thinking about a reconciliation project. We wanted to begin very gently. But a First World NGO came to say that they, too, were interested in reconciliation, and in a series of similar projects. Their ideas seemed very interesting... but then we had to change everything to fit in with them. Although we did this together and discussed everything,... the point is that they had funding for projects that fitted in with their ideas, and unless we went along with it, the money would not be forthcoming.

Development cooperation projects are meant to be endogenous and focused on the 'beneficiaries', who are supposed to be, or become, the central subjects of their own development; the protagonists. In theory, donors should take second place. But the inertia of almost 50 years of international aid shows us the opposite. It is rare to find cases where the recipients play the leading role. In fact, Northern NGDOs are seen simply as *funders* (to say nothing of the official aid agencies, which are more distant still):

> Who decides how the money for projects is to be spent? Basically, the Northern NGDOs. Some may consult [with us] on the real needs — if only because no-one is going to say they didn't do so. But in reality, decisions about how the funds are to be spent are more often made according to plans and budgets established in the North than on the basis of reality in the South.

We must stress here that this inertia is known about and fought against. The Spanish NGDOs know how easy it is to slip into it, which is why they are resisting this trend. They have done good work in terms of establishing priorities, and ensuring that their projects respond to real needs by spending time in the recipient communities. Despite this, however, another perverse inertia appears:

> It is true that there are Northern NGO people who come and stay with us, listen to us, examine the projects we are interested in, on the basis of which they draw up projects to present to their governments. They do a good job. But once done, the situation on the ground changes — and our reality does change a lot — and the project on paper no longer fits our needs. They cannot change it, however,

because the funds are approved for fixed purposes. Who is going to mess about with funds from the European Community? But if you can't change it in the light of new circumstances, then it's immaterial whether the project has been well-planned.

The bureaucratic, organised, and rigid rationales of most Northern institutions cannot be readily adapted to suit realities that are less structured — or, rather, which are organised in a different way. Most Northern NGDOs replicate the procedures of the institutional donors, which they are indeed concerned to follow. They know that they must answer to external audits, even at the expense of imposing these 'westernising forms of rationalisation':

> For example, when the refugees were returning, we planned for a project that would start immediately, with a second phase three years later. But as time went by, things changed. The reconstruction work was no longer needed. The project was no longer viable. But since not even a comma could be changed in the project document, the project was ineffective ... so that the aid that was intended to help a community to re-build had the effect of dividing it further. I'm painting a very black picture, but this often happens.

The project protocols are pre-defined in ways that do not allow for adjustments in response to changing circumstances. The need for flexibility in the design, follow-up, execution, and evaluation of development projects is one of the things that beneficiaries most demand. They do need collaboration and help, but they need this not like some kind of yoke around their necks, but as agile and effective cooperation. Experience shows that bureaucratic pressure compromises the optimum use of the resources invested.

The project culture

NGDO action has another kind of impact on the recipient population. Whenever assistance comes from outside, whatever the source, people's way of life is changed. Where aid policies are effected through the design and execution of projects, this compels people to start thinking in terms of projects and international aid:

> You see, people see aid coming in from outside and realise that they must organise themselves if they are to get anything. They see that assistance is given not to individuals but only to groups. So they

begin to organise — not only people such as returnees, who are used to it, but also local villagers. In other words, they begin to feel that what they have to do is to formulate projects for funding. They assume that this is why the returnees are better off than they are, for example. So the 'project culture' is generated — 'I have a need, so I must come up with a project to resolve it'. And since neither the state nor the local authorities are doing anything, we have to ask the white foreigners who are the ones with the cash. The result is 'projectitis' — the project culture.

This project culture, which aims to resolve problems through projects funded from abroad — either directly by Northern agencies or via their local 'partners' — tends to demobilise local citizen action, firstly because the State is relegated to second or even third place; and secondly, because people's own efforts are put 'on hold' as their trust is placed instead on the benevolence of the 'friends of international solidarity'.

And that's not all. After years of being involved in projects, other effects emerge — as in the case of refugees and returnees. In extreme cases, self-help is discouraged: as one respondent said: 'People see everything apart from looking after the fields or the home — whether building a house or sinking a well — as something that can only be done via a project'. However, those who receive (or endure) development aid are also aware, especially in El Salvador and Guatemala, that this is a temporary thing, that it will only last for a couple of years, so they must make the most of it. So they invent as many projects as they can — even if they are not needed:

> Let's give them poultry, a dozen hens each. Good. Twelve laying hens that you have to look after, and then you'll get eggs. So the poultry arrive. You have to make a proper chicken coop. But then you have a setting to which the chicken are not accustomed. They get up on the chairs, the tables, they get in the way. They're aren't strong like the local variety, so some of them fall sick and die. But the others are such a pest that the people end up killing and eating them. When the agency representative arrives, the people tell him or her that the tiger ate the chicken. The point is that this was not the right project in the first place.

Projects can be useful. When the circumstances, the people, and the resources are in synergy, and things work as they should: success. But it's quite the opposite when 'perverse inertias' are operating. If the project is ready-made, or pretty well decided beforehand without asking people what they really need, it is unlikely to engage them. Yes, consultation does sometimes take place. But it is also true that the pre-formed plans tend to carry more weight than the local realities. This means two things. Firstly, in a descriptive sense, a popular education process is needed to find out what people want and need: 'People say many things; perhaps some don't make sense, but out of these we can draw up a list of needs and then ask the community to prioritise...' Secondly, and prescriptively, projects should be flexible and able to adapt to changing realities: 'What happens isn't like this. It's obvious that there are some with the money, and others without. There are no two ways about it. It's not that people are stupid, rather they are grateful — and also know that if they are grateful they may get more money. So the project culture is deepened.'

This *projectitis* both encourages a mechanical approach to formulating projects: 'People develop the knack of coming up with projects — projects for anything under the sun'. And it also habituates people to the idea that money intended for projects actually gets diverted,

> ...for the war or whatever, or even for corruption ... Someone who used to be honest gets to manage US$100,000 then disappears with US$2,000. So, corruption is generated, along with power struggles, not over how to serve the community, but over access to money.

Living by the wound

The project culture is intimately bound up with living by the wound. It is both a parallel and a direct result:

> People think that have suffered so much and that more will be given to the one who suffered the most. Basically, this is not their fault. They have seen that masses of people have come to hear about their history, how they were slaughtered, how they were killed, and so on...and they see that after these testimonies, projects arrive. This has gone on since 1982... There comes a time when people feel very poor after having returned from exile with nothing ... and they automatically tell the first person who arrives how much they have suffered because they believe this is what they have to do to get help. This is what we call 'living by the wound'.

To live by the wound is to use one's personal narrative of suffering (or that of a loved one) in order to leverage resources, especially money, either via projects or gifts, whether as a means of survival or to meet a particular need. It is a vicious circle created by projectitis, and by the bad (or perhaps good!) conscience of the outsiders who come into contact with the reality of suffering.

If we ask what gives rise to that perverse inertia, the answer comes from the people who have lived through it:

> Who is responsible for projectitis and for living by the wound? They the ones who do it, but they didn't start it. The guilty ones are the international organisations, not only NGDOs, but also UNHCR, the Catholic church and many big agencies that have supported; for example, the Mexican government ... They encourage that kind of dependency, a dependency that has nothing to do with dignity. 'Here's some beans'. And although they are foul, you have to accept them. How can you say you don't want something that has been given to you? But people do recover their dignity at a certain point. 'I don't want any more weevil-infested old beans ...'. 'Right, you obviously aren't in need then, that's why you're turning them down', they say.

The challenge to NGDOs, as seen from this corner of the South, is to change these inertias. Procedures need to be clarified, and more flexible mechanisms adopted, so as to give the leading role to the beneficiaries and see how they behave. Donors and beneficiaries alike must distinguish between the various approaches to, and types of, cooperation. They need to get rid of the confusion that generates the situations we have described, and which also tends to undermine traditional community networks, and to introduce a certain lack of solidarity as a precondition for entering into the world of development projects:

> Before it took no time at all to build a community structure with everyone's input, and without any outside help. Now it is very hard to find volunteers to do any unpaid work. NGOs and international agencies pay for everything, including labour. So people say it is impossible to build a community hall, without having a project and without money: 'we have a lot to do; what will we eat? and so on'. This kind of aid has generated a lack of solidarity where previously people were willing to work for the common good, and were very organised.

True, without NGDOs, many things would not have been possible. But there comes a time when the NGDO reduces people's capacity to make political demands, because everything gets turned into projects. In the past, projects were used to support things like revolving funds. But today, the attitude is 'either you give it to me or I don't want it'. It is not that NGDOs are solely responsible for this change in attitude, but it is, neverthless, a natural consequence of the kind of aid they offer.

In emergency situations, such as those afflicting Central America throughout the 1980s, this loss of values is less obvious. But the same approach to aid continues in the name of development — but a development that is seldom sustainable and often creates dependency:

> These people ... arrived without any project, but with a lot of external help; enough to obtain land and things ... But after that, all the community houses, cooperative centres, the shops, were all built on a voluntary basis... even the runway, which meant bringing earth from several kilometres away. All this without a single project. Now we need to re-build, but no project means no reconstruction. Without a project and wages for the labourers, the runway will not be repaired. The very runway that is used by the tiny aeroplane that brings us help. Things are out of sync. But people have become innured to it.

Conclusions

We have explored the dark side of the fine NGDO words. Spanish NGDOs, like all the others, have adopted an impeccable rhetoric. But rhetoric and theory are one thing, practical results are another. Spanish NGDOs repeat the same internationally established development clichés. Development is to be sustainable, beneficiary-led, endogenous, human, participatory — all the best possible attributes. But the interpretation of these claims in practice shows some perverse inertias that should be fought against. The consequences of years of international development cooperation are felt in the two pathological trends explored above; pathological for two reasons. First, because they are an unintended effect of the prevailing discourse. Second, because they embed the intended beneficiaries in a situation that is both alienating and enslaving.

True, development projects have had mixed results. Some beneficiaries will be grateful for generations. But we must recognise that these examples have not helped to improve the living conditions of humanity overall.

The great majority of our interlocutors, who have been on the receiving end of development projects, feel the contradictions of their situation. The clearest among them adopt a bitter-sweet tone: they value others' efforts, their solidarity, but they also claim their dignity as intelligent human beings. Theirs is a fierce critique of the way in which their lives and their expectations of development are taken over by others in the name of international solidarity. They do not need a new set of parents or experts to explain to them how they must develop. The true protagonist is the 'beneficiary' and his or her community, not the intellectual vanguards who seek short-cuts to the 'truth'.

We need to fight against these pathologies, which are both socially demobilising and tend to blunt people's critical capacity — assuming, that is, that NGDOs want to be true to their rhetoric. The staff of Spanish NGDOs are largely aware of these perverse inertias. In trying to turn things around, the question is to participate, cooperate, and help to generate processes in which the recipients of development projects become the subjects of their own history. NGDOs must resist just being bureaucrats, and move towards where they say they want to go: 'To participate as equals with the peoples of the world in the common cause of development.'

Notes

1 The original Spanish verison of the paper is available on request from the Editor.

2 From the CONGD 1997 promotional leaflet 'Participate as Equals with the Peoples of the World in the Common Cause of Development'.

References

Coordinadora de ONG para el Desarrollo (1994a) Directorio ONGD 1994, Madrid: CONGD.

Coordinadora de ONG para el Desarrollo (1994b) Banco Mundial y Fondo Monetario Internacional, un análisis crítico, Madrid: CONGD: 53–93.

Coordinadora de ONG para el Desarrollo (1995) Memoria de actividades Coodinadora de ONGD 1994, mimeo.

Coordinadora de ONG para el Desarrollo (1996a) Memoria de actividades Coodinadora de ONGD 1995, mimeo.

Coordinadora de ONG para el Desarrollo (1996b) ONGD: Espacios de participación, Madrid: CONGD.

Marcuello, Ch. (1996a) 'El movimiento 0,7: un pulso colectivo, Acciones e Investigaciones Sociales 4: 201–218.

Marcuello, Ch. (1996b) 'Identidad y acción de las organizaciones no-gubernamentales', Revista de Gestión Pública y Privada 1: 103–122.

Whose terms? Observations on 'development management' in an English city

Richard Pinder

Contradictions

Are we witnessing in English cities the emergence of development management that makes for — because it is premised on — 'empowerment and participation'? More critically, even if this is what we are indeed witnessing, dare we hope that this will help shift the patterns of domination and deprivation that define those cities?

The answer, to both those questions, has to be: Yes, and No. I make that answer with reference to only one English city — Sheffield — though I have no reason to believe that, in this context, it differs significantly from any other such city. In Sheffield, certainly, it is the contradictory nature of how development is being managed that is its most striking feature: on the one hand, the explicit opening up of the process to a much wider set of players than traditionally has been the case; on the other hand, the continuing domination of a traditional top-down management style. We have the explicit espousal of equality as a central value in the council's vision for the city, and yet we see the continuing co-existence of wealth alongside poverty, of private affluence alongside public squalor, and of acceptance of this state of affairs.

I will look at the first of these contradictions, not least because I believe the introduction of new players, with different and differing values, may be precisely the stimulus required for a move against the inequality that is my main concern. The two stories I will tell revolve around the same two questions: *on* whose terms — a question of power — do those new players come to share in the management of development? and *in* whose terms — a question of language and culture — is their involvement framed?

User 'involvement'

The concept of 'user involvement' has been gaining currency in the increasingly linked fields of social and health care in the UK. The idea is a disarmingly obvious, and obviously virtuous, one: users of care services should be involved in the design, planning, delivery, and evaluation of the services they receive, not least as a vital means of improving the quality of those services.

In Sheffield, this idea's time seemed to have come in March 1996, when £240,000 was allocated by the local and health authorities to a three-year project to establish a *Sheffield Users Network* (SUN) that would promote 'the involvement of service users in decision making about care services'. The project would encourage the creation of groups of users around issues of particular importance to them, and would allow the statutory services to have better access to a broad and representative range of their views. The Network would promote a more coherent and powerful contribution on the part of users. The development of services would take on a different, more open character, would no longer be the exclusive preserve of statutory agencies. In September 1996, a Management Committee for the project was created and the process of recruiting workers began.

Eight months later, the SUN project was closed down, its Management Committee accepting a 'suggestion' from the lead officer in the Council that it 'consider the option of winding up in its current form'.

A complex of factors lay behind the closure: gender, 'race', ethnicity, class, culture; all of these caught up in relationships of cooperation and (increasingly) conflict between different groups of users, between users and professionals, and between different professionals. This is a complex that is difficult if not impossible to disentangle, and not immediately relevant to my interests here. Rather, I want to look at the statutory agencies' handling of the collapse, for this points to how fraught and fragile is the process of shifting the terms on which professionals and users meet, of shifting the balance of power between them.

The city council and health authority, through the Joint Consultative Committee (JCC) (which links the two public bodies for planning purposes), immediately commissioned a review into user-involvement in community care in Sheffield. This review was to explore the setting up and closing down of the SUN and 'make proposals for the development of user involvement in health and social care services planning, management and review'. Fieldwork took place between June and November 1997. A final,

66-page report — it starts with a 'HEALTH WARNING: This is a long report' — was presented to, and agreed by, the JCC in February 1998. Its recommendations as regards future funding for 'user involvement' (re-designating the SUN money) are now being implemented.

A number of aspects of the review suggest an attempt to take some of the risk — for existing management — out of extending user involvement. Three are of particular interest. The first has to do with the way in which the report's account of the rise and fall of SUN softened history, in particular by understating the element of conflict. Inter-personal politics, underpinned by, but not accounted for simply in terms of, ideological difference, had figured strongly. Yet the anger, venom, and bitterness that had characterised some exchanges between various interested parties were not reflected in the account.

This did more than simply reduce the dramatic intensity of the report. In playing down the conflict, the authors lost an opportunity to explore a wider political dimension. For all that they found particular, immediate form in the SUN development, the key conflicts were part of a much longer, local and national, history: years certainly, decades arguably. This relates to the post-war conflict between statutory agencies and black communities over equity and appropriateness in the provision of statutory services. There is also the no less long-standing conflict between statutory agencies and users of services over how needs are defined and, more pointedly, over who defines them. SUN turned into an arena in which both these conflicts were played out. This political dimension is not written into the account. In consequence, the conclusions drawn from the review focus more on the details of project management than on the dynamics of political process. A political problem becomes a technical one.

The second aspect is, again, about what is missing from the review. If the report de-contextualised SUN in this historical sense, it also de-contextualised it in an institutional sense. The authors had received evidence from the Disability Consultative Committee, a committee of disabled people set up to advise Council Departments on how they can effectively consult with disabled people. This they had not incorporated within their report, because the evidence referred to 'the wider organisational and cultural context of disability', which, they argued, did not come within their terms of reference. The Committee subsequently went on to make a number of critical comments on the draft report. It did not, they said, explain the social and political context of user involvement; it did not set out models of user involvement; it ignored understandings of user involvement which extend beyond the provision of welfare services, particularly those organised around challenges to disparities in power and status; and it ignored the vastly unequal power relations between users and service providers.

In referring to this in their final report, the authors acknowledged, 'that there are many shortcomings to the review', but went on to say that, 'despite all the acknowledged shortcomings of the report, we think that the evidence for our recommendations has been clearly presented by users and others involved, and we have no hesitation in presenting them to the Joint Consultative Committee'.

The third aspect relates to the recommendations themselves. I have already referred to conclusions which were more about project management than about political process. The recommendations that followed from these conclusions were essentially to do with tighter controls over the commissioning, management, and monitoring of user involvement projects. The review went further, and specified those areas where future investment in user involvement should be made. The most notable feature of these recommendations was the shift away from any large-scale, broad-based user-involvement movement and (back) towards smaller-scale projects organised around particular welfare categories — frail, elderly people with learning disabilities; people with physical disabilities — or around the needs of people in black and minority ethnic communities. As the Disability Consultative Committee observed, such 'recommendations may further compound the fragmentation of user groups and increase the domination by the statutory bodies'.

Re-generation partnerships

Just as it has become common practice for public officials to seek user involvement in the development of services, so it has become common practice for those officials to encourage people in the voluntary and community sectors to play a role in the city's social and economic re-generation. In this case, the process is presented in terms of 'partnership'.

'Partnerships' are being developed in a number of contexts. For some years now, there has been a statutory obligation upon local authorities to devolve a substantial amount of the provision of community care services to voluntary (and private) sector agencies. In Sheffield this has taken formal shape in the setting up of 'partnership contracts' between Social Services (as purchasers) and some 30–40 voluntary organisations (as providers).

With respect to urban economic and social re-generation, voluntary and community organisations are now being invited to join already existing 'partnerships' involving public, quasi-public, and private organisations. The major national and European funding regimes upon which re-generation projects draw increasingly require evidence of community involvement in projects before they will accept and approve bids for funding. And Sheffield City Council, recognising the need for allies in order to realise its vision for the city, has recently begun to promote an ethos of working 'in partnership with the community' — this after years in which the culture of the (locally) ruling Labour party was such as to encourage patron-client relationships between Council and community.

In all these contexts, there are ever-increasing opportunities for people in the voluntary and community sectors to take up more explicit roles in the management of re-generation in the city, and for the interests of their organisations to be recognised in planning processes. Indeed, it is commonly affirmed that no strategic working group, no project planning group, no development forum, should be without voluntary or community sector representation

For all this apparent openness to new players, it is clear that in many respects the change taking place is a matter more of an old order incorporating newcomers than of a new order being brought into being with, and through, the arrival of newcomers. In particular:

- New management bodies have been, are being, created, with a wider range of interests represented. However, these bodies function very much in the style of local authority committees, leaving newcomers either to learn this style, take on what may feel like an alien culture, or be left on the margins. And these bodies, for all that they have in their very composition the means of recognising and responding to the complex and conflictual reality of the city, come to be preoccupied with the management and allocation of their own resources.

- New strategies are formulated, with more of an inter-agency, inter-disciplinary, approach. However, they are very much the same 'strategies as blueprints' that have hitherto been produced by single agencies: these strategies are documents that pretend to map out the future, the future to which all interests will be expected to sign up. These are strategies, also, formulated by (and for) the few: short (externally set, the argument goes) time-scales prevent wide consultation; while length and language exclude scrutiny by the many.

- Accountability is newly stressed. However this is accountability of the many to the few, and of the people to the plan. This is accountability to strategies, expressed through the monitoring form, which specifies targets and milestones in boxes that necessarily distort and demean the work being reported. Quality is subordinated to quantity. And the longer the term under scrutiny, the more the 'evidence' becomes science-fiction.

- All is expressed in the language of new, wider and better, 'partnership'. However, this partnership is the partnership of centralised, pre-determined coordination, rather than of local emergent cooperation. This is partnership whose main object is efficiency. This is partnership which far from acknowledging diversity — the diversity which is at the heart of city life — submerges, seeks to subvert, it in common purpose. This common purpose, established by the few, is required of the many.

In all these ways, the potential added value of bringing new, diverse interests into play in the regeneration of the city is lost. Instead of reality — including the reality of inequality — being more faithfully reflected in the process of management, newcomers, particularly those from local communities, are expected to abandon their understanding of, and attachment to, local reality, and enter into the imaginary cityscapes of the city strategists.

What I have here set out in abstract terms can be illustrated from everyday experience. By way of example, at the time of writing (July 1998) our locality — along with two others — is being presented with a 'Development Framework' that is intended to set out a programme of 'sustainable development' stretching over the next 5–10 years. The Framework emerged from a study commissioned by the local Single Regeneration Budget Partnership Team, and undertaken by a private consortium involving no local people. The extract below presents the suggested 'Delivery Mechanism'.

> The Development Framework is designed to provide the context for concerted regeneration of the SRB area to the south of the city centre. It aims to bring together a set of strategic objectives and translate them into a range of integrated actions that will deliver sustainable regeneration over a 5–10 year period.

> The development framework and action plan relies [sic] on the effort of a variety of agencies, landowners, residents, businesses and funding bodies to enable it to move forward. Shared objectives translate into shared responsibility and a requirement for everybody to work together to achieve a set of shared goals. We would therefore

recommend that a new umbrella organisation led by the City Council be established to oversee the delivery of the framework and action plan. It is particularly important to engage the local community and business community in the delivery of the plan — they are integral to the successful delivery of regeneration within the area.

Clearly there are already a number of different partnerships/forums established in the area — and others are proposed. Without wishing to disrupt established working groups there is a requirement for an organisation acting as a driving force that can oversee integrated regeneration throughout the area. In our suggested organisation framework the City Council could fulfil this role.

There is also a requirement for dedicated groups to drive forward projects/strategies under the umbrella. This will enable teams/groups to remain focused on effective delivery and implementation. Our recommendation is that the existing and emerging forums, partnerships and development trusts, should become individual bodies geared towards the implementation of this framework and action plan.

Three points are remarkable, two evident from the extract, one not. The first is the acknowledgement of the importance of the local community. The second has to do with how local forums and so on — each an (imperfect) representative of a particular local community — are treated within this 'delivery mechanism' for the Development Framework. They are required to become agencies 'geared towards the implementation of this framework and action plan'. There is no sense of the legitimacy or significance of local interests that might lie outside the Framework, no recognition that the value of local bodies might lie as much as anything in expressing those divergent and other interests, or indeed that there is a city outside the Framework.

The third — all of a piece with the second — has to do with how local forums were treated within the study process. For at least two (covering two of the three localities involved) there was no consultation before, during, or (until demanded) after the undertaking of the study and writing of the report. And the onwards transmission of the Framework to the Regional Office of Government — to become, no doubt, another accepted representation of the imaginary city of Sheffield and its imaginary future at that 'higher' level of development management — was a reality local forums had to catch up with after the event.

Unfinished stories

In each of the two stories told above, there is a sense of new possibilities being opened up — and then being closed down: users of services having incipient freedom to manoeuvre severely curtailed; people in local community organisations, reflecting local interests, finding those interests count for little in the face of dominant re-generation management processes.

There is much in this to induce pessimism. The opening up of development management to a wider range of players does not seem to have changed the terms on which and in which development in Sheffield is taking place. On this view, little hope can be held out that development is likely to shift patterns of inequality.

It is, thus, more than usually important to say that in neither of the above cases has the full story as yet unfolded.

Information Technology and the management of corruption

Richard Heeks

Introduction

Corruption — 'inducement to wrong by bribery or other unlawful or improper means' — is a global problem and one that tends to stir strong reactions (adapted from Klitgaard 1984):

- corruption is a culture-bound concept: 'Your culture may say that X is corrupt; mine does not';
- corruption is a force for good: 'It helps the wheels of government and business to turn';
- corruption is too big to deal with: 'Corruption is everywhere. What can we ever hope to do about it?'.

All of these reactions can make it hard for corruption to be addressed by development managers. Yet it is an issue that many of them face, and which must be attacked for at least three good reasons (adapted from Davies 1987):

- it drains off valuable economic resources, particularly investment funds, into unproductive uses, and reduces the likelihood of development objectives being achieved;
- it siphons off another valuable resource — the time of development organisation staff — into unproductive use, and creates resentments and frustrations among staff, thus reducing organisational efficiency;
- because it is hidden and unaccountable, corruption is essentially undemocratic and hampers the development of democratic processes and institutions.

One currently-dominant paradigm of corruption control — termed the 'Panoptic vision' by Anechiarico and Jacobs (1994) — sees management techniques of rules and enforcement as the key to controlling corruption. Enforcement is, and has always been, a labour-intensive and information-intensive activity for which managers require assistance (Sparrow 1992). One model for such assistance is provided by Jeremy Bentham's nineteenth-century idea of the Panopticon: a constructed technology that allowed a single central unseen guard to observe the activity of all prison inmates. In the late twentieth century, information technology (IT) presents organisations with the possibility of creating their own Panopticon: one that would allow managers to gaze unseen upon the activities of their employees and thus monitor and control corruption (Roszak 1994; Ramasoota 1998).

But what of reality in development organisations: can information technology, in practice, help control corruption? Some thumbnail sketches are offered below to help provide initial pointers to an answer. The cases are drawn from the experiences of the author and of development managers studying at the University of Manchester.

Cases of IT and corruption

Case 1

Managers in a railway system were concerned about the efficiency of its seat and berth reservation system, and about corruption within the system. Booking staff had access to, and control over, the allocation of places on trains. A few would take a bribe (either directly or via a ticket tout) to provide a passenger with a reserved place; these being at a premium since all trains were over-booked. A computerised system was introduced, one objective of which was to eliminate corruption. To achieve this, allocation of reservations was handled automatically, including the particularly 'weak link' of moving passengers on the waiting list into places vacated by cancellations. Computerisation did make it harder for the clerical staff to be corrupt because the software, not the clerk, now decided — based on booking date — which passengers would fill vacated slots. However, corruption was not eliminated, and two aspects will be noted here.

First, station managers retained manual control over a certain proportion of the train places, supposedly to cover emergencies or last-minute travel by VIPs. Some continued to provide these places to nonemergency, non-VIP passengers in return for cash. Second, ticket touts showed how ingenious and resourceful they can be. Knowing that their best customers were businessmen in a hurry, they would book places well in advance on the main inter-city trains using a very common man's name, citing his age as 35 years. These places would then be sold at a premium to last-minute travellers, most of whom were men who could get away with appearing 35 years old to the ticket collectors.

Case 2

In a public works department, there was concern about the number of 'ghost workers' in the system. These are people listed on the payroll, and therefore paid, who do not exist in reality. Someone else collects the wages paid out under their names. The payroll system was computerised and, during this process, a check was made between listed and actual workers. Any non-existent staff were removed from the system.

This seemed to have solved the problem, assisted by the word being spread that the computer could make an automatic check between the payroll list and reality, and could automatically detect who was picking up ghost worker wages. Of course, it could do no such thing. An audit 18 months later uncovered a very well-to-do computer operator who was collecting his own wages plus those of 30 other workers he had entered into the payroll system.

Case 3

Examination marks at a university were previously kept on paper, with calculation of final grades and averages being done manually by a small group of trusted staff. Mark lists were kept locked in a safe when not being used. Given the large number of students, it was decided to computerise the marks and calculations. There was an assumption that information on the (un-networked) computer would be safe, though a password was added just in case, known only to a very few staff.

All seemed well until one lecturer noticed that a low-achieving student had obtained a spectacular final grade. Enquiries revealed that he was the son of one of the computer managers. The manager, knowing the importance of university grades for job prospects, had opened up the marks database and changed his son's mark. Unfortunately for him, instead of altering the figures slightly, he was over-ambitious and pushed them from the 40s up to the 70s.

Case 4

Computerisation was taking place in a (different) university, and it seemed obvious to turn attention to the admissions process, which was notoriously slow and corrupt. Computerisation of admissions involved entering the school-leaving exam marks of all applicants, and then producing a prioritised list, headed by the candidate with the best overall marks. Other factors might be taken into account but, if all other things were equal and there were 1,000 places at the university, the top 1,000 candidates on the computer-generated list would be the ones to gain admission.

This clearly represented a considerable threat to members of the admissions committee. These members could gain significant financial and political rewards by offering places to children of the rich and powerful who would not get into university if an entirely merit-based system were adopted. The committee therefore decided to accept the prioritised list merely as an 'advisory tool', and never made it public outside that committee.

Case 5

A customs department kept manual records with the names and addresses of overseas firms which had been involved in import or export transactions. These contacts were useful to local entrepreneurs, particularly those seeking export collaborations. The entrepreneurs therefore paid customs officials to provide them, illegally, with the contact details. The department, including its overseas firm details, was computerised and one computer was put into a front office where members of the public could access it. Entrepreneurs gained direct access to the contact details they wanted and payments were therefore no longer made.

Information about foreign businesses was a resource which local businesses required. Because the information was scarce and because it was kept as a private resource, customs officials (acting as information 'gatekeepers') were able to charge 'rent' for access to it. Once the information came into the public domain, no access charges could be made.

Impacts associated with introducing IT

From these cases, we can conclude that the impacts associated with the introduction of IT are quite varied:

Removal or detection of some corruption

Corruption in an organisation is possible because staff have access to a valued resource and to those who will pay for it. The valued resource could include provision of a service, legal permission to undertake some activity, or information of value. They also have the skills, confidence, and autonomy to make decisions about the provision of that resource.

Where IT can deny access to the resource or to relevant decision-making processes, this may remove corruption. Typically, this will occur if the processes are automated. For example, the clerical staff in Case 1 no longer had control over allocation of vacated reservations. In other cases, computerisation assists detection of corrupt practice, in line with the Panoptic vision. In turn, this reduces staff's perceived autonomy and so is likely to suppress some corrupt practices.

New corruption opportunities

In Cases 2 and 3, the introduction of IT provided new corruption opportunities for some staff. This phenomenon may often be related to closing down opportunities for other staff. Computerisation does so by creating changes in one or more of four aspects:

- *Skills*: computerisation is often associated with an 'up-skilling' of corruption, providing an opportunity for those with IT skills, and denying those without these skills.

- *Confidence*: borrowing from the Panoptic vision, a mythical image may be promoted of the computer as an objective, all-seeing, all-knowing machine. This may cause some corrupt staff to lose confidence and to refrain from corrupt practices. Those who understand computers are not put off (and will often spread the myth in order to reduce the likelihood of competition or detection).

- *Access*: in the cases described, computerisation of records was accompanied by closing down access to some staff but opening up access to all those operating the IT systems. With the advent of networked systems, such opportunities for access may greatly increase.

- *Control*: the mask of data quality and computer omnipotence makes some managers assume that IT removes the opportunities for corruption, i.e. that the Panopticon can operate without the need for human intervention. They may therefore fail to institute controls on computerised systems. This assumption provides greater autonomy for IT-literate staff.

No effect on corruption

In Case 4, and for the station managers in Case 1, computerisation had no effect on corruption. This is because computerised information systems were designed in such a way that key corruption-linked resources or processes were left uncomputerised, despite their possibly being surrounded by other computerised systems.

Factors determining the impacts of corruption

These different impacts can be explained by the different factors involved:

Information technology

Computers have no innate property related to corruption except that of their imagery. They do not automatically provide a Panoptic model of control — this only comes if they are deliberately and systemically designed to do so. The impacts described above, therefore, principally depend on the design of information systems and of wider organisational systems.

Information system design and management decisions

The way that computerised information systems are designed significantly determines the impacts of corruption. This design, in turn, depends on management design decisions. In Case 1, for example, it was a management decision that led to automation of clerical procedures and, therefore, to the removal of one opportunity for corruption. On the other hand, a management decision was taken to avoid computerising the station managers' allocation of emergency and VIP places.

To some extent, this latter design decision was part of the process of getting computerisation accepted: it was only able to proceed once the decision had been made that computerisation would not threaten these stakeholders' control and private incomes. Indeed, by removing sources of competition for corrupt earnings from the clerical staff, computerisation potentially offered an opportunity for station managers' incomes to be increased.

Other information system components will also affect the impacts of corruption. For example, the design of work processes will play a role. In Case 5, the presence of IT is largely irrelevant: the department could have made its manual records publicly accessible, which would have led to a similar result. What mattered was a management decision about the wider re-design of processes that changed the way information flowed in the organisation. Similarly, in Case 2, computerisation had little to do with the removal of ghost workers or claimants and the consequent (temporary) removal of corruption. This required the introduction of a process of physical checks, as was done both before and after computerisation.

Thus, it is management decisions about the design of an information system that shape the ultimate impacts. These decisions and designs do not always adhere to the Panoptic vision, with the consequent implications for corruption control.

Finally, there are other, wider systems components that play a role. For instance, the people involved must have some motivation to act corruptly. In part, this depends on fear of detection (which computers may affect), but in the main motivation relates to the wider context, as discussed below. Managers, and others charged with guarding against corruption, must also themselves have the skills, motivation, authority, and means to detect and act against corrupt activities. In part, this too depends on wider structures, strategies, and culture.

Organisational and environmental factors

Leaving aside the 'corruption of opportunity', such as that which arose in the payroll case, two particular types of corruption can be distinguished. 'Corruption of necessity' is practised by poorly-paid, low-level staff. Their incomes do not meet the many demands placed upon them, and they must find ways to supplement them. Computerised information systems may be designed to suppress some of their activities. However, these new systems will not extinguish the underlying motivation for additional income, because this arises from a wider context. Thus, corruption is almost bound to re-emerge, as it did with the ticket touts in Case 1. The Panoptic vision is a poor guide to this reality because IT cannot (yet) monitor all activities of all staff.

Alternatively, there is the 'corruption of greed' practised by senior staff. They have enough income to live on, but want and get more, because they are in a position to do so, and because it is seen as a natural activity for those in power. Given the power of these staff to determine their working environment, computerised information systems are unlikely to be allowed to have much impact unless imposed by a very strong external agency. Such staff will, therefore, remain aloof from any Panoptic gaze, exposing a further limitation of the vision as a guide to action.

In all cases, it can be seen that corruption arises from a combination of two sets of factors: the micro-level (the individual, his/her circumstances, needs, skills, access, confidence, and autonomy) and the macro-level (organisational and national management systems, politics, and culture). As we have seen, management decisions about computerised information systems may affect skills, access, confidence, and autonomy. However, they are most unlikely to affect the personal or environmental drivers behind corruption. Hence, the Panoptic ideal of corruption controlled by IT is, therefore, flawed.

To put this in simplified terms, IT-based systems guided by the Panoptic vision affect symptoms of a corrupt system rather than causes. Corruption is a phenomenon rooted in the cultural, political, and economic circumstances of those involved. IT does little to affect these root causes, remains limited in its surveillance potential, and so cannot eliminate corruption.

Development managers require a more holistic vision of corruption control to supersede the Panoptic vision. This would understand the roots of corruption, not just the symptoms. It would address corruption not through individual management techniques, but through strategies of institutional and contextual development. It would also see IT as having a potential role, but one which is limited and which forms only one small part of a much larger jigsaw.

Managing the introduction of IT in corrupt environments

Despite the preceding analysis of IT limitations, experience suggests development organisation staff often perceive that introducing IT is going to have a significant effect of reducing corruption. These perceptions will feed into the process of planning any new information system. The effect of these perceptions is likely to be particularly marked where a new computer system is being introduced in the presence of practices that are currently corrupt.

In one government's pensions office, for example, computerisation was roundly resisted. Many factors were at first seen to underlie the resistance including:

- fears of loss of jobs;
- fears that staff would not have the necessary skills;
- health and safety concerns.

What emerged during investigation, however, was that the main fear lay around the issue of corrupt incomes. Pensions staff had the power to deny claimants access to pension payments or to provide claimants with access to certain types of higher-income pension. The staff were using this power to extract bribes from pensionable claimants. They feared that computerisation would remove this power; hence their true reason for resistance.

Where resistance and corruption are linked in this way, there are three possible reactions that can be drawn from the case-studies above:

- if the computerised system will not have an effect, make this (subtly) clear;
- if the computerised system will affect corruption and the stakeholders are not that powerful, then 'tough it out', i.e. push on in the likelihood that resistance can be overcome;
- if the computerised system will affect corruption and the stakeholders are powerful, change the design plans so that the key corrupt processes are not computerised or are not exposed to monitoring by IT.

'Toughing it out' can also be tried in the last case, and this would seem to be the morally-correct route to take. However, it will greatly increase resistance to IT and the risks of information system failure.

Whatever the reaction, it is clear that the link between IT and corruption will have to be recognised in the planning of some information systems. This link must also be teased out as a component of resistance to computerisation.

References

Anechiarico, F. and J. B. Jacobs (1994) 'Visions of corruption control and the evolution of American public administration', *Public Administration Review* 54(5): 465–73.

Davies, C. J. (1987) 'Controlling administrative corruption', *Planning and Administration* 2: 62–66.

Klitgaard, R. (1984) 'Managing the fight against corruption: a case study', *Public Administration and Development* 4: 77–98.

Ramasoota, P. (1998) 'Information technology and bureaucratic surveillance', *Information Technology for Development* 8(1): 51–64.

Roszak, T. (1994) *The Cult of Information*, Los Angeles: University of California Press.

Sparrow, M. K. (1992) 'Informing enforcement', *Informatisation and the Public Sector* 2(3): 197–212.

Petty corruption and development

Stephen P. Riley

The Connaught Hospital is the main hospital, indeed the only real hospital, in Freetown, Sierra Leone's capital city. An inscription on the oldest part of the building reads: 'Royal Hospital and Asylum for Africans. Freed from Slavery by British Valour and Philanthropy, AD 1817.' Leaving aside the irony of the inscription, in modern times, in that run-down hospital, hard-pressed, irregularly and poorly paid nurses demand bribes before they will feed or give injections and medication to patients.

The bribes paid in Freetown's hospital are an example of the petty corruption which is often pervasive in poor societies. It involves small sums of money or favours. It benefits the holders of junior positions in the public services. Petty corruption is a common problem where public officials have considerable discretion in their dealings with citizens, and little accountability.

This form of corruption is not, of course, confined to poorer societies, as recent scandals in western Europe — in London's Metropolitan Police, for example — demonstrate (Naim 1995; *The Times* 1998). Nevertheless, petty corruption can be particularly pervasive and damaging for the poorest in poorer societies. In the former Zaire, corrupt payments were necessary to enrol children in schools, to visit public health clinics, to get licences and permits. Zairians developed an elaborate terminology to describe it: 'beans for the children, a little something, an encouragement, an envelope, something to tie the two ends with, to deal, to come to an understanding, to take care of me, to pay the beer, to short-circuit, to see clearly, to be lenient or comprehensive, to put things in place, to find a Zairian solution' (Gould 1980).

Petty, incidental, or low-level corruption is a difficult, complex, morally ambiguous, and intractable issue. Workers in low or irregularly paid positions may have to resort to corrupt behaviour in order to feed their families. Greed, obligation to family, other cultural factors, lax administrative procedures in a post-colonial setting, and opportunity: all contribute to petty corruption.

But petty corruption is not an isolated difficulty that can be solved by a 'quick-fix' solution of a smaller, higher paid and more regulated or more professional workforce (*The Economist* 1997). It is linked to higher level systematic and systemic forms of corruption. Mrs Imelda Marcos, 'First Lady' of the Philippines until 1986, has finally admitted that there is at least US$ 800 million salted away in Swiss bank accounts (Dougary 1998). Estimates of former President Suharto's family wealth range from US$5 billion to US$30 billion — or about one-seventh of the entire economy before Indonesia's economic collapse and political crisis (Cornwell 1998).

Visible high-level corruption encourages petty corruption. As one Turkish saying has it: 'A fish rots from the head first'. Mobutu Sese Seko, Zaire's former President, also once described his state bureaucracy as 'one vast marketplace': everything was for sale for a corrupt payment, with Mobutu leading by example.

How serious is petty corruption?

Some observers, therefore, argue that we should concentrate on reducing high-level, or grand corruption. Petty corruption is deemed trivial. It doesn't do much long-term harm to economic development. Academic economists writing in the 1960s claimed it could actually speed up the state bureaucracy and have a 'humanising' effect upon relations between public officials and citizens.

I would suggest, however, we should judge petty corruption from the point of view of the poorest people in poor countries.

If you are a slum-dweller in India, you have to pay more, more often, than does the general population (Paul and Shan 1997). In Bangalore, 33 per cent of slum dwellers had to pay a bribe averaging Rs 850 (about £13 compared to the average Indian income of £2.30 a day).

Petty corruption in Ecuador is tied to some of the state's political dramas, including the popular uprising against the regime of Abdala Bucaram in February 1997. Corruption affected public works, reduced the adequacy of service provision, and politicised justice. Electricity 'black-outs' of up to eight hours a day were a product of corruption (Larrea-Santos 1997).

In Tanzania, a public service delivery survey found that petty corruption was widespread in the police, judiciary, and revenue services (PCC/EDI l996). Extra payments to service workers were common if not universal: 35 per cent in the case of the police, for example. The Tanzanian respondents voiced anger and frustration at having to give petty bribes, and argued strongly that it denied justice, disadvantaged the poor, destroyed local economies, and divided communities. The Commission held public hearings across Tanzania during 1996 and actively investigated all complaints.

The following examples, taken from the Executive Summary of the Commission's report, summarise its findings regarding petty or low-level corruption (PCC/EDI 1996:1–4):

- Bribes are demanded and paid to register children in schools and to pass examinations. In addition, teachers give bribes in order to get promoted or transferred.

- Patients pay bribes in hospital to get treatment, be allocated a bed, or operated upon.

- Policemen get bribes to protect criminals and to arrest the innocent. Traffic policemen accept bribes to forget traffic offences, and immigration officers accept bribes to issue passports, visas, and residence permits to foreigners. Prison warders solicit bribes to give prisoners favourable treatment.

- Income Tax Department officials accept bribes to alter tax assessments. Ministry officials demand bribes to authorise payments. Auditors demand bribes to conceal financial discrepancies in accounts. Retired people are forced to offer bribes to obtain their pensions.

- In the judicial services, Court Clerks demand bribes to open, process or hide files. Magistrates accept bribes to reduce penalties, withdraw charges or give bail.

- In the Lands and Natural Resources Departments, officials demand bribes when surveying or allocating plots of land. They demand bribes to allow businessmen to fell more trees than allocated, and to let off poachers.

- Water Department employees demand bribes to connect new applicants and to show favouritism when there are water shortages.

- Works Department employees receive bribes for showing favouritism in awarding tenders and concealing the weaknesses of contractors. Telephone operators receive bribes for allowing businessmen to make calls without charge, or are charged to the government.

- Labour Department officers receive bribes to reinstate dismissed workers. Foreigners give bribes to obtain work permits.

- Journalists accept bribes to conceal incriminating information and to glorify individuals.

- Local Government officials receive bribes during staff recruitment, promotions procedures, and the allocation of tenders and permits.

Petty corruption is obviously not petty to those who experience it. Far from humanising relationships between citizens and officials, petty corruption is often profoundly alienating. The poorest don't get the public services — such as health care — they desperately need. There are delays, or bias, in service provision. Richer citizens will be advantaged. Poorer people may have far fewer expectations of the state, and may opt out or avoid using its services.

It is a 'Robin Hood in reverse' phenomenon: instead of robbing the rich to give to the poor, the relatively rich public officials and others gain, while the losers are often the very poor and marginalised living on the periphery of society. Petty corruption is inegalitarian and redistributive. It reinforces the current unequal distribution of opportunities and undermines basic human rights.

Reducing petty corruption

How can petty corruption be reduced or minimised? I would argue that you have to mainstream the control of corruption as part of a strategy to reduce or eliminate poverty. There is a clear link between corruption and poverty, although some have until recently shied away from addressing the issue because it is seen as too politically sensitive, too difficult to deal with, or a product of differing cultures and traditions. I recently tried to interest a British NGO in this issue but was told 'we're interested in poverty', not corruption. But in order to reduce poverty, you have to be interested in corruption, particularly petty corruption, which afflicts the poorest most immediately and most directly.

Many international organisations argue that it is important to reduce the centralised power and extractive nature of the state, and of the state's employees, who are a principal cause of petty corruption. This is exceptionally difficult to do. There are many suggested solutions: economically liberalising, democratising, decentralising, reducing the discretion of officials, and encouraging popular participation, particularly by those on the political margins of society, such as women.

It is also argued that the solution lies in a strong or stronger civil society, or in increasing the autonomy, strength, and competence of professional groups, such as lawyers, accountants, and investigative journalists, who can create the means to empower citizens, spread information, create scandals, and more easily expose petty corruption.

However, increasing literacy, and especially political literacy, is the key strategy to reducing petty corruption in poor countries. Poor citizens need to know their rights and know what is wrong. One of the conclusions of the 1996 Presidential Commission on Corruption in Tanzania was that it was important to remind or educate citizens to complain about corruption and to revive or create a public ethic of honesty, impartiality, and competence. A 'whistle-blowing' ethos was needed.

Political literacy should be supplemented by organisation and collective awareness of the poor in both rural and urban contexts. Many have pointed to the examples of micro-credit schemes, such as the Grameen Bank, and environmental movements, which give voice and collective strength to small or larger groups and provide an avenue to achieve positive change. These and similar movements, such as the Public Affairs Committee (PAC), which is active in Mumbai and several Indian states, can have the by-product of improving public integrity by spreading knowledge and holding public officials to account. The PAC conducts service-delivery surveys and generates public awareness of public integrity issues.

Corruption is often the subject of jokes, rumours, and scandals. But having to make a corrupt payment is not much of a joke if you're living on less than US$1 a day. Reducing the damaging impact of petty corruption ought to be central to improving life chances, eliminating poverty, and reclaiming the public realm for the poorest.

References

Cornwell, R. (1998) 'The secretive ruler who turned his country into a family business', *The Independent,* 15 May 1998.

Dougary, G. (1998) 'The dictator's dictator', *The Times Magazine,* 9 May 1998.

The Economist (1997) 'Reasons to be venal', 16 August 1997.

Gould, D. J. (1980) *Bureaucratic Corruption and Underdevelopment in the Third World: the Case of Zaire,* New York: Praeger.

Larrea-Santos, R. (1997) 'The Experience of Ecuador', paper at the Conference on Corruption and Integrity Improvement Initiatives in the Context of Developing Economies', UNDP / OECD Development Centre, Paris, 24–25 October 1997.

Naim, M. (1995) 'The corruption eruption', *The Brown Journal of World Affairs* 2(2): 245–261.

Paul, S. and M. Shan (1997) 'Corruption in public service delivery', in S. Guhan and S. Paul (eds.) *Corruption in India: Agenda for Action,* New Delhi: Vision Books.

PCC/EDI (1996) *Service Delivery Survey: Corruption in the Police, Judiciary, Revenue and Lands Services,* Dar es Salaam: Presidential Commission on Corruption, Government of Tanzania/Economic Development Institute, World Bank.

The Times (1998) 'Corruption crusade running out of time in the Metropolitan Police', *The Times,* 16 May 1998.

The need for reliable systems: gendered work in Oxfam's Uganda programme

Lina Payne and Ines Smyth

Introduction

Despite the familiarity of gender as a development issue, it is still not always apparent that bringing a gender perspective into development interventions means fostering fundamental social change.

This paper looks at the findings of a Gender Review of Oxfam GB's programme in Uganda.[1] The Review found that the work directed towards integrating gender relied on a conventional approach which could not effectively bring about change. This, and other limitations of the programme, were the result of a lack of appropriate and reliable systems.

Oxfam GB's effort to place gender concerns at the core of its management practices is widely recognised. This has been attempted through the creation of a specialised team of advisers, the formulation of a Gender Policy, and the development of implementation strategies. The Gender Policy recognises the links between poverty and gender relations. Country offices are given the freedom to interpret and adapt this to their own contexts. However, results remain chequered across the organisation and among its local counterparts, with different impacts being achieved in different regions, countries, and sectors. This is, to a great extent, because the Policy is not supported by a more systematic and binding approach to planning, monitoring, and evaluating gender-sensitive work.

Background

The Review was initiated by the Uganda Office to aid the implementation of institutional changes, namely the recent emphasis on advocacy work (in particular on land and debt issues) and, at the international level, the shift towards more decentralised regional programmes. The aim was not to evaluate the impact of the programme work on gender relations, but to learn what approaches had been adopted in theory and in practice, and how these could be improved.

The Review was carried out in two main stages: a desk review in the UK, followed by field work. In Uganda, the team consisted of two people from the Country Office and two from Oxfam headquarters. The process included discussions and workshops with staff, local counterparts, and representatives of other organisations. A visit was also made to the refugee settlement of Imvepi where Oxfam has carried out operational work.

The Uganda programme covers several activities. A range of local NGOs are funded, in the areas of community-based health care, disability, and food security. Oxfam has also initiated operational programmes with agro-pastoralists in Karamoja, and a long-term development programme in Kitgum district, although activities in both areas are constrained by ongoing security problems. The Office has also been running a large settlement programme for Sudanese refugees in Arua District (north Uganda) since 1994.

Advocacy work has expanded greatly over the past four years, with significant demands on staff time. There have been important achievements, most notably on the issue of debt relief and structural adjustment policies. Oxfam has also worked on land issues, where it has supported the Uganda Land Alliance, which lobbies for legal reforms.

Initially, the Uganda programme followed a conventional approach to gender concerns, 'targeting' women, in particular the satisfaction of their immediate daily needs. A change in emphasis came after 1992. This meant moving away from small women-only projects, and in theory towards appropriate strategies that would be the outcome of an in-depth social, and thus gendered, analysis. In 1994, the decision was taken to eliminate the post of the Gender and Development Programme Officer (GADPO), which had been in place since October 1988, because it was felt that the position risked exonerating other staff members from taking responsibility to address gender concerns. In reality, this decision also resulted in the loss of opportunities for proactive interventions, and also of safeguards against gender-blind or insensitive work.

Managing change

The Review found a number of interrelated problems: poor understanding of key concepts; unwillingness to challenge what were defined as traditional roles and attitudes; the deployment of *ad hoc* initiatives; and the failure to interact with a broader constituency. At the root of these was the absence of procedures through which understanding, performance, and outcomes could be planned systematically, and evaluated.

For instance, while staff were familiar with notions of gender as social relations, and had a good grasp of 'gender language', this understanding remained at an extremely broad and abstract level. In some cases, Oxfam's local counterpart organisations still understood gender in an extremely out-dated sense, and referred to separate 'gender programmes', which were seen as 'the soft parts' (in the words of the representative of one of these) of otherwise more serious activities.

Poor understanding, accompanied by lack of confidence, led staff and partners to take a defensive stance, based on an expressed concern that 'culture' would cause negative reactions from communities (especially men) to any explicit attempts at confronting gender inequalities. For example, Oxfam's approach to the land reform issue ignored the different implications for women and men, in the belief that explicit advocacy on women's access to land, for example, would alienate male supporters and hence be divisive. This preoccupation with an unspecified notion of culture was never addressed or properly managed, and as a result, it has led to pursuing activities that are intended not to challenge dominant gender norms and practices. For example, the continued support to many local groups and organisations for loans and credit activities to women, despite their widespread and long-term bad performance, or to activities which assume that gender concerns are being addressed simply on the basis of having a numerical equality in the representation of women in committees and groups.

While a preoccupation with safeguarding the cultural integrity of local communities is commendable and sometimes strategically advisable, it should not become a constant excuse for tame approaches that relegate women to stereotypical roles, or that promote gender awareness simply as a means to sustainable development. These may even be counter-productive in creating the false impression that 'gender issues have been addressed'.

In addition, Oxfam has failed to interact with the broader environment of organisations (both national and region-wide) that are engaged in gender-related activities. In other words, it failed to explore the opportunities for mutual support, information exchange, and lobbying, offered by the growing women's movement in the country. Very often, this has been the outcome of management decisions not to engage with particular organisations on the basis of a fairly vague and limited idea of what they stood for or could offer. For example, Oxfam Uganda kept at arm's length the government's Ministry of Gender and Community Development, because it perceived it as 'focusing on training and workshops and limited practical work'. In fact, like many similar organisations, the Ministry is a complex and multi-layered body, which includes many capable and creative people with whom fruitful exchanges are possible.

Integrating a gender perspective in the programme relied on *ad hoc* approaches, often based on a single initiative or activity. Furthermore, gender-based initiatives had been left to chance, and were overly dependent on individual personalities. For example, a major shift in the management of the refugee camp in Arua, which significantly improved the representation of refugee women, was the unplanned outcome of a short-term secondment.

Gender considerations were, instead, constantly treated as 'add-ons' to the main part of programmes or projects, both by staff and local counterparts. How this contributes to minimising the value of gender issues is acutely illustrated by the claim of one senior manager that insecurity and time pressures had prevented the programme from looking 'at the finer details, such as incorporating gender'.

At the core of all these problems, lies the absence of reliable systems and binding procedures to support and monitor how work of this type is identified, planned and executed, what technical and other support is needed to ensure it effectiveness, and whether any impact can be established.

This was most evident among Oxfam's local counterparts, with whom relations had never entailed stringent reporting requirements that featured gender as a criterion. There had been no demands for accountability on the basis of established and agreed systems, even though some of the Ugandan counterparts felt that, on gender in particular, this would have been a helpful way of monitoring their own progress and of receiving support.

This was mirrored more generally by a lack of support, either to local organisations, or to Oxfam staff in operational programmes, for developing social analysis and in building practices emanating from it, in accessing information, and in communicating appropriate messages to communities. A key mechanism that could have been in place would have been the presence of an individual or working unit with responsibilities for gender issues.

It is not only the effectiveness and reliability of the systems in place that determine how change is managed, but also the sensitivity with which mechanisms are employed. The Review found that in many instances senior managers had demonstrated scant regard for the different needs of male and female staff, especially those working in the difficult circumstances of operational programmes. For example, while the harsh and insecure living conditions were inevitably not conducive to bringing in families, there was little attention given to compensating staff for this. This also acted as a disincentive — discouraging female staff from applying for or remaining in such positions. The Review also found that Oxfam had made little effort to monitor the stress and strains that are inevitable in situations of insecurity.

Conclusions

The obvious solution suggested by the Review was to develop a clear and binding strategy. This would contain a statement of the broad goal of the type of social change that the Uganda programme is trying to achieve, integrating gender concerns. It would also contain a detailed outline of mechanisms for monitoring and evaluation, for external support to local counterparts, for capacity-building among staff, and for interaction with women's organisations and other relevant bodies. Putting such mechanisms in place would entail the necessary leadership from senior management at all levels, as well as financial commitments. It should also entail the appointment of a person or advisory group leading on gender, to ensure a systematic and reliable approach.

At another level, the Review pointed to the need to take a more political approach to gender concerns. Oxfam GB's known stance on rights would offer it the ideal point of entry to participate in public debates, with a clear and progressive voice on gender issues, supportive of organisations and individuals more hampered by political and other constraints. Networking, and a stronger gender emphasis in its advocacy work, would be practical ways in which this could be realised. This kind of innovative approach can only be adopted if the organisation is prepared to recognise and grasp opportunities as they present themselves, and to confront possible risks.

Notes

1 There are several affiliates to Oxfam International. Oxfam GB, previously known as Oxfam (UK and Ireland), is the British member.

Domestic violence, deportation, and women's resistance: notes on managing inter-sectionality

Purna Sen

Introduction

Southall Black Sisters (SBS) s a small women's organisation in London which combines campaigning, lobbying, activism, and casework. We have worked for over 15 years on issues of relevance to the (predominantly) Asian women who come to seek advice, support, and counselling, most commonly on domestic violence and the associated practical difficulties of ensuring housing, money, and safety. Of course, there are also issues relating to emotional distress, fear, and trauma with which abused women and their children have to deal. However, for many Asian women this constellation of problems is not the full story — the British state and the women's families (both in the UK and in the sub-continent) too often act in ways which restrict the choices available to abused women, continue to threaten their safety, or force the women out of the UK, back to their country of origin, against their will.

SBS is intolerant of domestic violence and the conditions in which it thrives. We challenge and seek to change the context and experience of abuse, including at the hands of the state which can, and does, deport women facing domestic violence. Our work cuts directly across a number of social cleavages — those of race, gender, and poverty — and we seek to increase the influence women can assert over their own lives, partly through changing the conditions which give rise to those deprivations. We now handle an average of about 1,000 enquiries per year — the majority of which concern domestic violence, sexual abuse, family problems (such as young girls being forced into marriage), and immigration difficulties. Our staff speak a number of south Asian languages and are thereby accessible to women who do not speak English and who have been disenfranchised from other services. Our advice always prioritises safety for the women and children with whom we work, and this brings us into conflict with organisations with other priorities (discussed below).

We engage in deliberate actions for change in individual cases and in the contemporary UK policy context. Over the 19 years of SBS' existence, our casework has provided the anchor for our lobbying and campaigning work: the problems faced by the women who seek our help illustrate failings in mainstream services, policies, and legal provisions. Our work for social change includes challenges to:

- the cultural climate in which women are systematically denied control of their own lives, especially through the endemic practices of violence against women;
- the construction and delivery of services to abused women which are poorly geared to the needs of Asian women, particularly those with little or no English;
- the legal and policy context (at local and national levels) which undermines the ability of Asian women to resist violence and take control of their lives.

Many of our clients who leave their husbands find themselves plunged into poverty. Those who do leave home become economically responsible for themselves and their children, although they may have been dependent on their husbands, families, or in-laws. Employment opportunities are few, especially for women who speak little English and have childcare constraints. Many of our clients find paid work in a twilight zone, untouched by employment legislation and protection, similar to women in informal sector activity elsewhere in the world.

UK immigration rules contain a restriction (the 'one year rule') on incoming spouses whereby residency status is dependent upon the marriage lasting at least one year. It means that the incoming spouse is liable to deportation if the marriage does not last for the specified year and effectively ties women to husbands, no matter how good or bad the relationship. Further, during the 12-month period the incoming spouse is denied access to state welfare provisions — such as housing benefit, the means by which women fund their stay in safe houses (refuges) if fleeing domestic violence.

SBS works in many ways, including casework, lobbying, campaigning, policy work, publications, and public speaking. Our casework includes giving advice, counselling, making clients aware of the possible consequences of certain decisions, arranging alternative safe accommodation, finding appropriate legal counsel, and supporting them through legal proceedings. Legal cases commonly relate to obtaining injunctions (for example, to prevent violent men from harassing their wives), child custody arrangements, and divorce. However, our casework can also take us into pioneering areas. For example, in March 1998 one of our clients won a case against her husband for marital rape (the first by an Asian woman). She also took her in-laws to court for false imprisonment and actual bodily harm and won her case. While this client's success is significant, she now has to fight the British state which seeks to deport her as she is caught by the one-year rule. We continue to support her in fighting this injustice by state agencies. This is an illustration of the way in which our casework is the basis for, and link to, our campaigning work.

The 'community' and the state

It is rarely easy for women to speak out about domestic violence, no matter who they are. Quite apart from their own (perhaps conflicting) emotions, they may face disbelief or even disapproval from those whom they tell about the violence. For black and ethnic minority communities in the West there are a number of particular pressures which may be brought to bear upon women — most commonly the potential for internal criticism to be used to strengthen racist stereotypes or actions against their communities (see, for example, Mama 1989; Bryan et al. 1988). These dangers have been constructed as constraints to action and discussion, both against individual women and against organisations — such as Southall Black Sisters. The construction of knowledge on racial oppression has been allowed to contest the construction of knowledge of gender oppression, and means that only those voices and issues which are not critical of the community are sanctioned for public discourse. This allows male 'community leaders' successfully to impose an agenda of race over one of gender (see Sahgal and Yuval-Davis 1992; Trivedi 1984); and some black women themselves have declined to expose 'their men' to further harassment from racist institutions such as the police (Mama 1989; Bryan et al. 1988). Isolated and abused women are denied the first step towards seeking help — speaking about abuse. The feminist imperative to 'break the silence' is at odds with the minority community imperative to maintain a silence.

SBS has refused to be silenced on issues of gender, male power, and violence within the Asian community and on discriminatory actions of the state. This has brought considerable antagonism from within the 'community'. We have been accused of wrecking the fabric of Asian culture, and our funding has been threatened because of the nature of our work (Southall Black Sisters 1994a; Sahgal and Yuval-Davis 1992). SBS is known in certain circles as 'home-wreckers' , a nervous reading of our efforts to support abused women, including their decisions to leave home. Men escape censure for their actions: how sad and significant it is that the men (and their families) who abuse women are not named as home-wreckers — a title of which they are undoubtedly worthy. Nor are violent husbands commonly subjected to calls to protect the community image in the context of racism — if men were to stop using domestic violence, this would both strengthen their own relationships and be a step towards reducing racist-inspired criticisms of the community.

Our campaigning and lobbying work arises from the casework we do — both in terms of supporting individual clients, and in terms of seeking policy change. We have run a campaign against the one-year rule which has included commissioned research — it found 512 women caught in this situation in 1995–6 (Southall Black Sisters 1997) — and we have given evidence to parliamentary investigations and lobbied politicians. We have had to educate politicians about domestic violence and the particular impact on Asian women both in terms of cultural context and in the immigration legislation. The current government recently faced questioning in parliament on the need to review and change this law. In his reply the Immigration Minister acknowledged SBS' campaigning efforts:

> I pay tribute to the work of SBS who brought this matter to the attention of Ministers and the House.... The evidence given by SBS was described by the then Minister — and I endorse the description — as moving and poignant...I have worked closely with SBS to see how we can change the law ... (O'Brien 1998).

We expect an announcement soon on changes to the legislation, but we anticipate that these will not include the abolition for which we have pressed. We intend to encourage a range of organisations to monitor the impact of any changes; we will make shortcomings known to the government; and, we shall continue to press the government for abolition.

Zoora Shah

Campaigns may also be built around the need to gain support for an individual client. A current case involves Zoora Shah who is currently serving a life sentence for the murder of a man who exploited her sexually and economically for over twelve years, while he was married to and living with another woman. Having been brought to England to marry, Zoora suffered domestic violence from her husband and was later abandoned by him, along with three young children; another two children had died. She was illiterate, spoke no English, and found herself homeless and extremely poor. At this time of heightened vulnerability she was befriended by Azam, a man from the criminal underworld, who provided her shelter in return for sexual services. Destitute, Zoora felt she had no alternative and began to live in a house bought by Azam, for which she made the mortgage payments. Azam's sexual demands were relentless — sometimes he would demand sex four or five times in a day, sometimes he would take her to the cemetery where Zoora's children were buried and demand sex there. Zoora was not free of Azam's influence even when he was imprisoned for drugs offences — he sent former prisoners to her in the expectation of getting sex. As Zoora's children grew older Azam began to express his sexual interest in her daughters.

Zoora did try to get help during her years of abuse, including turning to Sher Azam — Azam's brother and then head of the Bradford Council of Mosques — but her appeal was unproductive and her ordeal continued. On one visit to Pakistan, Zoora obtained *neela thotha* (arsenic), which she was told would render Azam impotent, and brought it back to the UK. She used the poison in Azam's food and found relief from his sexual demands for a short period. Azam's interest in her daughters continued to distress Zoora and eventually she gave him a second dose of poison, which killed him. At her trial she said nothing of her history of abuse or of Azam's sexual interest in her daughters. She was sentenced to life imprisonment for murder, with a tariff (minimum period to be served) of 20 years. Zoora made contact with SBS from prison; we appointed a new legal team and over five years we pieced together her history of abuse and exploitation. In July 1997 Zoora won leave to appeal against her conviction for murder. Her appeal — that she was wrongly convicted for murder and her offence should be reduced to the lesser charge of manslaughter (which does not carry a mandatory life sentence) was heard, and dismissed, in April 1998: the judges did not believe Zoora's history of abuse.

Zoora's case exemplifies some of the difficulties discussed above. The nature of community dynamics and power relations severely limit the degree to which Pakistani women in Bradford are able to raise their voices, particularly in relation to the thorny issue of domestic violence. Discourses of shame and honour denied Zoora support within the community and severely limited her access to support elsewhere. The sexual nature of much of the abuse was deeply embarrassing for Zoora to discuss, but sexual matters are, anyway, beyond the limits of respectable discussion in her social milieu. This shows how effective is male power and control over what enjoys legitimacy as public discourse and what is denied that recognition. Failure to give public space to abuse serves to silence women's voices and to deny abused women recognition of their experiences and support to enable them to change their situation. The Appeal Court decision turned Zoora's reality upside-down by claiming that her relationships with men showed that she was not behaving as Asian women should, and that she thus had no shame left to salvage by remaining silent about domestic violence.

Intersections: challenging many fronts at once

SBS recognises that state and patriarchal systems interlock; and this makes our work difficult, as we have to unravel these without becoming simplistic or reinforcing gender/cultural stereotypes. We sometimes strike alliances in our work — with women's groups on gender issues and with anti-racist groups, for example, against deportations. However, alliances are not always straightforward, as a recent example in Zoora's case illustrates.

Leaflets about this case were sent to various groups for distribution and in all but one instance this was unproblematic. However, one group (a well known anti-racist organisation) refused to distribute any leaflets as they thought the literature fuelled racist stereotypes of Asian/Muslim/Pakistani communities. They wanted SBS to re-write some of the leaflet and remove the references to patriarchal forces within Zoora's community. This (predominantly white) organisation told Southall Black Sisters (a black group) that our leaflet strengthened racist understandings by saying that Zoora's culture is patriarchal. Their argument displays a lack of understanding both of the nature of minority women's oppression (especially in the intersection of race and gender inequality) and of the need strategically *to take on* multiplicity, rather than dealing with only one issue at a time. Their response subscribes to the silencing of women which patriarchal dynamics in all cultures seek to impose, and highlights the discomfort of strands of anti-racist thinking in dealing with oppression within minority communities as opposed to oppression from external sources.

The changes they asked for would have decontextualised Zoora's experiences and left us referring only to the inter-personal dynamics of a single relationship. SBS understands the nature of male violence — that it is institutionalised in community and social practices — and we seek legal recognition of the context in which Asian women experience and respond to domestic violence. Like women across the world, we strive to keep gender on the agenda alongside other forms of oppression (e.g. Jayawardena 1986) and do not subscribe to a linear approach. Parallels can be found with the 'poverty-first-gender-later' argument and the cultural relativism which de-legitimises challenges to gender oppression. In the UK context, the struggle is to maintain challenges to gender oppression alongside anti-racist struggles. Our history of, and commitment to, challenging both forms of oppression strengthens our work and brings tensions into partnerships with other organisations. SBS is not afraid to take on difficult cases (although we do so with care) and we work with both Muslim and Hindu women (as well as others); we take a clear stand against communalism and against abuses of male power in all communities. There is enough evidence on the widespread prevalence of domestic violence to put any community (not only Muslim or south Asian) to shame for institutionalised abuse of women.

Concluding thoughts

Unlike many other groups in the UK, SBS works against gender and racial oppression (including religious fundamentalism and communalism) and we operate at the level of the family, the community, and the state. There is the possibility and need for work with other groups on various aspects of this work, or on specific campaigns. However, our commitment to challenging the simultaneity of oppressions has brought tension (even conflict) into those alliances and partnerships, and ours is a constant struggle to raise and keep a focus on gender in the face of pressure to privilege cultural /religious identity.

I have sought to highlight three key strategies in our work. Firstly, maintaining a strong and dynamic link between our casework and the macro view of policy and social practices which impinge upon women's options in dealing with violence. This grounding facilitates informed and relevant work at the level of the individual, the family, the 'community', and the state, and shows a clear relationship from the individual to the macro level. Secondly, we maintain a view on the simultaneity of various forms of oppression, including gender or race/ethnicity relations, communalism, and state practices. Thirdly, working across these areas means that we can, and do, link up with a range of other organisations as appropriate to the specific work we are doing. However, both cooperation and tension can mark these relationships.

We continue to campaign and lobby for individual women and for policy changes which would benefit women. Sometimes we find our voices isolated, but we remain determined in our pursuit of justice for women in the UK. Perhaps our greatest strength is our knowledge that our work is both productive and necessary. The constant flow of cases with which we deal reminds us of the need to continue seeking the best possible conditions for south Asian women to be free from both racial and gendered oppression: it is our grounding in the daily lives of women from which our vision, strategies, and determination derive.

References

Bryan, B., S. Dadzie and S. Scafe (1988) *Heart of the Race: Black Women's Lives in Britain*, London: Virago.

Jayawardena, K. (1986) *Feminism and Nationalism in the Third World*, London: Zed Books.

Mama, A. (1989) *The Hidden Struggle: Statutory and Voluntary Sector Responses to Violence against Black Women in the Home*, London: London Race and Housing Research Unit.

O'Brien, M. (1998) Reply to Margaret Moran MP from Mike O'Brien, Parliamentary Under-Secretary of State for the Home Department, House of Commons Hansard Debates for 24 June 1998 (pt. 17).

Sahgal, G. and N. Yuval-Davis (1992) *Refusing Holy Orders: Women and Fundamentalism in Britain*, London: Virago.

Southall Black Sisters (1994a) *Domestic Violence And Asian Women: A Collection Of Reports And Briefings*, London: Southall Black Sisters.

Southall Black Sisters (1994b) *Against The Grain: A Celebration of Survival and Struggle 1979–1989*, London: Southall Black Sisters.

Southall Black Sisters (1997) *A Stark Choice: Domestic Violence or Deportation? Abolish the One Year Rule!*, London: Southall Black Sisters.

Trivedi, P. (1984) 'To deny our fullness: Asian women in the making of history', *Feminist Review* 17: 39–52.

A day in the life of a development manager

David Crawford, Michael Mambo,
Zainab Mdimi, Harriet Mkilya, Anna Mwambuzi,
Matthias Mwiko and Sekiete Sekasua, with
Dorcas Robinson

Introduction

What does development management mean to development managers on a daily basis? Seven such managers in an NGO in Tanzania were asked to write a diary of one day in their working life.[1] This paper presents extracts from these diaries. They are only snap-shots of a more complex picture. But whether presented as bullet points, descriptive narrative, or more personal reflections, they provide insights into the routines, challenges, and concerns which shape the working days of many managers.

Writing diaries can serve a number of purposes: from individual managers realising how they actually spend their time and using this as a tool for time management; to information-sharing and building under-standing within teams; to providing a collective memory or organisational record for future reference.

These managers particularly enjoyed the opportunity to read each others' diaries. They began to see, committed to paper, the issues which provide the substance of 'informal' thinking and talking; issues that rarely get written into reports or minutes of meetings. For them, the question then arose of what this might mean for the way they work and communicate with each other on a regular basis.

Clearly, even on the most 'operational' of days, these development managers are grappling with significant, and at times apparently overwhelming questions. As one manager pointed out, mostly these diaries reveal the endless stream of 'problems' which bombard you in your daily work: 'problems' which you have to filter and resolve in some way. Thus, most days of the development manager are about how managing feelings about the bigger picture, in the face of one's own limitations, at the same time as dealing with the day-to-day nitty-gritty.

Michael Mambo

One of my duties is to visit villages. On Friday, for example, I went with my colleagues to Usinge village. The journey took about four hours on the train (the road is not open at the moment).

On arriving in the village, as usual you are met by village officials. Always they want you to talk about *your* plans; that is what they want to hear. I try to change their expectations by explaining that we have the following areas to look at: meetings with the building committee to review a way forward *together*; with the village assembly to discuss, among other things, each one's role in the project; and with the Community Based Health Care committee (CBHC).

As usual, you discover that people want to know more about the organisation. They want you to talk in the village assembly. But what exactly do they want me to talk about? I thought that the Community Extension Worker (CEW) in the village would have done this. Am I not doing her job? My colleagues and I ...discuss this among ourselves...and decide it is not a problem as it was in our plan to meet the village assembly anyway.

Meeting with the CBHC committee was very interesting. About 18 people met, half of whom were women, which was quite unusual. The chairman opened the meeting in only two sentences: '...the meeting is opened and I welcome Mr Mambo to tell us what he has come with'. My first reaction is to think 'I don't live in Usinge, so what do I say?' All of a sudden I made up my mind and decided to talk. I said, 'this is an opportunity for us all to discuss what has happened to the plans you developed at your CBHC meeting last year. What do *you* want to talk about, based on the real situation in your village?' It was agreed, and our discussion went very well.

What else!

When you are in the village you also discover a lot. For example, a new doctor has been appointed and sent to the village. He is a Medical Assistant — a higher rank than the Rural Medical Aid (RMA) who managed the dispensary before. Good news. But he does not have accommodation. He wants an upgraded type of accommodation. Some villagers think he should stay anywhere but he is reluctant. All of a sudden you discover it is a problem and they want you to be part of it. They start asking you a lot of questions. But what do you say?

You go round the village and talk with some people. You discover that a lot of people in the village have malaria; some children are anaemic when they are brought to the dispensary. I go to the dispensary and find the Medical Assistant with a child who will only survive if it gets some units of blood. According to the Circular from the Ministry of Health, only District and Regional hospitals are allowed to give blood to patients, so the case is then referred to the District hospital. Now a problem arises. The child's mother does not understand why the Medical Assistant does not just give drugs. 'What kind of doctor is this?' she asks, 'People say that he is more qualified than an RMA'. The child's mother does not want to go to the hospital. Some people are saying it is because the transport is too expensive, and she is very poor because she is not married. They tried to persuade her, but the child passed away while we were in the village. Now people are talking: some are abusing the doctor; some are accusing the woman. Some come to you complaining, and they want you to comment and maybe 'deal with the doctor'. I end up smiling, as usual. I don't want to comment on anything. This leaves them surprised.

I left Usinge feeling quite frustrated. When you think about your work in your head you expect that when people in a village start to use the CBHC approach (problem analysis, dialogue and so on), the problems of anaemia, of relationships with the dispensary and so forth, will be dealt with through discussions about prevention and community action. But what I found in Usinge was the CBHC committee has not been active, and that there are new problems with the Medical Assistant. Now how do I deal with this?! During their discussions, the CBHC committee planned to make house-to-house visits to discuss malaria and clearing swamp areas, because child deaths have been increasing. I think that the CEW and the CBHC committee need more support, so I begin to plan more visits.

PS: Usinge is located about 210km from Tabora town, in the middle of the forest reserve. Villagers are kind and they offer accommodation, clearing a room for you. For god's sake, how are you going to deal with the mosquitoes? You realise that you didn't remember to bring your sleeping bag or bed net....

Sekiete Sekasua

Read book on methods of financing health care for one hour; held planning meeting for one hour to sort out the problem of the government Community Development Technician (CDT) for Usinge village, who was after the increase in government site allowances which the district government cannot afford to pay; went to Tanzania Telecommunications and Tenesco to clear office bills; half an hour on lunch break. Went to [the Regional] hospital to organise a training session about working in partnership on community health, for next week. This took one hour, and was followed by attending two cases for a co-worker who was in a training course. I joined the course and conducted a session about community games for improving communication skills while working with communities. This exercise took one and a half hours. I returned to the office to write this report and finalise the lesson notes for the planned training on partnership.

Anna Mwambuzi

Today I visited the Community Extension Worker (CEW) in Ufuluma Cluster. The villagers were breaking stones to make *kokoto* [aggregate] for the construction of a village primary school. The CEW was busy with the women in doing the same job, and others were carrying stones. So what I did is join those with hammers and start breaking stones. I talked with the CEW to see if she could arrange a meeting with the women in the afternoon.

At the meeting we discussed about how a woman can participate in the projects whilst it is the same woman who is needed in the family/home activities. Does the woman feel that she is overloaded instead of getting relief? How does she feel when she can discuss/participate in decision-making in front of her father/brother/husband and fellow women?

The women also said that they are very happy that their children will have a modern school, and this assures them that their children will get a good education, as competent teachers will be willing to come to the school as it is modern with good quality staff quarters. One woman said that 'one day, one of my daughters will be working as a doctor to the village dispensary which honourably was opened by the President, as she will pass her examinations because of the good quality classrooms'.

They discussed how they can find a market for their groundnuts. They agreed to make oil from the nuts, and use some in their daily cooking and sell the rest to their fellow villagers. The women asked if we can find a refinery machine to help. I told them that in town there is someone who sells different machines. I will go there and see if there any and then I will tell them how much it costs so they can decide/plan how to buy it.

I went to see the building committee chairman to talk/enquire about women's participation in the project. He said in fact women are the ones who initiated the school and well construction, and now every villager is benefiting.

I thanked the CEW, and came back to the office.

Matthias Mwiko

'Last year we had a problem in raising funds to pay local *fundis* [craftspeople] because we had poor crop yields from our fields' — a lament from a village chairperson. 'This year', she continued, 'there is too much rain which is not good to our crops either'. Another person can be heard complaining like this about rains — a truck was not able to ferry sand and rocks for a school project because it was very difficult to reach places where these materials are located. The story continued like this. 'These are national trunk roads and you are calling them water trenches — how unkind!' Anyway, let us stop these endless complaints and get our heads into our PRA and CBHC and Child-to-Child workshops.

Back to the office — where …it is no longer possible to come through the front, with the Singidan lake about to encroach on our office. What surprises people is that by late November there was no water in the lake and people from different corners of Singida District came to collect salt from the dried water.

But what is on my mind? The question is whether our approaches suit, and are appropriate to, such communities. Techniques and tools like PRA, CBHC etc might sound OK …but are they jargons that have nothing to do with actual needs of people? This El Nif Singhlights the level of development of the communities we are working with, in relation to their capacities and capabilities in handling issues. For example: 'Last year we had no rains, so we ended with poor harvests. This year we are in the same situation because of too much rain.' Most people have not been able to cope with the situation, unable to utilise the rain by growing something else instead of traditional crops. … But a few farmers were able to grow different crops and they are very proud of their performance, while the majority are blaming El Nieen able

On days like this (and there are many), I am left thinking, how is it possible to suit or meet community needs, and to be acceptable to them, at the same time as trying to retain reputation from outsiders such as donors? Or are we just using such communities for our own learning ...while poor villagers are left off helpless.... with a lot of semantic and sweeping statements. It was said by Jules Feiffer 'I used to think I was poor. Then they told me I was needy. Then they said it was self-defeating to think I was needy instead I was deprived. Then they said deprived had a bad image; I was really underprivileged. Then they said underprivileged was overused; I was disadvantaged. I still don't have a cent, but I have a great vocabulary'.

The list of catch-phrases includes participation, democratic process, working partnership, decentralisation. But does it end up with grassroots people with access to decision-making machinery ... or ... are they still more dictated to by the participatory facilitators? On a day like this you are faced with people's immediate problems, but have gone to conduct PRA. You talk about flexibility, but have to worry because your year's schedule must be modified because the roads are inaccessible!

Harriet Mkilya and Zainab Mdimi

We set out for the monitoring of Child-to-Child activities in the nine neighbouring primary schools of Kaselya ...and of course we got stuck twice due to the muddy roads. ... After two Child-to-Child workshops last year, the four schools responded with an action plan of activities ... which included rehabilitation and construction of pit latrines, growing shade trees in the playground and nutrition projects like growing vegetables. ...The last monitoring in December showed a good start to these activities. ...Then there were the holidays, and after these the roads were impassable until April.

What do you think we found? A promising progress of Child-to-Child activities? But alas! The El Nig shade trees in the playground and nutrition projects like growing vegetables. ...The last monitoring in December showed a good start to these activities. ..ng well, but in others people are just busy trying to maintain damaged houses. .... Village fund-raising for the projects is an issue until harvest time...

David Crawford

8.00   Arrive at office, say good morning to everyone, talk with Sek about break-in the night before last.

8.10   Straight to the Administration Manager's office to talk about reconciling the cash. I am trying to get her to make Friday a day for financial matters. She finds it difficult to package the week like this because she has a lot of work and the staff are constantly asking her about admin and money matters.

8.15   Start on SUN (accounting software).... Need to analyse SUN data to make an invoice for April to GiftAid.(2)

8.30   An entrepreneur from Urambo looking for GiftAid money to expand his business. He had been in Dar and 'a woman' told him that we would help. Our agreement with GiftAid is very clear. We only support community-based health and education projects. I think he has a good idea ...but have to tell him no...

10.00   Phone (Singida Programme Manager), talk about programme matters. ...It looks like his block making machine is working now ... Discuss again about working/training/capacity building with District government. It's hard to be optimistic about this, partly due to experience, partly due to cynicism...Why are we here?

10.30–11.00 Shoot the breeze with Farajala (mechanic). The Landrover won't be ready for Monday.

11.00   Need confirmation from GiftAid that they will fund Ifucha school project. (Last month I found out that they will not, as it was not in our original agreement — I also found out that the guy who said they would fund it has been sacked. The goalpost for me has moved again. Lesson learnt.) Phone the new GiftAid Technical Director. He tells me he never received the fax requesting funds. ...I was told to send it to his HQ as he was on leave. He tells me off for sending it there! I say sorry. I suggest that he send someone to help us prepare our new agreement as this will avoid misunderstanding in the future. He says he is coming at the end of May ... he will never come, of course, as Tabora is out of Mobitel range! I fear, not for the first time, that the GiftAid projects unit will soon implode anyway, and start to worry about funding.

11.30   Go shopping....

12.30–2.00 Make lunch, cake, talk business ideas, argue badly with my children in Mandinka.

2.15   Meeting with Sek and Mambo. They have produced a coherent training proposal with budget and well thought out training plan. Suggest this is definitely the way forward and that we have the makings of a training manual. I ask how they will know if their target group in the training will learn and translate it into their work. There is talk of supporting CBOs and supporting the national policy on participatory development. So I rephrase the question and link it to 'bite size projects', 'costing money' and 'who pays'. I tell them that in order to justify this kind of training to [funders] I need to be able to show 'it can work because....'. Also it needs to be finite, so vague notions of 'follow-up' are not good enough...

4.00 Chali has made some blocks with the new block-making machine. Nice ones too. Think about how this would affect our 'appropriate technology' policy...

4.15 Back into office. Neat piles of paper, articles etc (neat because the cleaning lady has been in and I have not) all over desk and shelves. No idea where to start, so don't. Realise I haven't been in my own office all week and this is Friday. Do something about it on Monday.

Notes

1 Health Projects Abroad, a British NGO which has programmes in two regions in Tanzania. It uses the Community Based Health Care (CBHC) approach to promoting community health and development. CBHC seeks to enable communities and groups within communities to undertake a continuous process of participatory problem analysis, dialogue, and resource mobilisation in the interest of taking action to improve community health. As part of this programme, the NGO also works with primary school teachers and pupils, extending Child-to-Child, an approach to developing health awareness among children, and to promoting learner-centred education more generally. This group of managers includes those employed full-time by HPA and those who are seconded to it from their government posts.

2 Pseudonym for a programme donor.

Funding preventive or curative care? The Assiut Burns Project

Norma Burnett

This case-study examines the achievements of a small Egyptian NGO, the Assiut Burns Project, and the problems it faces in becoming financially sustainable. Burns injuries, despite their prevalence in developing countries, are given low priority by governments and aid agencies alike, as medical care is expensive and the poor are unable to pay for treatment. Yet neglected burns produce crippling disfigurement and deformity which may leave men unemployed and women and children as social outcasts. Current development policy favours primary preventive health care, according curative care low priority even where this involves wider development issues. Assiut deals with issues central to development management, including:

- the right of the poor to basic health care;
- women's rights and access to health care;
- the integration of medical, preventive and social care;
- social and economic rehabilitation of the disabled;
- local capacity-building through:
  - appropriate research and training;
  - building links with other key providers, including the state.

This innovative programme faces problems in raising funds because the work rests on medical care which is unattractive to many donors who prefer low-cost preventive work, and refuse core costs, especially salaries, in the name of sustainability.

The Assiut Burns Project: a victim of funding policy?

Poverty and accidents

Throughout Upper Egypt, the poor are at high risk from burns and scalds. Domestic accidents are the major cause of injury for women and children. Women squat to cook, using badly designed Kerosene stoves placed on uneven dirt floors amid free-ranging goats, chickens, and children. Scalding is common when children or animals overturn large, unstable cooking pots, and ill-fitting wicks can cause the stove's fuel-tank to explode. Women and girls also wear long, inflammable dresses of synthetic fabric, cotton now being too expensive. Butagaz is gradually becoming affordable, and leaking cylinders cause dramatic accidents often injuring a whole family. Men are injured both in the home and at work in conditions which pay scant regard to health and safety. Finally, punishment and suicide by burning is prevalent throughout Egypt, with young women being the main victims.

Access to treatment

State medical care is theoretically free, but in practice patients must pay towards their treatment. Even so, chronic under-funding results in low standards of care. Doctors and, in particular, nurses receive nominal salaries which they supplement through 'tips' from patients. There are few drugs and little equipment, even basic items such as dressings, rubber gloves, sheets, and waterproof mattresses being in short supply.

The position is even worse for burns patients, who need scrupulous care. Most public hospitals offer only palliative care in grossly unhygienic conditions where infection is the norm. Difficult cases may be refused admission, or patients may be discharged early with suppurating wounds and left to die or survive as best they may. Despite the high burns injury rate, (over four cases per thousand per year), the Assiut University and District Hospitals are the only ones in Upper Egypt with specialised burns units; and they have just 46 beds to serve a population of over 15 million. The University Hospital, which has the best facilities, limits in-patient admissions to two days per week and takes only burns less than 24-hours old, to reduce infection rates.

Even these service standards are declining as government funding fails to keep pace with inflation and World Bank structural adjustment policy moves resources to the already large free-market sector. Given the poor facilities and the cost of treatment, it is hardly surprising that, although the immediate treatment of burns is vital, the poor commonly resort to folk remedies, or the pharmacist, going to hospital as a last resort. This combination of delay and poor quality care means the poor have a high risk of suffering permanent scarring and disability.

Disfigurement and disability

Neglected, infected burns fail to heal or accept grafts, which results in permanent disfigurement and painful scarring. Malnourishment increases the risk of infection. Only the specialist hospitals offer compressive dressings or grafting or any physiotherapy, yet without this muscles and skin contract resulting in major disability, including:

- necks sealed to the chest wall, so that the head cannot be raised;
- fingers sealed together and the hand contracted to a useless claw;
- arms sealed to the chest wall;
- lower leg contracture, making walking impossible.

Disability and disfigurement carry harsh consequences. Women, especially, may end up as social outcasts; divorced and denied custody of their children, or unable to marry in a society where this carries a heavy stigma. Those who die, and many do, may suffer a protracted and agonisingly painful death. It must be stressed that the disfigurement and deformity that result from poor treatment are avoidable and rare in most developed countries.

Good medical care is not simply curative, it *prevents* deformity. Furthermore, provided old injuries are caught within about ten years, then operations, grafting, proper dressings, and physiotherapy can restore some mobility to the disabled. Much of the Assiut's work involves the treatment of such neglected burns.

The Assiut Burns Project

The Assiut Burns Project (ABP), a small independent NGO, was set up in 1990 by two remarkable men as a direct humanitarian response to this unnecessary suffering. Phillipe Macchi, a Swiss national, regularly encountered burns victims while working as an administrator with a trachoma project in Upper Egypt. Unable to ignore their plight, he began taking individual children to the private clinic of Dr Mahmoud el Oteifi, a skilled plastic surgeon and burns specialist at Assiut University Hospital. The children were treated free or at nominal cost and funds were raised on an *ad hoc* basis, often from friends.

However, both men were acutely aware that this barely touched the sea of need. They developed a proposal for a Burns treatment centre for the poor, particularly women and children. Initial support came from Oxfam UK/I (now Oxfam GB), Médicins pour Tous les Hommes (MPTH), and a Swiss support group, Fondation en Faveur des Enfants Brulés, (FEB), founded by Phillipe's friends. MPTH and FEB continue to support the work.

The Project's formal charter stresses human rights:

> Access to medical treatment of a certain standard, and efficient rehabilitation, is the right of every human being. This right takes into account the whole person; not just physical needs, but also psychological, social and economic needs.

The programme operates from a cramped seven-bed unit in a converted flat in Assiut, a major provincial capital in Upper Egypt. The surrounding rural areas are some of the most impoverished in the country. They now treat over 800 patients a year in their own centre, and improve treatment for hundreds more through their collaborative work with Assiut University and District Hospitals, and charitable dispensaries run by Christian nuns in neighbouring rural areas. Sectarian strife is a fact of life in Upper Egypt, yet ABP employs both Christian and Muslim staff, and treats patients irrespective of religion. They operate with about 50 core staff, and need a budget of over £100,000 a year to cover general running costs.

More than a medical programme

The ABP has pioneered treatment which integrates medical, social, and community work. It has also developed innovative training courses and a successful programme of health education and accident prevention which is markedly reducing the incidence and severity of burns in the villages in which it is being piloted. The key elements of the ABP, which are almost unique in Egypt, are:

- high-quality surgery and nursing care plus compressive dressings, and physiotherapy to prevent scarring and contractures;
- protein supplements and protein-rich food for in-patients to ensure survival and good response to treatment;
- financial support through subsidised fees;

- social work support to help patients maintain lengthy and painful treatment programmes;

- rehabilitation work to help families and individuals cope with the consequences of burns injuries and, where possible, find jobs;

- social support groups and income-generating projects for the poorest and those rejected by their families;

- health education, both intensive in selected local villages, and mass through school programmes, stressing, 'Pour water on burns, and get treatment quickly';

- prevention programmes in selected villages to test out ways of reducing burns accidents ;

- collection of statistics from local hospitals and pharmacies on numbers of burns, causes, and mode of treatment (basic research);

- provision of basic and upgrading training for doctors, nurses, physiotherapists, dressers, social workers, health educators, and village outreach workers. Training is also offered to collaborating centres, including local hospitals and dispensaries;

- outreach work, providing training, personnel, and essential supplies (including dressings and food supplements) to support and upgrade the work of other centres, including government hospitals and charitable dispensaries.

It is difficult to encapsulate the achievements of this complex programme, which has broken new ground in almost every respect. The integration of social and medical work, and the support given to women, illustrate its quality.

Social support

The doctors were not initially convinced of the value of dealing with social and economic problems, but now recognise the importance of this work in helping patients regain the will to live and endure the long treatment. Social workers keep surgeons informed of the progress of patients which in turn motivates the surgical team. This holistic approach is at the heart of true Primary Health Care (PHC).

Social workers, who are trained by the centre, assess the family situation and ability to pay, and provide care, counselling, and practical support, from the patient's first contact with the programme. Two key elements of their work are:

- Counselling: Burns cause great physical and psychological trauma. Social support can re-kindle the will to live, without which treatment is ineffective. Reconciliation work with families is particularly valued, as it is virtually impossible to live a normal social life outside the family setting.

- Out-patient support: successful treatment is dependent on completion of out-patient programmes, which may involve over a year of painful dressings and physiotherapy. Many people are tempted to give up, depressed and frustrated at the slow progress. The social workers give practical support, for example through transport subsidies, and moral support through their sheer stubborn refusal to forget the patients and allow them to give up.

Helping women

Given the abject poverty in the region, the family acts as an economic unit; children work from an early age and women's work is essential. A disabled, disfigured woman is, in many cases, an unwanted burden, being of no economic use and unmarriageable. Men take the key decisions in the family and women are bound by strict traditions which limit their freedom of travel and association and right to work outside the home. Apart from giving them priority in admission, the ABP takes account of women's special needs many ways. For instance:

- attempted suicides, who are mostly young females, do not pay any fees;

- if, after persuasion, a family refuses to pay for a woman's treatment, the case is treated free;

- families may bring young girls or elderly women as 'willing' skin donors. In such cases, the centre refuses and tries to persuade healthy adult males to give skin;

- facial disfigurement, although not technically disabling, is regarded as such for females and given high priority;

- families may object to females travelling for follow-up treatment. The centre helps with costs and 'safe' arrangements, and may treat in the home if persuasion fails;

- the centre provides a temporary refuge for women who are rejected by their families, and counselling to promote re-conciliation, or to face the future outside the family if necessary;

- legal advice to help rejected women claim their rights to economic support and child custody;

- help with finding work and income-generation schemes, which also involve rebuilding social confidence;

- disfigured children, especially girls, find it hard to face their peers and continue at school. Priority is given to counselling these children and their families.

Funding: 'selling the programme'

Assiut has built a programme of integrated care which offers lessons not just for other burns programmes but for health work in general. Despite this success, the ABP now faces problems in securing future funding. Although it has attracted funding from several major international NGOs, these donors tend to see themselves as catalysts, giving grants for an initial period after which they expect the project to become 'financially self- sustainable'. As it comes to the end of this 'honeymoon' period, ABP faces a major problem, common to many health projects: How do you finance good health care for the poor, when the clients cannot cover the cost and the state is unwilling or unable to do so?

Currently, the ABP raises about seven per cent of its budget from fees, which are index-linked to inflation. But it can never hope to recover more than a small minority of the costs given the poverty of the clients and the nature of the treatment. Assiut uses the simplest techniques and has no specialist laboratories or intensive-care unit, but the costs of burns care are high. Even dressings and physiotherapy are expensive when treatment lasts for months. Two examples:

High-cost case: 35 per cent burned area costing £1,800 for 100 days in hospital + four operations + dressings + 72 out-patient physiotherapy sessions

Low-cost case: 16 per cent burned area, an old burn costing £115 for one day in hospital + dressings + 25 out-patient physiotherapy sessions.

International donors are driven by their own logic and development rhetoric, which pose a number of problems for projects such as Assiut. Firstly, many donors are unwilling to fund core running costs preferring to support capital costs which do not commit their future budgets. And secondly, there is a general focus upon PHC, which tends to exclude specialist medical care even when combined with social and educational objectives.

Selective funding

The ABP has a good record for obtaining funding for capital items which do not entail a long-term commitment. Covering core-costs, especially treatment costs and staff salaries, is much more difficult. Yet development depends on people, not just things, and Assiut's real achievement is to have built a team of skilled, committed, local staff. The Project has secured most of the costs of building and equipping a new centre, a formidable achievement for a small local group, but cannot go ahead without the ability to support staff salaries. For Phillipe this selective funding policy made no sense:

> I fought hard for percentage contributions instead of funds for
> special activities; we do not wish to sell little pieces of our work, but
> to find partners who will share with us in our care for the whole
> programme.

Primary Health Care (PHC)

Many NGOs give priority to PHC programmes, with the stress on low-cost, preventive care, health education, and outreach work, often using low-paid or volunteer labour. Only simple curative care is likely to be accepted as part of PHC. This means that many donors look at the Assiut project in simplistic terms, labelling the majority of its work as medical and curative simply because it deals with burns. They are happy to fund the village preventive work which is much cheaper and fits with their priorities. Phillipe wrote:

> since most of the organisations consider that prevention work is
> intelligent and curative stupid, I feared many times of having far too
> much for preventive work and no money at all for curative.

For Assiut, the integrated nature of the programme is crucial; springing from the right of the poor to proper care, not just health education. They believe that their preventive work is successful because it is part of a wider programme. Villagers accept the ABP community workers because they know and respect the project's work in providing the poor with good medical treatment. One key element in PHC, and one which donors readily support, is the idea of the poor defining their own priorities. There is little doubt that good curative treatment is a priority for the poor, as for all of us. Prevention is better than cure, but Utopia belongs to the future, while disease and accidents are a reality today. It is this reality which fuels Assiut's commitment to an integrated programme.

If donors could cast away their simplistic view of curative care, they would see that Assiut, with its complex web of research, health education, practical prevention work, training, medical, paramedical, social and economic support, directed at the family, not just the patient, is the very essence of quality PHC.

Assiut has been called an 'island of excellence', and in the eyes of donors who seek to measure impact in numbers and readily replicable projects, this is damning with faint praise. But quality is important too, and Assiut shows what can be done using basic techniques and giving local people the skills, motivation, and opportunity to deliver good care to the poor, something which is not possible within the state system at present. In Egypt, radical reform is on the agenda but is unlikely to yield positive results within this decade. In this context, the ABP should be seen as a beacon of light, to be tended until other beacons can be lit. Unfortunately, the fuel for this beacon is money, and if neither the state nor major donors will fund humanitarian care for the poor, then the prospect is truly bleak.

Postscript

At my first evaluation meeting with Assiut, I was briefed to express 'my' donor's policy that money should be directed towards preventive care and treatment of medium to mild burns. Representatives of FEB were shocked that any aid agency could suggest this. The arguments raged furiously, and there was much puzzlement over what this concept of 'development' was if it excluded the seriously ill. Then Phillipe was called away. On his return he said he had admitted a woman burned from the chest down and almost gangrenous, having been 'treated' for several weeks in a small hospital which had then discharged her when her money ran out. They had heard there were honest people in Assiut, and travelled 250 kilometres to reach help. I was asked if I would have refused her. My answer was 'No'. The view from the ground looks different.

Small enterprise opportunities in municipal solid waste management

John P. Grierson and Ato Brown

Waste is a resource in the wrong place at the wrong time.

Mustapha Tolba, former UNEP Executive Director

Servicing growing cities

Rapid urbanisation is a dramatic reality in most developing countries. Small towns are becoming cities, and big cities are getting bigger as growing and increasingly mobile populations crowd into urban areas. Expanding urban populations, with their ever greater needs and expectations, are fuelling a relentless growth in demand for more and better urban services; services that many municipalities cannot hope to provide in the current climate of stagnant municipal budgets and decreasing external support. The staff, equipment, and budgets — and more importantly, the systems and methodologies — needed to service growing cities are simply not available within the public sector (UMP/SDC/SKAT1996a). One of the most obvious manifestations of this reality is that small enterprises are moving in to fill the vacuum left by the contracting public sector capacity. These early and imperfect, yet innovative and successful, private sector initiatives have often prevented problems from becoming crises. But more importantly, they have demonstrated that private sector enterprises have an important role to play in meeting the demand for municipal services.

It is now broadly recognised that 'public-private partnerships' — that is, municipal authorities working together with private enterprises to fulfil public sector responsibilities for urban municipal services — can help meet the growing demand for these services. Waste collection and processing is but one area where there is clear evidence both of the benefits of private sector participation and of the need for closer cooperation between municipal authorities and private entrepreneurs (Bartone1995). This report looks at the progress to date of the component of an action-research initiative led by the Collaborative Group on Municipal Solid Waste Management in Low-income Countries that is developing best practice guidelines for expanding the involvement of micro- and small enterprises (MSE) in municipal solid waste management (MSWM).

The Collaborative Group on MSWM in Low-income Countries

This group is an informal international network encompassing multi-lateral agencies, including the UNCHS (Habitat), the World Bank, and the UNDP (working together as the Urban Management Programme), and WHO; bilateral agencies, including the Swiss Agency for Development and Cooperation (SDC) and Deutsche Gesellschaft für Technische Zusammenarbeit GmbH (GTZ); and a number of foundations, NGOs, research groups and institutions, and professional specialists in the field of MSWM. Its first meeting was held in April 1995 in Switzerland (UMP/SDC/SKAT1995), followed by a workshop held in Cairo in October 1996. The theme of this workshop was 'expanding enterprise involvement in MSMW', and participants were charged with the task of developing practical guidelines to support effective public-private partnerships.

Expanding enterprise involvement in MSMW

Public-private partnerships are a relatively new and innovative approach to municipal service provision, particularly in Africa. Documented experience is modest; relatively little is known about how the public and private sectors can work together effectively, or about how public-private partnerships will affect the evolution of public sector responsibilities. A very large part of the current private sector involvement in municipal services is the result of the private sector simply moving in to grasp the opportunities created by growing demand, a phenomenon readily apparent in the field of waste management. MSWM responsibilities are increasingly being abandoned to market forces, with informal, irregular, and even illegal enterprises often in the lead in taking advantage of these opportunities. This dramatic and imperfect process has served to demonstrate both the potential of the private sector to supply MSWM services and the need to co-opt and focus this potential through a greater degree of 'partnership' between the public and private sectors (Schübeler et al.1996). There is an emerging realisation that there is at hand the opportunity to move beyond merely allowing the private sector to 'rush in', towards working with the private sector in order to expand overall capacity to 'reach out'.

The private sector has the capacity to raise capital, to mobilise latent material and personnel resources, and to apply these quickly and efficiently to the market for MSWM services. The public sector has the opportunity — indeed, many argue, the responsibility — to attract and co-opt these capacities while continuing to provide the strategic direction, the policy framework, and the context of societal values that must stimulate and shape the growing market for MSWM services.

The nature of the need is clear and visible. Cities, municipalities, neighbourhoods, and squatter areas are being overwhelmed with waste. As Mustapha Tolba has succinctly implied: many of those who are idle or under-employed amid this waste could be productively employed in collecting, sorting, transporting, and processing it. The eyesore of ill-managed urban waste is but the tip of a well understood environmental iceberg: efficient and sustainable natural resource use, and acceptable standards of public health, are threatened by inadequate and inefficient municipal waste management.

The nature of the partnerships needed to address such problems and capture the attendant opportunities is much less clear. What, indeed, is a 'public sector-private sector partnership'? What are its characteristics and practical realities? What effect will these new relationships have on existing responsibilities? The urban management initiative reported on here, and the practical experiments of many municipalities worldwide, are seeking to clarify and document the answers to these difficult questions. While expert knowledge is admittedly still modest, there is a broad-based recognition of the need to determine best practice. A firm base has been established; statements of basic principles and useful practical guidelines are beginning to emerge in support of efforts to evolve effective 'partnerships'.

Public-private partnerships

Consensus and clarity should not, however, be taken for granted. Misunderstandings persist. One area of uncertainty is the effect on public sector responsibilities. It can be stated unequivocally that public-private partnerships are *not* about the abdication of public sector municipal responsibilities. Public sector responsibility cannot be abandoned or delegated. Because of the embedded social, environmental, and public health aspects, urban municipal services will remain the responsibility of the public sector. A growing array of 'means' are needed to reach an expanding array of 'ends'. Public-private partnerships are one of the means municipalities can use to expand their capacity to meet their expanding public sector responsibilities.

Three defining characteristics of public-private partnerships have emerged:

1 *synergy* (private sector capital, capacity and efficiency)
2 *combined with* public sector policy and administrative oversight in order to meet the
3 *public sector responsibility* to provide efficient, equitable, environmentally-sound municipal waste management services.[1]

Large and growing need, set within a wider context that emphasises economic adjustment and transition and greater environmental awareness, has resulted in a high degree of acceptance of the principle of public-private partnerships. This acceptance is not, however, matched by a similar degree of understanding of how and when to bring such partnerships to bear on MSWM issues. A much better understanding is needed of the institutional, financial, and environmental issues affecting private sector involvement in MSWM, and of the practical aspects of structuring and administering effective partnerships. There is a clear need to develop and make widely available the practical 'tools' that will be needed to build effective partnerships arrangements at the local level (UMP/SDC/SKAT 1996b).

Putting partnerships into practice

The types of enterprises that are likely to participate in MSWM partnerships are, for the most part, well known and readily available. In general, these will be businesses with common capacities and flexible resources that can be applied to waste collection, sorting, consolidation, transportation, recycling, processing, and re-use. Many of the new business opportunities that are emerging, particularly at the primary collection and sorting stages, offer little in the way of economies of scale, and hence favour small and micro-enterprises (Bartone 1995). Many of these enterprises are by nature labour-intensive and can be used to generate economic activity and employment in the neighbourhoods they serve. In many cases, MSWM partnerships will generate opportunities for community- and group-based small enterprises. MSWM partnerships can help improve overall economic efficiency by stimulating the business linkages that will result from the commercial relationships among the many enterprises that make up the private sector component of the MSWM chain.

The commercial mechanisms these partnerships will use are standard and well established; their strengths and weaknesses are clearly understood. Most MSWM partnerships will use only one or two of a limited range of basic commercial mechanisms, of which there are four that are used in one form or another for virtually all MSWM partnerships (adapted from Cointreau-Levine 1994):

1 *Contracting:* whereby a municipality awards a contract to one or more firms to provide services. Service contracts are used for waste collection, transportation, and landfill management.

2 *Concession:* whereby a municipality gives an enterprise the right to build and operate a waste facility. Concessions are usually awarded on a build-own-operate (BOO) or build-own-operate-transfer (BOOT) basis. Concessions are commonly awarded for transfer stations, landfill development, recycling plants, and incinerators.

3 *Franchise:* whereby a municipality awards, usually via competitive tendering, a limited monopoly in a defined area for a limited time. Franchises are commonly used for residential waste collection.

4 *Open competition:* whereby a municipality registers or licenses a number of enterprises as 'approved service providers' and then encourages the approved providers to compete freely to provide a defined range of services. Open competition is often used for industrial waste collection.

The Cairo Declaration of Principles

There is little mystery surrounding the respective component parts of public-private partnerships. Public sector responsibilities, resources, and procedures are apparent and understood, as are the types of private sector enterprises likely to be involved and the commercial mechanisms they will use. The mystery — and the challenge — lies in the nature of the interface between them, that is, in the details of the partnership itself. Hence, the immediate task facing those with MSWM responsibilities, as well as those concerned with environmental, economic development, and employment creation, is to develop and disseminate practical tools for building and managing successful sustainable public–private MSWM partnerships. Taking the mystery out of 'partnering' proven and positive aspects of the public and private sectors will result in greatly enhanced overall MSWM capacity, increased employment, enhanced overall economic productivity, and reduced negative environmental effects.

The Cairo Workshop on Micro and Small Enterprise Involvement in Municipal Solid Waste Management in Developing Countries produced a Declaration of Principles to stimulate and guide the process of developing sustainable MSWM partnerships. These Principles identified five key areas that must be addressed if there is to be both the enabling environment and the local capacity needed to create and maintain effective MSWM partnerships:

1 *Legitimisation of MSEs and contractual commitments*: national policies will need to be developed, and local by-laws amended, to facilitate private sector involvement in MSWM. Contracting arrangements will need to be fair and transparent; contracting periods will need be of sufficient duration to attract the private sector's capital and commitment.

2 *Finance and cost recovery*: cost-recovery models must be clear and transparent. Financial systems should reflect an overall 'willingness and ability to pay'. Standards of accountability must be high and apply equally to all parties involved. Support for micro-institutions and guarantee funds might be needed to stimulate micro- and small enterprise involvement.

3 *Capacity building in technical skills*: municipal authorities need to understand the working practices, and the strengths and limitations, of their private sector partners if they are to design and administer efficient sustainable partnerships. The private sector will need assistance in recognising and capturing the opportunities that partnership possibilities generate, and they will need support if they are to work to the technical, environmental, and social standards mandated by the public sector.

4 *Citizen responsibility and public cooperation*: MSWM becomes more efficient in both environmental and economic terms when informed citizens insist upon and participate in responsible waste management practices.

5 *Scaling up MSE participation*: national policy and municipal-level strategic plans should provide for large-scale MSE involvement in MSWM. Public sector institutions and departments should expand their degree of active interface with MSEs to both raise capacity and monitor performance. NGOs and enterprise development agencies should be encouraged to support the introduction and diffusion of best practice among MSEs involved in MSWM. (UMP/SDC/SKAT 1996b)

Conclusion

The public sector will need to learn about the workings and motivations of the private sector if the mystery is to be taken out of the public-private interface. If the growing populations of the world's cities are to be well served, the public sector must learn how to bring the power of the private sector to bear on MSWM responsibilities. To do this effectively, they must acquire the skills to design and supervise programmes that enable the private sector to participate as an active partner in all stages of MSWM. The Collaborative Group for MSE involvement in MSWM will continue to encourage and support this process.

Note

1 This definition is derived from the findings of a workshop on 'Business Opportunities for SMEs in Urban Environmental Fields' for African municipal executives and administrators, sponsored by the International Training Centre of the ILO, Turin, Italy, 9–13 December 1996.

Bibliography

Bartone, Carl (1995) 'The role of the private sector in developing countries: keys to success' in ISWA (15 September 1995) 'Waste Management: The Role of the Private Sector', Proceedings of a conference held at Singapore 14–15 September 1995, International Solid Waste Association (ISWA).

Cointreau-Levine, Sandra (1994) 'Private Sector Participation in Municipal Solid Waste Services in Developing Countries', Volume 1, *The Formal Sector,* UMP Discussion Paper No. 13, Washington DC: World Bank.

Pfammatter, Roger and Roland Schertenleib (1996) 'Non-governmental Refuse Collection in Low-income Urban Areas: Lessons from Asia, Africa and Latin America, Sandec Report No. 1/96, Duebendorff, Switzerland: EAWAG/ SANDEC.

Schübeler, Peter with Karl Wehrle and Jürg Christen (1996) 'Conceptual Framework for Municipal Solid Waste Management in Low-Income Countries', *UMP Working Paper Series, No. 9,* St Gallen, Switzerland: UMP/SDC/SKAT.

UMP/SDC/SKAT (1995) 'Proceedings: Ittingen International Workshop on

Municipal Solid Waste Management', report of a workshop held in Ittigen, Switzerland 9–12 April 1995, St Gallen, Switzerland: SKAT.

UMP/SDC/SKAT (1996a) 'Workshop Report: The Promotion of Public/Private Partnerships in MSWM in Low-income Countries', report of a workshop held at Washington DC, 22–23 February 1996, St Gallen, Switzerland: SKAT.

UMP/SDC/SKAT (1996b) 'Micro and Small Enterprise Involvement in Municipal Solid Waste Management in Developing Countries', unpublished report of a workshop in Cairo, 14–18 October 1996, St Gallen, Switzerland: SKAT.

An innovative community-based waste disposal scheme in Hyderabad

Mariëlle Snel

Introduction

A community-based voluntary waste disposal scheme, implemented in 1992 in Hyderabad, is one of the first of its kind in India being launched by an urban civic body with the assistance of NGOs and community-based organisations (CBOs).[1] Its purpose is to help keep neighbourhoods (or colonies, as they are often called in India) clean, as well as to make it quicker and more effective to lift waste with the help of employees of local organisations; *to involve waste-pickers* who collect the waste; and in order to develop a favourable social climate within which to educate citizens on the importance and economic value of waste.

The inclusion of waste-pickers from the informal recycling sector provides a main linkage to the formal sector of Municipal Waste Management (MWM).[2] They are not only capable of handling the collection of waste from each household (where Municipal Corporation of Hyderabad trucks cannot reach it) and transporting it to the municipal waste bin, but also of integrating the collection of waste with the existing recycling activities of the informal sector. This scheme could, therefore, potentially provide a large portion of these waste-pickers with sustainable work that is both economically and environmentally viable.

Labour-intensive segregation of waste by informal sector workers for recycling by factories, as well as the establishment of compost plots at the local level, designed and organised by the Municipality and the NGOs or CBOs, represent realistic steps towards the use of more ecocentric approaches in future MWM which are at the same time cost-effective in terms of natural resources.[3]

Hyderabad's community-based waste disposal scheme

The economic objectives of the scheme are not only to make waste management more effective, and to link up with the informal recycling activities, but also to increase the utilisation of biodegradable waste collected for the production of compost by introducing vermiculture and composting methods.

The Municipality was estimated to produce around 660 tonnes of organic manure per day during 1994; by 1999, this will rise to 1,800 tonnes per day. Other possibilities, such as the future production of fuel pellets are also being examined. Social objectives include the rehabilitation of between 10,000 to 20,000 of the approximately 35,000 waste-pickers in Hyderabad by providing them with work, free medical treatment, allowing them to sleep in night shelters, and providing non-formal education and vocational training (*Newstime* 1994).

The scheme started in June 1993, and is managed by community- or neighbourhood-based organisations (NBOs) within middle and upper income areas. At present, 167 colonies with around 100,000 households, are involved in such programmes. The scheme is also taking place in 217 slum areas, some of which are managed by the former Overseas Development Agency (ODA, now called Department for International Development. For simplicity's sake all these areas are called *ODA slum areas*). This type of scheme also functions with the help of CBOs or NBOs and comprises a total of 190,000 households (MCH 1994). In addition to colonies and slums involved in the scheme, twelve vegetable markets with biodegradable waste have been selected to take part.

The present waste disposal scheme entails recruiting one or two unemployed youths (or adults) in each residential area, usually local. Currently, they are drawn from among unemployed people and not yet from existing waste-pickers. Every day, between 6 a.m. and 9 a.m, the 'waste collector' visits the homes involved in the scheme to collect their waste. This is dumped in a box (200kg capacity) that has been fitted onto a tricycle, (the scheme therefore is often called the Tricycle scheme). Once all the waste is finally collected from each household it is dumped in one of the MCH bins or in one of the 'garbage houses' (at present an extra 100 are being constructed). The waste is then cleared daily by the MCH conservancy staff.

To encourage the residents in middle- and upper-income areas to join the scheme, the MCH pays a subsidy of Rs.5/- per household per month as an incentive to the CBO or NBO for maintaining daily operations. An average of about Rs.10/- per month is charged to each household as a membership fee, and Rs.5/- at the time of enrolment as an admission fee. The monthly fee plus subsidy gives the CBO or NBO an income of Rs.0.50 per day from each participating household.

No subsidies for the waste disposal scheme, however, are given for households in any of the ODA slum areas. These must pay the additional fee of Rs.5.00 per household themselves, but neither the ODA nor the MCH give funds for the waste disposal scheme in these areas. Officials say that these areas are not paying any property taxes and that already enough additional finances are being funnelled into them.

The proposed scheme also intends that households should segregate their waste into two containers, one for non-biodegradable and one for biodegradable waste. The former will be disposed of in the 'garbage house' in the residential area. The latter (organic) waste will be taken to a plot in the residential area, usually half an acre in size, for the production of compost. This is made with the help of earthworms given by the MCH free of charge. The organic manure produced in each of these plots will be brought to a central unit, which will be under the supervision of the Street Children Work Coordination Federation, where it will be collected, packaged and marketed (see Figure 1).

Figure 1 Flow chart of Hyberbad's waste disposal scheme

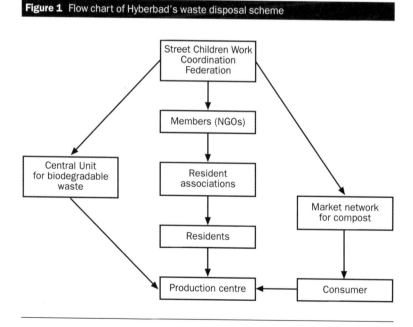

A total of seven vermiculture centres have been identified where biodegradable waste collected from residential areas will be turned into organic manure. Successful pilot studies for vermiculture have taken place in one of these.

At present, in the middle- and upper-income Municipal areas, a total of 301 people have been appointed by the various NGOs or CBOs to collect waste from households using the tricycles. The Municipality has estimated the annual saving in the collection of waste from households to be approximately 8.04 million R/s (after subtraction of subsidies). Within the ODA slum areas, the scheme has employed a total of 217 people with annual estimated savings of 13.63 R/s (MCH 1994).

Survey conclusions

In order to assess the potential success of the scheme, a survey was conducted in Hyderabad, focusing on whether or not community participation is a realistic response to solving the problems involved in MWM.

Two surveys were administered to monitor the effectiveness of the schemes within the seven administrative districts (or circles, as they are often called), each of which contains some areas in which NGOs or CBOs are involved in the waste disposal scheme. In the first year of surveying only a certain number of questionnaires were administered in each of these circles. The first, which took place in October 1993, was a pilot study. A total of 100 questionnaires were administered, of which 50 were to households which were part of the scheme (participants), and another 50 to households who did not participate (non-participants), as a control group. The same methodology was used for the ODA slum areas in which a total of around 25 surveys were administered each to the participating (experimental) group and to the non-participating (control) group.

The second survey was administered in September 1994 on a larger scale with additional questions. During the second year of the survey a total of around 210 questionnaires were administered around the MCH areas and 122 to the control group. Within the ODA slum areas a total of 100 surveys were undertaken, but only to those who were part of the waste disposal scheme.

Conclusion

This Practical Note has raised a number of diverse issues regarding municipal solid waste management based on the integration with informal recycling activities in waste disposal schemes. It has briefly addressed the attitudes of citizens with respect to the scheme; and although it is impossible to reveal all the survey results here, evidently most respondents in both areas seem enthusiastic and willing to assist in the scheme, provided the Municipality itself takes the leading role in MWM. Therefore, the essential point is that — provided the Municipality remains primarily responsible — citizen participation through the waste disposal scheme seems to represent a realistic approach to the solution of the solid waste management crisis in Hyderabad.

During the survey it became clear that much preparatory work was still necessary to integrate informal recycling activities, such as the vermiculture project for the recycling of bio-degradable waste, and for the employment of waste-pickers. Since this part of the project has not yet been successful, residents have become less enthusiastic about it, although they have become more aware of the potential of recycling in general, as well as the employment of street waste-pickers in particular.

The prospect of the waste disposal scheme linking up with existing recycling activities seems promising, but can only be realised after initial problems have been overcome. In ODA areas, however, less of a recycling base exists due to their own re-use of old materials. Educational campaigns have been found useful in gathering sufficient support from citizens for making the link with the recycling activities as beneficial for them as possible.

The overall conclusion is that community participation is a realistic response to solving the problems involved in MWM. However, if the Municipality of Hyderabad and citizens want to solve its waste-management crisis and to clear away its backlog of uncollected waste, it has to abandon its conventional methods of waste management and its 'old' mainly technocratic model. That approach relies largely on the public bureaucracy and on complicated and costly technologies, such as machinery, to provide its services. Although the Municipality needs to adjust its organisation to changing demands and to alter its financial management, especially by extending its tax structure, it can surely save financial costs by applying more appropriate technologies, a move towards a 'new' model in solid waste management based on community participation. Applying this 'new' model — although still at an experimental stage — reflects the official acknowledgement of the importance of the recycling sector, and implies a more ecocentric approach for solid waste management services combined with more effective labour-intensive means of providing them.

Notes

1   The expenses for the project are funded by the Municipal Corporation and UNICEF, although the work depends largely on the cooperation of local NGOs, CBOs and, citizens.

2   The informal sector of MWM is 'associated with unregistered, unregulated activities, individual and family enterprises, small-scale and low capital inputs, local materials and labour-intensive techniques' (Furedy 1989:14)

3   Ecocentric in this context refers to self-reliance, self-sufficiency, small-scale production, low-impact technology, and recycling.

Bibliography

Furedy, C. (1989) 'Social considerations in solid waste management in Asian cities', *Regional Development Dialogue* X(3): 13–41.

MCH (1994) 'Pilot Project for Solid Waste Management for Hyderabad', unpublished paper.

Newstime (1994) 'MCH to launch ragpickers rehabilitation project', 11 June 1994: 2.

Annotated bibliography

Development management is an umbrella concept that encompasses many specialised areas, from theories of what constitutes 'development' through to a range of schools and practices in the field of management studies, all within the context of prevailing political, economic, social, and cultural realities. The setting will differ significantly according to local circumstances, such as whether these are primarily rural or urban economies, or whether countries have devolved or centralised systems of government. The focal point of development management, however, is that of value-based public action in order to achieve a set of social goals that favour equity and inclusion. In establishing the boundaries for this selective bibliography, we have therefore focused on the intersections among development actors, be these official aid agencies, governments, the private sector, NGOs, civil society organisations (CSOs), academic or policy research institutions, or other entities rather than on abstract development theories, or on management textbooks. Nor have we sought to include more than a tiny sample of the many universities and training institutions working in this field, since readers will tend to explore local or regional options in the first instance; similarly, we have excluded the various UN organisations and all but a few bilateral aid agencies since their materials are widely disseminated and readily accessible. Rather, we have concentrated on publications that explore the problematic nature of social institutions that operate within the development context, for instance in terms of their public accountability, their gendered nature, their handling of power, and the assumptions they embody about the needs and perspectives of those cultures and social sectors whose worldviews do not shape the mainstream policy framework.

The bibliography was compiled by Deborah Eade and Nicola Frost, Editor and Reviews Editor respectively of Development in Practice, *with some input from staff at The Open University.*

Books

Raymond Apthorpe and Des Gasper (eds.): *Arguing Development Policy: Frames and Discourses,* London: Frank Cass in association with EADI, 1996.
Public policies are not simply statements of intention but also incorporate values, considerations of legitimacy, and assessments of constraints, all of which combine to shape a chosen course of action. The chapter by Gasper assesses various tools to analyse policy arguments and reveal the components that structure them, the core ideas that 'frame' them, and to judge how policies are presented and structured. He argues that since 'tactics build structures', the systematic reading of policy can help illuminate the broader conceptions that underpin particular arguments.

Robert Chambers: *Whose Reality Counts? Putting the First Last,* London: IT Publications, 1997.
A sequel to the 1983 *Rural Development: Putting the Last First,* this book urges development professionals to reconsider the power relations at work in their engagements with people in the South, and to develop 'new approaches and methods for interaction, learning and knowing'. It also reflects on the development of participatory rural appraisal (PRA)-based techniques, examines the challenges of bad practice, and explores how a new professionalism could continue the change in behaviour and practice. Chambers has published widely on participatory approaches to development.

Emma Crewe and Elizabeth Harrison: *Whose Development? An Ethnography of Aid,* London: Zed Books, 1998.
Drawing on their experience with both UN agencies and small NGOs, the authors examine the underlying assumptions about issues such as progress, culture, partnership, and social diversity in the theory and practice of development; and at how these understandings are rooted in inequitable power relations. Conflicting value systems within aid agencies, and between these and the diverse values of the societies within which they intervene, call for a far more nuanced account of policy and practice than the dominant discourse is willing to accommodate.

Anthony Davies: *Managing for a Change: How to Run Community Development Projects,* London: IT Publications, 1997.
The author offers a straightforward overview of the key stages of planning and running a community development project and looks first at problem identification and analysis, moving on to mobilising a group, planning, resource identification, project funding, basic book-keeping, project supervision, and implementation. There is advice on all aspects of the process including decision making, leadership, employment of contractors, and evaluation. For more information about IT Publications' management list, see the entry for Bookaid International.

Jean Drèze and Amartya Sen: *Hunger and Public Action,* Oxford: Clarendon Press, 1989.

This is an influential and intellectually rigorous study, which examines the complex causes of and reaction to chronic hunger. It notes the positive role that political pluralism and participation can play in eradicating hunger and deprivation, urging a perception of the public, 'not merely as "the patient" whose well-being commands attention, but also as "the agent" whose actions can transform society.'

Michael Edwards and David Hulme (eds.): *NGOs, States and Donors: Too Close for Comfort?,* Macmillan, 1997; *NGOs — Performance and Accountability: Beyond the Magic Bullet,* London: Earthscan, 1996; *Making a Difference: NGOs and Development in a Changing World,* London: Earthscan, 1992.

These volumes emerged from two conferences that were organised by the editors in 1992 and 1994 and thus reflect the preoccupations of Northern and large Southern NGOs in the early 1990s. *Making a Difference* looks at different ways to 'scale-up' NGO impact, for instance by partnering with governments, by becoming service-providers, by expanding the scale and scope of their programmes, or by undertaking advocacy work whether to shift public policy or to influence public opinion. *Too Close for Comfort?* and *Beyond the Magic Bullet* seek both to re-define what NGOs are best at (and against whose criteria to prove this) and to explore the opportunities and risks inherent in becoming dependent on acting as channels for official aid — both volumes focusing on questions of downwards or two-way versus upwards accountability.

Patrick Fitzgerald, Anne McLennan, and Barry Munslow (eds.): *Managing Sustainable Development in South Africa,* 2nd edn, Capetown: OUP, 1997.

South Africa has a wealth of practical experience in attempting to transform the old-style public administration into a more developmental management culture and has also sought to encourage critical thinking on development management by NGOs, consultants and trainers, and several university departments. The Graduate School of Public and Development Management at the University of the Witwatersrand was largely responsible for this volume, in which over 30 researchers and practitioners explore what sustainable development means, and how it can be managed in post-apartheid South Africa. The contributions together have something to say about virtually all aspects and sectors of development, and the lessons can be applied in any context of reconstruction and development.

Alan Fowler: *Striking a Balance: A Guide to Enhancing the Effectiveness of NGOs in International Development,* London: Earthscan, 1997.

NGOs face multiple and often conflicting demands and expectations that come from a wide range of stakeholders, usually based in the North as well as in the South. The author of this reference and source book argues that to be effective, NGOs must be able to balance these tensions. First, their internal systems need to be appropriately linked with those of relevant external bodies. Second, their own structures and organisational culture must be coherent in themselves and consistent with their purpose. Third, NGOs must be able to deal with the 'ambiguities and dilemmas' that are inherent in the aid system and intrinsic to development processes.

Anne Marie Goetz: *Getting Institutions Right for Women in Development,* London: Zed Books, 1997.
The author offers a gendered analysis of a range of development organisations, looking both at the state and at multilateral organisations and at less formally bureaucratised institutions such as NGOs and women's organisations. Goetz builds a conceptual framework for exploring the gendered politics and procedures internal to the institutions which design and implement gender policy, and applies this to the analysis of case studies from around the world.

Naila Kabeer: *Reversed Realities: Gender Hierarchies in Development Thought,* London: Verso, 1994.
Development can be seen simply as a planned process by which resources are put together for specific ends, or in terms of processes of social transformation unleashed by the attempts of several agencies to achieve various and often conflicting goals. Charting the process of development in this broader sense requires an awareness of the hierarchies, constructs, and assumptions that underpin the work of these agencies, and of the often unintended, and gender-differentiated, consequences of their interventions. Kabeer argues that hierarchies of knowledge and ideas conceal entrenched hierarchies of interests, giving rise to particular representations of disadvantaged groups, and translating into organisational forms, rules, and practices that reinforce these representations. A significant challenge to entrenched gender biases can emerge from women's collective action over self-identified interests.

Allan Kaplan: *The Development Practitioners' Handbook,* London: Pluto Books, 1996.
Despite the title, this is not a 'how to' manual but a series of reflections on the nature of development practice and the role(s) of practitioners (whether agency personnel, external consultants, or community activists) in facilitating change processes. While the author regards this work as systematic and not simply haphazard, if development is essentially about growth, the qualities most prized in the practitioner who seeks to accompany and nurture that growth are those of flexibility, imagination, and the ability to work with ambiguity and contradiction. This calls for guidelines, principles, and value-based criteria rather than for rules and bureaucratic procedures.

Carol Miller and Shahra Razavi (eds.): *Missionaries and Mandarins: Feminist Engagement with Development Institutions* London: IT Publications with UNRISD, 1998.
In this collection of seven essays on various aspects of feminist engagement (or disengagement) with development bureaucracies in different national settings, whether multilateral, governmental, or non-governmental, contributors examine both the discourse of development (how women's presumed interests and needs

are translated into policy), the rules and procedures that govern decision-making and resource-allocation, and the ways in which 'femocrats' seek to influence policy and practice. The overall message is that while development institutions are gendered (i.e. they reflect and reproduce gender power relations), they are neither monolithic or impermeable, nor are they static.

Martin Minogue, Charles Polidano, and David Hulme: *Beyond the New Public Management: Changing ideas and practices in governance*, Cheltenham: Edward Elgar, 1998.
A critical enquiry into the 'new public management' (NPM) model, as applied in both developed and developing countries, the authors provide an overview of the current theoretical debates in public management, drawing on material from development studies, economics and political science as well as management studies. They conclude that NPM most closely lives up to its revolutionary claims in developed countries, whereas in developing countries a closer examination of alternative strategies, rather than simple criticism, is needed.

Gareth Morgan: *Images of Organization,* new edn., London: Sage, 1997; *Imaginization: The Art of Creative Management,* London: Sage, 1997.
Morgan is a management thinker whose views are relevant to any kind of organisation and who does not assume that business-based values should apply elsewhere. In *Images of Organization* he uses various metaphors to explore different views of what organisations are (organisations as machines, as brains, as political systems, as psychic prisons). In *Imaginization* he suggests practical ways to use metaphors in management situations in order to explore creative possibilities for action. His unconventional ideas, cartoon drawings, and group activities are backed up with theory arguing why such methods are necessary within an unpredictably changing world. See the website at www.imaginiz.com for more information.

David Mosse, John Farrington and Alan Rew (eds.): *Development as Process: Concepts and Methods for Working with Complexity,* London: Routledge, 1998.
This book considers a process approach to information management in development, both as a method of monitoring and participatory appraisal, and as a new perspective on the development project as a whole. It acknowledges an increasing emphasis on longer term behavioural changes over immediate concrete products. Contributions consider aspects of inter-agency partnerships, policy reform, and organisational learning, in relation to process documentation.

Nici Nelson and Susan Wright (eds.): *Power and Participatory Development,* London: IT Publications, 1995.
The contributors demonstrate that participatory development and research generate power relationships between institutions and communities and also affect power relationships within communities. The concepts of power, participatory development, and community are critically analysed by drawing on debates within anthropology, feminism, and development studies. These themes underpin detailed case studies

of participatory interventions in both North and South. The book argues that shifts of power between agencies and beneficiaries, and within recipient communities, are necessary for participatory research and development to be effective.

Mike Powell: *Information Management for Development Organisations*, Oxford: Oxfam, 1999.

In the context of an exponential growth in the rate of information flows, and the new opportunities afforded by electronic communication, the author argues that development managers and practitioners along with other social actors need to review their own information needs as well as re-considering how they might best generate, store, and use information in order to shape and sharpen their work in the years to come. The book includes an annotated list of print and web-based resources.

Dorcas Robinson, Tom Hewitt, and John Harriss (eds.): *Managing Development: Understanding Inter-Organizational Relationships*, London: Sage, 1999.

Changing institutional imperatives, terminology, and political agendas have created spaces for new types of relationships to emerge between groups and organisations. This book asks how such relationships can be managed so as to build the intended public action and outcomes of development interventions. This book examines the challenges and opportunities presented by the current interest in the partnership approach to development cooperation. It explores the diversity of inter-organisational relationships, and the sometimes contradictory array of relationships promoted by policy makers, noting how forces of competition, coordination, and cooperation constantly influence these relationships.

Mark Robinson (ed.): *Corruption and Development*, London: Frank Cass and EADI, 1998.

The current interest in corruption is fuelled by the prevalent 'good governance' and democratisation agenda of donors and by the major shifts in relations among social actors that have been fostered by economic globalisation. There are crucial differences, however, in what is understood to constitute corruption; the explanatory framework that is used (e.g. whether it is assumed to be motivated by self-interest, permitted by a weak civil society, or reflects the political power associated with groups and resources allocated by the state); and in terms of how best to tackle it depending on whether it is as incidental (individual), institutional (e.g. the police service), or systemic (i.e. entrenched or societal). The volume constitutes seven essays on corruption, international development, and anti-corruption strategies in Asia and Africa and concludes that in each setting, complementary strategies are needed in order to tackle corruption on all fronts.

Chris Roche: *Impact Assessment for Development Agencies: Learning to Value Change*, Oxford: Oxfam and Novib, 1999.

Using in-depth case studies from Oxfam and Novib and their counterparts in developing countries, this book considers the process of impact assessment and shows how and why it needs to be integrated into all stages of development programmes from planning to evaluation. Its basic premise is that impact assessment should refer not to the immediate outputs or effects of a project or programme, but to any lasting or significant changes that it brought about. From a theoretical overview, the book moves on to discuss the design of impact-assessment processes and a range of tools and methods, before illustrating its use in development, in emergencies, and in advocacy work. It ends by exploring how different organisations have attempted to institutionalise impact assessment processes and the challenges they have faced in doing so.

Peter Senge et al (eds.): *The Fifth Discipline Fieldbook: Strategies and Tools for Building a Learning Organization,* London: Nicholas Brealey Publishing, 1994.
The ideas and techniques presented in this book are all rooted in actual practice and experience. Defining a 'learning organisation' as one that is 'focused on marrying the development of every member with superior performance toward the organisation's collective purpose', the contributors believe that the more its members increase their ability to learn collaboratively, the more they can accomplish, the higher their performance, and the more effectively they can hope to change the world for the better. Learning organisations may be corporations, small businesses, schools, hospitals, government agencies, non-profit organisations – any enterprise where people gather to accomplish something they could not create alone.

Ian Smillie: *The Alms Bazaar: Altruism Under Fire – Non-Profit Organizations and International Development,* London: IT Publications, 1995.
An honest and wide-ranging study of international development agencies, looking at their origins and motivations, and tracing their development since 1945. The book focuses on the implications for NGOs' independence of changing relationships between them and donors, UN agencies, and governments. It goes on to look at how NGOs themselves are evolving, with the advent of transnational mega-charities. (For other publications in which Smillie has been involved, see the entries for INTRAC and the OECD Development Assistance Committee.)

Naoki Suzuki: *Inside NGOs: Learning to Manage Conflicts Between Headquarters and Field Offices,* London: IT Publications, 1998.
Drawing on both personal experience and interviews, the author examines the internal dynamics of NGOs. She highlights the tensions between field and head office, recognising that the former deals largely with beneficiaries, while the latter often has more contact with donors. The book provides insights on how to create a framework for action that would reconcile an NGO's objectives with those of the programmes it supports. It looks at how to balance staff diversity with organisational unity (although while most NGO field workers are women, there is no attempt to assess these issues through a gender framework), and the similar tensions between systems and flexibility. The author makes practical suggestions for promoting understanding and openness.

Alan Thomas, Joanna Chataway and Marc Wuyts (eds.): *Finding Out Fast: Investigative Skills for Policy and Development* London: Sage (in association with The Open University), 1998.

Aimed at practitioners who want to investigate policy issues and policy processes, those who commission research, and those who want to become better at assessing research, this book, with contributions from 19 diverse authors offers practical approaches, but is not a simple set of guidelines. It includes a chapter on journalists' approaches to investigation, and one in which the use of case studies is discussed. Other sections discuss qualitative and quantitative methods, and the limitations of 'quick and dirty' investigations, as well as practical guidance on how to conduct literature searches and analyse institutional accounts.

Tina Wallace, Sarah Crowther and Andrew Shepherd: *Standardising Development: Influences of UK NGOs' Policies and Procedures*, Oxford: Worldview Press, 1997.

In the wake of the general shift among Northern development NGOs towards more formalised systems of planning and evaluation, this book provides insights into the working of UK-based NGOs. The book draws on interviews with donors and NGO staff, as well as the proceedings of a joint workshop, and emphasises the complexity of many large agencies. It examines the impact of these changes on ways of working both in the UK and in developing countries, and includes an assessment of the growing 'contract culture' between agencies and donors.

Marshall Wolfe: *Elusive Development*, London: Zed Books, 1996.

In this 'insider' critique of global development as a project and specifically of the international development agencies within which he worked for almost 50 years, the author describes a series of benighted and increasingly jargon-ridden efforts to discern (or impose) a rational and benevolent order on reality, essentially through financial and technical means. The problems range from mandate shift as agencies seek to respond to the immense complexity of their task by taking on ever more roles and priorities (the Protean effect), to the difficulties even in properly defining such basics as poverty (be it absolute, extreme, abject, or merely relative) and its eradication. If change happens, it is through 'the interplay of values, priorities, prejudices and apathies' rather than through formal development interventions.

Marc Wuyts, Maureen Mackintosh and Tom Hewitt (eds.): *Development Policy and Public Action*, Oxford: OUP/Open University, 1992.

This core text in development studies and development management courses is innovative in treating development policy as an activity of many different types of public institution — public action. It thus moves away from public/private dichotomies and opens up development policy to a wider public sphere that includes case studies of street children and child labour, the emergence of private interest among civil servants, the ambiguous public/private nature of NGOs, the implications for public action of women's organisations and empowerment, and virtuous circles of social development within a responsive state. The book questions classic concepts of the public sphere and expands the notion of public action, both exploring the negative impact of structural adjustment while also emphasising the possible range of new forms of conscious activity of people and organisations in effecting change.

World Bank *World Development Report 1997: The State in a Changing World*, Oxford: OUP, 1997.

This issue of the Bank's annual report examines the changing role of the state, taking into account issues such as privatisation, service provision, and globalisation; and emphasises the importance of good governance for development. The Report goes on to explore the economic implications, but also looks at issues of decentralisation, accountability, participation, and consultation. It advocates new forms of partnership with civil society to enhance state effectiveness.

Journals

Public Administration and Development: published by John Wiley and Sons, ISSN: 0271-2075, Editor: P. Collins.

Focusing on the practice of public administration at all levels where this is directed to development in less industrialised and transitional economies, *PAD* gives special attention to investigations of the management of public policy formulation and implementation that have transnational influence, including the management and policy of para-statal organisations or corporations. The journal also examines the implications for state administration of NGOs and private corporations involved in development activities. Volume 17 is especially relevant to management debates involving the voluntary sector.

Development in Practice: published in five issues per volume by Carfax Publishing Ltd on behalf of Oxfam GB, ISSN: 0961-4524, Editor: Deborah Eade.

A forum for practitioners, policy makers, and academics to exchange information and analysis concerning the social dimensions of development and humanitarian work. As a multidisciplinary journal of policy and practice, it reflects a wide range of institutional and cultural backgrounds and a variety of cultural experience. Thematic compilations of papers published in the journal are also available in the *Development in Practice Readers* series. Titles of particular relevance to development management include *Development and Patronage* (1997), *Development with Women* (1998), and *Development, NGOs and Civil Society* (forthcoming).

Journal of International Development: published in six issues per volume by John Wiley and Sons in association with the Development Studies Association, ISSN: 0954-1748, Editors: Paul Mosely and Hazel Johnson.

Aiming to publicise the best research on development issues in an accessible form, regardless of which particular school, analytical technique or methodological approach it represents *JID's* focus is on the social sciences — economics, politics, international relations, sociology, and anthropology — but papers that blend the approach of the natural and the social sciences in relation to a development problem are also published. Volume 8(1) includes Alan Thomas' paper 'What is Development Management?', and volume 11(5) focuses on New Public Management.

World Development: published monthly by Elsevier, ISSN: 0305-750X, Editor: Janet L. Craswell.
Recognising 'development' as a process of change involving nations, economies, political alliances, institutions, groups, and individuals, the journal seeks to explore ways of improving standards of living, and the human condition generally, by examining potential solutions to problems such as: poverty, unemployment, malnutrition, disease, lack of shelter, environmental degradation, inadequate scientific and technological resources, international debt, gender and ethnic discrimination, militarism and civil conflict, and lack of popular participation in economic and political life. Volume 24(4) includes Joel Samoff's 'Chaos and Certainty in Development'.

IDS Bulletin: published quarterly by the Institute of Development Studies ISSN: ISSN 0265 5012, Editor: guest editors for each issue.
Intended for all those involved in development work — field workers, administrators, planners, students and teachers — the *Bulletin* is designed to bridge the gap between professional journals and journalism. Each issue is guest-edited and features a theme, which is explored from a variety of angles. Volumes 23, 24, and 26 include articles of particular relevance to development management.

New Leadership: published quarterly by the Caribbean and African Self-Reliance International (CASRI) in Canada. This new journal takes a bottom-up approach to leadership for community transformation within its primary constituency of 'people of Caribbean and African heritage' worldwide.

Organisations

Asian NGO Coalition for Agrarian Reform and Rural Development (ANGOC): An association of national and regional NGO networks from 10 Asian countries engaged in food security, agrarian reform, sustainable agriculture and rural development activities. ANGOC's efforts to strengthen the voluntary sector in Asia include hosting an annual Asian Development Forum on key development themes, enabling the provision of specific services in areas such as NGO management, and information sharing for more effective advocacy work. ANGOC also facilitates practical exchanges and internship arrangements among NGO personnel. E-mail: angoc@angoc.ngo.ph; Web: www.angoc.ngo.ph/

Bookaid International/Intermediate Technology Publications: Bookaid International produces a user-friendly list of resources relating to the management of NGOs, available through Intermediate Technology. The collection includes titles covering training and participation, research and evaluation, and finance, as well as more theoretical topics. Entries provide guidance on language complexity. More practical titles include the two-volume *Manual of Practical Management for Third World Rural Development Associations*, 1997. Web: www.bookaid.org/resources/ngo/index.html

Centre for Voluntary Organisation, London School of Economics: A teaching and research centre, interested in problems and issues arising from the work of voluntary agencies and NGOs and the implications for public policy. Research findings are tested and disseminated through publications, postgraduate teaching, and applied research projects. With the Mandel Center at Case Western Reserve University in Cleveland, Ohio, the CVO also sponsors the journal *Nonprofit Management and Leadership*. A series of International Working Papers, available online, includes: 'NGOs and participatory management styles: a case study of CONCERN Worldwide, Mozambique' by James Sheehan; and 'Are expatriate staff necessary in international development NGOs? A case study of an international NGO in Uganda' by Sarah Mukasa. E-mail: cvo@lse.co.uk; Web: www.lse.ac.uk/Depts/CVO/

CIVICUS — World Alliance for Citizen Participation: An alliance of organisations committed to strengthening citizen action and civil society worldwide, Civicus believes that private action for the public good can take place either within the civil sphere or in combination with government or with business and that a healthy society needs an equitable relationship among these different sectors.

Two recent publications include Kumi Naidoo (ed.) *Civil Society at the Millennium* (co-published with Kumarian), 1999; and Laurie Regelbrugge (ed.) *Promoting Corporate Citizenship: Opportunities for Business and Civil Society Engagement*, 1999. CIVICUS also produces a useful newsletter, available on e-mail. E-mail: info@civicus.org; Web: www.civicus.org/

Community Development Resource Association (CDRA): A non-profit NGO which works throughout sub-Saharan Africa to promote a just civil society by offering consultancy services (training, accompaniment, facilitation) to build organisational capacity, and by publishing materials arising from its experience. Its annual reports, which are available on its website, are particularly thought-provoking and are generally critical of the technocratic and project-based view of development. E-mail: cdra@wn.apc.org; Web: www.cdra.org.za/

Harvard Institute for International Development: A multidisciplinary centre for coordinating development assistance, training, and research on Africa, Asia, Central and Eastern Europe, and Latin America. Training programmes tend towards economic issues, as does the extensive collection of working papers. A recent book from the Institute is *Getting Good Government: Capacity Building in the Public Sectors of Developing Countries*, Merilee S. Grindle (ed.), 1997. E-mail: info@hiid.harvard.edu; Web: hiidgate.harvard.edu/

Indian Institute of Management, Bangalore: One of the premier management schools in the Indian sub-continent, with a strong focus on development and gender issues with the presence of Professor Gita Sen, one of the founding members of the Southern feminist network DAWN. The Institute publishes a quarterly journal, *Management Review*. Web: www.iimb.ernet.in/

Institute for Development Policy and Management, University of Manchester (IDPM): A multi-disciplinary unit specialising in management and development in developing and transitional economies, IPDM offers various postgraduate degrees and short professional courses, including some in-country training. Several series of full-text working papers are available online, covering human resources, policy, information technology and finance, among others, e.g. 'Participation, "process" and management: lessons for development in the history of organisation development', William N. Cooke IDPM Human Resources in Development Group Working Paper No. 7, 1996. E-mail: idpm@man.ac.uk Web: www.man.ac.uk/idpm

Instituto Brasileiro de Análises Socias a Econômicas (IBASE): One of Latin America's largest social research NGOs, IBASE maintains an extensive 'citizens' website' with information and bibliographies (works written in and translated into Portuguese) on subjects of major concern in development management, including citizenship, gender, the environment, and social movements. E-mail: ibase@ibase.br; Web: www.ibase.org.br/

International Development Research Centre (IDRC): A public corporation created by the Canadian government to help communities in the developing world find solutions to social, economic, and environmental problems through research. An extensive publishing programme includes many French-language titles, and some also in Spanish. Many publications are available in full online. IDRC's research programme supports or facilitates research into a wide range of development challenges. Working web sites provide ongoing information about current projects. E-mail: info@idrc.ca; Web: www.idrc.ca

International Institute for Environment and Development (IIED): Promotes sustainable patterns of world development through collaborative research, policy studies, consensus building and public information. A number of research programmes are hosted by IIED, many of which involve management or planning. The resource centre can organise worldwide document delivery and can help with literature searches. A CD-ROM database of documents on participatory learning and action (PLA) is available free to those from non-OECD countries (as are many of the documents themselves). Publications include an NGOs and Institutions list, with papers such as: 'NGOs and the Informal Sector in Africa: what links and for what purpose?' 1998. E-mail: mailbox@iied.org; Web: www.iied.org

International Institute for Sustainable Development (IISD): IISD seeks to promote sustainable development in decision making internationally and within Canada, through contributing new knowledge and concepts, analysing policies, disseminating information about best practices, and building partnerships to amplify these messages. IISD works with businesses, governments, communities, and concerned individuals, using Internet communications, working groups, and project activities to move sustainable development from concept to practice. An excellent website has hundreds of documents relating to all aspects of IISD's work, and conference and workshop reports from its reporting services. E-mail: info@iisd.ca; Web: iisd.ca/

International Institute of Rural Reconstruction (IIRR): IIRR seeks to strengthen the institutional capacity of government and NGOs to serve better the needs of the rural poor through training, consultancies, technical advisory services, publications, and audiovisuals. An annual international course is run on rural development management. Web: www.panasia.org.sg/iirr/

International Training and Research Centre (INTRAC): INTRAC is primarily an NGO support organisation that offers training in capacity-building and institutional development. INTRAC is also involved in ongoing programmes in Central Asia and Malawi. Its research and training programmes feed into publications ranging from newsletters to occasional papers and co-published works, substantial summaries of which are available on its website. Relevant titles include: 'People's participation in development projects', Peter Oakley, 1995; 'NGOs and the private sector: potential for partnerships?' Simon Heap, 1998; and 'Partners or Contractors? Official donor Agencies and direct funding mechanisms' Ian Smillie et al., 1996. E-mail: intrac@gn.apc.org Web: www.intrac.org

New Economics Foundation (NEF): NEF works to construct a new economy centred on people and the environment and combines research, advocacy, training, and grassroots practical action in furtherance of this aim. As well as providing advice to UK government and NGOs, it also supports the work of partner organisations in developing countries. E-mail info@neweconomics.org Web: www.neweconomics.org/

Development Assistance Committee (DAC), Organisation for Economic Cooperation and Development: Part of OECD, the DAC's current work concentrates on supporting partnerships and cooperation. Two publications examine some of the implications for NGOs identified in the research: *NGOs and Governments: Stakeholders for Development* Ian Smillie and Henny Helmich, Development Centre of OECD, 1993; and *Stakeholders: Government-NGO Partnerships for International Development*, Ian Smillie and Henny Helmich (eds.), in collaboration with Tony German and Judith Randel, London: Earthscan, 1999. OECD's website includes many additional documents looking at development cooperation. Web: www.oecd.org//dac/

Participatory Research in Asia (PRIA): This Delhi-based organisation is dedicated to providing opportunities for sharing information between NGOs and other civil society groups, promoting inter-sectoral dialogue, and analysing social and development trends and policies. Its resource centre plans to make some of its information available online. The website is well organised and informative, with an extensive list of publications (unfortunately without dates), including several titles in Hindi. PRIA publish two periodicals, *Journal on Institutional Development* and *Bulletin on Participation and Governance* as well as *Global Alliance News*. PRIA's topics extend also to occupational and environmental health, literacy, and women's empowerment. PRIA is a member of the NGO Working Group on the World Bank, chairs the sub-group on Participation, and is also the secretariat for the International Forum for Capacity Building (IFCB). E-mail: pria@sdalt.ernet.in Web: www.pria.org

The World Bank: The Bank has an NGO/Civil Society website, which aims to keep civil society organisations (CSOs) informed of opportunities for interaction with the Bank. It includes a number of key policy documents, as well as practical guidelines. Web: www.worldbank.org. A number of Northern government agencies have recently published guidelines or reports on their partnerships with NGOs. **AusAid's** paper, 'Working with Australian NGOs' (1999), outlines a framework for ongoing partnerships. Web: www.ausaid.gov.au/. **USAID's** New Partnerships Initiative promotes 'strategic partnering for collective problem-solving at the community level'. Web: www.info.usaid.gov/. The Swedish International Development Cooperation Agency (**SIDA**), among other Scandinavian governments, has also recently produced a evaluation of development cooperation through NGOs. Web: www.sida.gov.se.

Addresses of publishers and other organisations

ANGOC, PO Box 3107, QCCPO 1103, Quezon City, Metro Manila, Philippines. Fax: +63 (2) 9207434.

Bookaid International, 39/41 Coldharbour Lane, London SE5 9NR, UK. Fax +44 (0)20 7978 8006.

Nicholas Brealey Publishers, 21 Bloomsbury Way, London WC1A 2TH, UK. Fax: +44 (0)20 7404 8311.

Carfax Publishing Ltd., PO Box 25, Abingdon OX14 3UE, UK. Fax: +44 (0)1235 401550.

CASRI, Centretown Services, 130 Slater Street #750, Ottawa ON, Canada K1P 6E2. Tel: +1 (613) 598 4661.

Frank Cass, Newbury House, 900 East Avenue, Newbury Park, Ilford, Essex IG2 7HH, UK. Fax: +44 (0)20 8599 0984.

Centre for Voluntary Organisation, London School of Economics & Political Science, Houghton Street, London WC2A 2AE, UK. Fax: +44 (0)20 7955 6039.

CIVICUS, 919 18th Street, N.W., Third Floor, Washington, DC 20006 USA. Fax: +1 (202) 331 8774.

Clarendon Press, Walton Street, Oxford OX2 6DP, UK. Fax: +44 (0)1865 556646.

Community Development Resource Association (CDRA), PO Box 221, Woodstock, 7915 South Africa. Fax: +27 (21) 462 3918.

Development Assistance Committee, Organisation for Economic Co-operation and Development, 2, rue André-Pascal, 75775 Paris Cedex 16, France. Fax: +33 (1) 45 24 82 00.

Earthscan Publications Ltd., 120 Pentonville Road, London N1 9JN, UK. Fax: +44 (0)20 7278 01142.

Edward Elgar Publishing Ltd., 8 Lansdown Place, Cheltenham, Gloucestershire GL50 2HU, UK. Fax: +44 (0)1242 262111.

Harvard Institute for International Development, 14 Story Street, Cambridge, Massachusetts 02138, USA. Fax: +1 (617) 495 0527.

Indian Institute of Management Bangalore, Bannerghatta Road, Bangalore 560076, India. Fax: +91 (80) 6644050.

Institute for Development Policy and Management (IDPM), University of Manchester, Crawford House, Precinct Centre, Oxford Road, Manchester M13 9GH, UK. Fax: +44 (0)161 273 8829.

Institute of Development Studies, University of Sussex, Brighton BN1 9RE, UK. Fax: +44 (0)1273 621202/ 691647.

Instituto Brasileiro de Análises Socias a Econômicas (IBASE), Rua Visconde de Ouro Preto, 5/7 andar, Botafago, 22250-180 Rio de Janeiro, RJ Brazil. Fax: +55 (21) 2860541.

Intermediate Technology Publications, 103–105 Southhampton Row, London WC1B 4HH, UK. Fax: +44 (0)20 7436 2013.

International Development Research Centre (IDRC), PO Box 8500, Ottawa, ON K1G 3H9, Canada. Tel: +1 (613) 236 6163.

International Institute for Environment and Development (IIED), 3 Endsleigh Street, London WC1H 0DD, UK. Fax: +44 (0)20 7388 2826.

International Institute for Sustainable Development (IISD), 161 Portage Avenue East, 6th Floor, Winnipeg, Manitoba, Canada R3B 0Y4. Fax: +1 (204) 958 7710.

International Training and Research Centre (INTRAC), P.O. Box 563, Oxford OX2 6RZ, UK. Fax: +44(0)1865 201852.

Macmillan Press Ltd., Houndmills, Basingstoke RG21 6XS, UK. Fax: +44(0)1256 330688.

New Economics Foundation, Cinnamon House, 6–8 Cole Street, London SE1 4YH, UK. Fax: +44 (0)20 7407 6473.

Oxfam Publications, Oxfam, 274 Banbury Road, Oxford OX2 7DZ, UK. Fax: +44 (0)1865 313925.

Oxford University Press, Walton Street, Oxford OX2 6DT, UK. Fax: +44 (0)1865 556646.

Participatory Research in Asia (PRIA), 42,Tughlakabad Institutional Area, New Delhi 110062, India. Fax: +91 (11) 6980183.

Pluto Press, 345 Archway Road, London N6 5AA, UK. Fax: +44 (0)20 8348 9133.

Routledge, 11 New Fetter Lane, London EC4P 4EE, UK. Fax: +44 (0)20 7842 2302.

Sage Publications Ltd., 6 Bonhill Street, London EC2A 4PU, UK. Fax: +44 (0)20 7374 8741.

Verso, 6 Meard Street, London W1V 3HR, UK. Fax: +44 (0)20 7734 0059.

John Wiley & Sons, Ltd., 1 Oldlands Way, Bognor Regis, West Sussex PO22 9SA, UK. Fax: +44 (0)1243 843 232.

WorldView Publishing, PO Box 595, Oxford OX2 6YH, UK. Fax: +44 (0)1865 201906.

Zed Books, 7 Cynthia Street, London N1 9JF, UK. Fax: +44 (0)20 7833 3960.

Oxfam books on management issues in development

Impact Assessment for Development Agencies: Learning to Value Change

Chris Roche

This book shows how and why impact assessment must be integrated into all stages of development programmes, from planning to evaluation. Its premise is that impact should refer to lasting or significant changes that development work brought about.

From a theoretical overview, the book discusses the design of impact-assessment processes and a range of tools and methods. Case studies show a variety of approaches to impact assessment —qualitative, quantitative, and participatory — used in development work, in emergencies, in advocacy work, and in organisational assessment.

1999 An Oxfam Development Guideline, co-published with Novib
0 85598 418 x paperback 160pp £9.95/$15.95
0 85598 424 4 hardback 160pp £24.95/$39.95

The Oxfam Handbook of Development and Relief

Deborah Eade and Suzanne Williams

1995 0 85598 274 8 paperback 1,200pp
(3 volumes, slipcased) / £24.95 / $39.95
1995 0 85598 273 x hardback 1,200pp
(2 volumes) £49.95/$39.95

Information Management for Development Organisations

Mike Powell

This book aims to help managers of non-government and community organisations to think critically about what kinds of information they, their organisations, their staff, and their project partners need. It discusses how they can access such information, manage it, and communicate it in the most effective and equitable way. It is illustrated with case studies

from Oxfam's experience and other sources. Practical tools are offered to help managers relate the ideas to their own situations.

1999 Oxfam Skills and Practice
0 85598 410 4 paperback 160pp £8.95/$14.95

A Guide to Gender-Analysis Frameworks

Candida March, Ines Smyth, and Maitrayee Mukhopadhyay

This guide to the best-known analytical frameworks for gender-sensitive research and planning offers step-by-step instructions and summaries of the frameworks' advantages and disadvantages in particular situations. An introductory section places the frameworks in the context of gender-transformatory development work and research.

1999 A Skills and Practice Guide
0 85598 403 1 paperback 96pp £6.95/$11.95

Capacity-Building: An Approach to People-Centred Development

Deborah Eade

This book considers specific and practical ways in which NGOs can contribute to enabling people to build on the capacities they already possess, while avoiding undermining such capacities. Capacity-Building reviews the types of social organisation with which NGOs might consider working, and the provision of training in a variety of skills and activities, for the people involved and for their organisation. The particular importance of using a capacity-building approach in emergency situations, and the dynamic and long-term nature of the process, are emphasised.

1997 An Oxfam Development Guideline
0 85598 366 3 paperback 226pp £9.95/$15.95
0 85598 392 2 hardback 226pp £24.95/$39.95

**For details of all our books and how to order, call BEBC Distribution on
+44 (0)1202 712933 or visit www.oxfam.org.uk/publications.html**

Postgraduate study in International Development Management

The Open University

Are you a development professional? Would you like to be? Do you want to gain skills in managing development programmes in an international context?

The Open University's Global Masters and Postgraduate Diploma in Development Management offers innovative and challenging courses with an open entry route.

Recommended introductory course

◆ *Development: Context and Practice* addresses key contemporary issues in international development and development policy.

Core courses

◆ *Capacities for Managing Development* provides frameworks and skills for planning and evaluating development programmes.

◆ *Institutional Development: Conflicts, Values and Meanings* focuses on institutional change, its role in development, and how to work with some of the practical issues of institution building.

◆ The *Development Management Project* enables students to carry out some independent research on development management and write a 10,000 word dissertation.

All courses can be studied alone or as a credit towards the MSc degree.

Through OU supported open learning

Our unique method of teaching lets you study wherever you like and in your own time. The Open University uses a multimedia and interactive approach with teaching texts, readings, case studies, audio and video cassettes. You will also receive support from your personal tutor and Regional Centre.

Courses are offered twice yearly in May and November. For further information, fill in the coupon below or telephone 0870 900 0314, quoting reference GDM9J, or visit the Open University website at: www.open.ac.uk.

Complete and send this coupon to:
The Open University, PO Box 625, Walton Hall, Milton Keynes MK7 6AA
☐ Tick if you have contacted the OU before
☐ Please send me *The Global Programme in Development Management*
☐ Please send me *Higher Degrees from the Open University 1999/2000*   GDM9J

Title   Initials   Surname

Address

Postcode

Tel   Date of Birth | | 19

☎ 0870 900 0314

THERE'S NO SUBSTITUTE FOR THE OU EXPERIENCE